# ANNE LINDSAY'S LIGHT KITCHEN

*More easy and healthy recipes from the author of the bestselling* Lighthearted Everyday Cooking

**United Way**
of Canada

**MACMILLAN CANADA**
Toronto

**Canadian Cataloguing in Publication Data**

Lindsay, Anne, 1943 -
  Anne Lindsay's Light Kitchen : more easy and healthy recipes from the author of the bestselling lighthearted everyday cooking

Includes index.

ISBN 0-7715-9029-6

1. Low-cholesterol diet - Recipes.  2. Low-fat diet - Recipes.  I. Title.  II. Title: Light kitchen.

RM219.L55 1994   641.5'638        C93-095143-3


Macmillan Canada wishes to thank the Canada Council and the Ontario Ministry of Culture and Communications for supporting its publishing program.
Macmillan Canada gratefully acknowledges the support of Canada Trust.


Macmillan Canada
A Division of Canada Publishing Corporation, Toronto, Canada


1 2 3 4 5  BP 98 97 96 95 94
Printed in Canada

*Cover photograph:* Michael Mitchell
(Hoisin Sesame Chicken Platter; Chinese Vegetable Fried Rice; Easy Berry Flan; Nectarine and Orange Compote): Yellow print fabric, blue napkin, servers, blue platter and blue bowl, all from *En Provence*, Toronto. Glass compote and glass pedestal cake plate from *The Compleat Kitchen*, Toronto.


*Design:* Andrew Smith

*Page Composition:* Joseph Gisini / Andrew Smith Graphics, Inc.

*Food Photography:* Doug Bradshaw / Bradshaw Photography Inc.

*Illustrations:* Penelope Moir

*Food Styling:* Olga Truchan

*Prop Coordination:* Janet Walkenshaw

*Nutrient Analysis:* by Info Access (1988) Inc., using the nutritional accounting component of the CBORD Menu Management System. The nutrient database was the 1991 Canadian Nutrient File supplemented when necessary with documented data from reliable sources.

*This book is dedicated to my husband,*
*Bob Lindsay, with love.*

∾

*It is also to the memory of*
*Wendy Buda and Sarah Martin.*

# ACKNOWLEDGEMENTS

I was very fortunate to work with a wonderful team to produce this book. I appreciate and thank all the people who were involved, and give special thanks to : Shannon Graham, dietitian, friend and co-worker, for helping with recipe testing for all four of my cookbooks. Nancy Williams, my sister-in-law, for her help with the book. Denise Schon, at Macmillan for the many extra hours she has put into all aspects of this book and to Bob Dees, Kirsten Hanson and everyone else at Macmillan for their patience and enthusiasm for this book. Bev Renahan for her expert editing of the recipes. Barbara Selley and Sharon Joliat for the nutritional analysis, their advice and extra work. Elizabeth Baird, food director, and Daphna Rabinovitch, test kitchen manager at *Canadian Living*. Many recipes first appeared in articles I wrote for the magazine. I'm very fortunate to have had Olga Truchan do the food styling for this and my *Lighthearted* cookbooks. Thanks also to Doug Bradshaw, photographer, and Janet Walkenshaw, props coordinator, for the great photographs and enjoyable week spent in the studio. Kerry Dean and Lynn Roblin for their help with the introductory material. Andrew Smith for his great design. Linda Alexander Leonard for reviewing the entire book.

The following reviewed the introductory material. Thank you for your advice and comments, they were most helpful:

Fran Berkoff, R.P.Dt., Dietitian, Mount Sinai Hospital
Leslie Berndl, M.Sc., R.P.Dt., Lipid Clinic Dietitian, St. Michael's Hospital
Anthony Graham, M.D., F.R.C.P. (C) Chief, Cardiology Division, Wellesley Hospital
Linda Alexander Leonard, M.H.Sc., R.P.Dt., Corporate Nutritionist, Nestlé Canada
Lynn Roblin, R.P. Dt., Nutrition Consultant
Barbara Selley, R.P.Dt., Consulting Associate, Info Access (1988) Inc.
Judy Wilkie, R.P.Dt., Public Health Nutritionist, North York

I'm very pleased to be working with United Way Canada. I hope this book will raise funds so United Way can help more Canadians improve their quality of life. Thanks to Judith John and Marilyn Michener for being so enthusiastic about this joint project.

I would like to thank Canada Trust for their generous support.

---

## CANADA TRUST MESSAGE

Canada Trust has built its business on the concept of community banking. As such, we look for opportunities to enhance the health, strength and vitality of the cities and towns where we live and work.

By sponsoring *Anne Lindsay's Light Kitchen*, we are providing much needed support to United Way and the millions of Canadians who rely on their services.

We are pleased to help United Way continue their valuable work as changemakers in the community, mobilizing local volunteer and financial resources in a common cause of caring.

Every contribution counts. Thank you for doing your part.

# CONTENTS

# United Way Foreword

United Way Canada is delighted and proud to be involved in the publication of *Anne Lindsay's Light Kitchen*. The cookbook's message echoes United Way's mission: building healthy communities. Healthy eating, after all, is about prevention. Through careful nutrition, people can lead healthier lives. Studies have convincingly demonstrated the importance of creating a healthy environment—nutritionally and psychologically—early in life.

United Way, too, is about prevention and taking responsibility for our own well being. Since the turn of the century, United Ways across Canada have been connecting individuals and groups in the common cause of building stronger, healthier communities.

In 124 United Ways across the country, volunteers and staff strive to meet urgent needs in their neighborhoods through a unique partnership with leaders from government, labor, business, special interest groups and individuals. They work with local social service agencies to help them develop and deliver innovative, high-quality and effective programs to meet the needs of individuals and families. Last year alone they recruited and trained hundreds of thousands of volunteers to raise $224 million.

From coast to coast, United Way is a focal point for gathering community resources—volunteers, fundraisers, planners—working in partnership to enhance the quality of life for those around them. This unique partnership supports 4,000 Canadian charities:

- agencies devoted to assisting **children and youth**, like boys and girls clubs, Big Brothers and Big Sisters, help telephone lines and counselling services;

- agencies helping **families**, like women's shelters, self-help groups, crisis phone lines and family service associations;

- agencies dedicated to improving the lives of the **disabled and the challenged**, from the Red Cross, Canadian National Institute for the Blind, and the Canadian Hearing Society to job training programs and guidance;

- agencies for **older adults**, offering counselling, visiting services, meals on wheels, respite care, community and employment centres;

- **social and community planning** agencies building better and healthier communities.

Across Canada annually, hundreds of thousands of people get involved in United Way. Millions of dollars are raised, thousands of agencies provide services, and millions are helped through their efforts. But however enormous and impressive these statistics, we must remember, those people are helped one person at a time.

# THE MEANING OF THE UNITED WAY SYMBOL

During campaign time, the United Way symbol is seen everywhere—but what does it mean? It's called the helping hand symbol, and it is used by United Way organizations all across Canada, the United States, and many other countries around the world.

The rainbow represents the hope for a secure and happy future which comes from the valuable services provided through your gifts. More than a hand out, United Way is the hand up to a better life.

The person at the centre represents the giver of help—you the donor—as well as the people receiving the services they need from United Way agencies.

And the hand is the hand of help extended by the donors, whose gifts ensure a helping hand to the millions of people who count on United Way services to make their daily lives easier, productive and more comfortable.

The United Way Helping Hand—a symbol of help, of service, and of hope. For more information about United Way, please call this toll-free number: 1-800-267-8221.

# INTRODUCTION

## HEALTHY EATING, DELICIOUS FOOD

Most people don't think about healthy eating until their doctor tells them they have to. Oh, no! cry household cooks, fearing they'll have to change their way of cooking, and that no one's going to like it. This negative perception of healthy eating is very common. After all, "healthy" cookbooks in the past had their faults. The good ones could be forbiddingly earnest, for instance. And vegetarian cookbooks often defeated their own purposes by balancing the virtuous brown rice with high-fat cheeses, nuts and oils. Spa cookbooks offered picture-pretty dishes that enslaved you in the kitchen for hours. Cookbooks on the fringes of good sense took sparse regimens to dangerous extremes. Well, that was then. Now, we know more.

We know that variety, not self-denial, is the key to healthy eating. We know that moderation works better than fad diets. Most of all, we know that just because people want to eat healthy doesn't mean they want to enjoy their food any less.

My philosophy of healthy eating is that food should appeal to the senses: it should taste delicious and look fabulous. Healthy eating, in my view, is not just for when the doctor says so—it's for all times, and for all ages.

It's even, believe it or not, for when company's coming. For some reason, people have always thought they had to throw good sense out the window when they entertained. The healthy cookbooks stayed on the shelf, and out came the special-occasion volumes calling for gallons of heavy cream and rich oils. But all this is changing. I know Canadians are already interested in reforming their eating habits because of the way they have embraced the recipes in my previous three healthy-eating cookbooks, and are still asking for more. They have especially requested entertaining menus that aren't overloaded with fat and calories.

For this book, I have responded by working out whole menus (see pages 27 to 31)—many of which I have served to friends—as well as individual recipes, following both the recommendations in Canada's Food Guide to Healthy Eating (see pages 10 to 13 and 246 to 247), revised in 1992, and my own creed that everything must taste and look good. (I just get there by different routes from the butter-and-oil brigade.)

In the 1990s, creating good taste the healthy way is easier than ever. In decades past, when produce wasn't great at all times of the year, the temptation was to cover things up with creamy sauces. But now all sorts of great new food products are available.

• Herbs and spices are my trademark, and happily, thanks to growing ethnic influences in Canada, a wider-than-ever variety is available. I like to use lots of fresh garlic and ginger, of course, and lemon and mustard; beyond these, fresh coriander, sun-dried tomatoes, hot chili peppers (fresh, bottled and dried) and rice vinegar—all things that can make food taste great without fat.

- When I wrote my first cookbook, *Smart Cooking*, in 1984, light versions of high-fat foods such as mayonnaise, sour cream and cheeses were almost unheard of. Today's light versions have cut the fat in half, and with sour cream we have a choice of lights: 7% butterfat, or even 1%. In 1984, only a couple of low-fat cheeses existed, and they were about as tasty as rubber balls. Now, a good deli might stock half a dozen cheeses at less than 15% butterfat, and three or four at 7%—and, yes, many of them taste great. Add to this a truly low-fat version of ice cream at 1% butterfat. New products are coming on the market all the time. Brand-new extra-thick and pressed yogurts are just reaching supermarket shelves, and I can hardly wait to start experimenting with them as low-fat alternatives in creamy dips, salad dressings and desserts.

- Meats are getting leaner, even since my 1991 cookbook, *Lighthearted Everyday Cooking*. New feed and grading systems for pork and beef have resulted in much leaner cuts—which in turn require new cooking methods.

- Better-quality frozen fish is now available across the country.

- Improved transportation and storage techniques make good-quality produce—those fruits and veggies we keep being reminded to eat more of—plentiful year-round.

All these great new developments are reflected in these pages, as is the way our cooking habits have changed for the better. Where the cook in the '50s fried in bacon drippings, and the cook in the '70s fried in butter or oil, the cook in the '90s is not frying, period.

When creating recipes, I've also kept the busy person in mind. Recipes are fast and easy to prepare, and use only ingredients I believe to be widely available. If an ingredient seemed unnecessary, I deleted it; if a recipe could be made as easily in one bowl as in two, I made it in one. And you have my busy sister-in-law Linda Elliott to thank for the make-ahead information that accompanies each recipe. She pointed out that my books were no good to her without it.

Who needs to eat healthy? Every single member of the family!

Young children need the right kinds and amounts of foods to help them grow and develop properly. Healthy foods help them establish positive eating habits that may reduce their chances of nutrition-related diseases later in life.

Healthy eating during adolescence can be challenging. Male teens are okay—they usually satisfy their nutrient needs by eating lots of everything. But the more complex eating habits of a teenaged girl often result in a lack of basic nutrients in her diet. Her social life may involve hanging out at the local burger joint eating fries; at the same time she desperately wants to stay pencil-slim.

Women who hope to become pregnant or who are pregnant or breast feeding require an increase in specific nutrients. Women in general have to be careful to choose balanced, nutrient-packed meals.

Finally, healthy eating is important for all adults concerned about nutrition-related illnesses such as heart disease and cancer. Since about 50% of adult Canadians have higher than desirable levels of blood cholesterol and half of adult Canadians face potential health risks because of their weight, preventive eating habits are a must. I've also included diabetic food choice values at the back of the book.

I know from experience that many of these different dietary needs and concerns can easily reside in a single household. But that doesn't mean you have to prepare a lot of separate menus every day. Look at my family: my husband has elevated blood cholesterol; my university-age sons eat mountains of food; my teenaged daughter has a good appetite yet worries about her weight; I am constantly trying to exercise away the results of the business I'm in—and we all love to eat. So I make the main courses of our dinners low in fat for my husband. This also suits my daughter and me because they're lower in calories. My sons make up the difference in snacks and other meals. In the fridge, we keep low-fat and regular choices in certain foods: 2% milk and skim; regular Cheddar and skim milk cheeses; regular ice cream and the 1% option.

Healthy eating reduces everyone's risk for all disease. It helps you feel better, perform your best, handle stress and maintain a healthy weight. No single miracle food or pill can do this for you. This book will provide you with valuable nutrition information and wonderful recipes and menus to help you and your family continue on the road to healthy and happy eating.

ANNE LINDSAY, DECEMBER, 1993

# ABOUT CANADA'S FOOD GUIDE TO HEALTHY EATING

For the healthy person and average Canadian, healthy eating means making food choices that will contribute to your nutritional health and help you feel great. That means choosing a variety of foods from each food group in Canada's Food Guide to Healthy Eating*. Healthy eating also involves eating less fat and including more carbohydrates and fibre in your diet. Healthy eating doesn't mean avoiding your favorite foods. It means enjoying your food, but being careful with the amount of higher-fat foods you choose.

*How Do You Begin Healthy Eating for Life?*

The easiest way to adopt a healthy-eating pattern for you and your family is to follow Canada's Food Guide to Healthy Eating (see pages 246 to 247 for the Guide itself). This food guide is the result of years of research about foods, nutrients and the way people eat and their health. It translates all that nutrition knowledge into one practical, easy-to-use healthy-eating guide. I don't worry about getting enough of this vitamin or that mineral, or what foods are high in what, I just try to follow the Food Guide. Even my daughter will check to see if she has all the food groups in her lunch when she packs it.

*Canada's Food Guide to Healthy Eating Tells Us To:*

**ENJOY A VARIETY OF FOODS FROM EACH GROUP EVERY DAY**
Your body needs over 50 different nutrients every day. You won't find that in a meal replacement shake or bar! In order to make sure you are getting all the nutrients you need, choose different foods from each food group and vary your choices within each group. The easiest way to get variety in your diet is to include different food groups at each meal.

* Published by Health and Welfare Canada, 1992.

## CHOOSE LOWER-FAT FOODS MORE OFTEN

Everyone needs to eat some fat to stay healthy, but the reality is that most people eat too much. Dietary fat is linked to the development of chronic diseases such as heart disease, cancer, hypertension and obesity. In 1986, data showed that 38% of the calories that the average Canadian ate came from fat. This appears to be decreasing. Current nutrition recommendations suggest that adults* get no more than 30% of calories from fat.

## About the Food Groups

There are four food groups in Canada's Food Guide to Healthy Eating: Grain Products, Vegetables & Fruit, Milk Products, Meats & Alternatives. The new Food Guide tells us to eat more foods from the Grain Products and Vegetables & Fruit groups than ever before. That's because foods in these two groups are high in carbohydrates, fibre and nutrients. Milk Products and Meats & Alternatives are also important, but they should make up a smaller part of your healthy eating pattern and most of the choices you make should be lower in fat.

## What and How Much from Each Group?

The number of servings you need from each group varies depending on your age, sex, size, activity level and if you are pregnant or breast feeding. The Food Guide is for all Canadians over the age of four. Young children and older women can choose the lower number of servings. Male teenagers and very active people can choose the higher number of servings from each group.

A word of warning: don't throw up your hands and say the Food Guide suggests more than you could eat before you note the size of servings. A plate of pasta can equal 3 to 4 servings of Grain Rroducts, 2 Vegetables & Fruit servings and 1 Meat & Alternatives serving, for instance.

### GRAIN PRODUCTS: 5 to 12 servings per day

*Choose whole grain and enriched products more often.* Whole grain products made from whole wheat, oats, barley or rye are suggested because they are high in complex carbohydrates and fibre. Enriched foods such as bread, cereal and rice are recommended because they contain vitamins and minerals that were removed in processing. Try multigrain breads and bagels, enriched pasta, cold bran cereals or cooked oatmeal.

**1 serving** = 1 slice bread; 30 g cold cereal; $\frac{3}{4}$ cup (175 mL) hot cereal
**2 servings** = 1 bagel, pita or hamburger bun; 1 cup (250 mL) pasta or rice

### VEGETABLES & FRUIT: 5 to 10 servings per day

*Choose dark green and orange vegetables and orange fruit more often.* These foods are high in important nutrients such as vitamin A (beta carotene), C and folate. Choose broccoli, spinach, squash, sweet potatoes, carrot, cantaloupe or orange juice.

**1 serving** = 1 medium-sized vegetable or fruit (apple, banana, orange, potato, carrot); $\frac{1}{2}$ cup (125 mL) cooked vegetables or juice; 1 cup (250 mL) salad with leafy greens

### MILK PRODUCTS: 2 to 3 servings per day, children 4 to 9 years; 3 to 4 servings per day, youths 10 to 16 years; 2 to 4 servings per day, adults; 3 to 4 servings per day, pregnant and breast-feeding women

*Choose lower-fat milk products more often.* Lower-fat milk products

* For fat guidelines for infants and children, see ** page 17.

provide protein and calcium essential to healthy eating with less fat and calories. Look on the labels and choose milk, yogurt or cottage cheese with 2% milk fat (m.f.) or less; for cheese choose 15% or less m.f. (milk fat) or b.f. (butterfat).

**1 serving** = 1 cup (250 mL) milk; ¾ cup (175 mL) yogurt; 2 slices (50 g) cheese or 3" x 1" x 1" (50 g) piece of cheese

### MEATS & ALTERNATIVES: 2 to 3 servings per day

*Choose leaner meats, poultry and fish, as well as dried peas, beans and lentils more often.* Many leaner choices of meats, poultry, fish and seafood are now available to help you eat less fat without losing important nutrients. Trim visible fat and try baking, grilling, roasting or microwaving instead of frying. Remove extra fat after cooking. Choose a meat alternative such as baked beans or pea soup to help you eat less fat and more fibre.

**1 serving** = 2 tbsp (30 mL) peanut butter; ⅓ cup (100 g) tofu; ½ to 1 cup (125 to 250 mL) baked beans; 1 to 2 eggs; ⅓ to ⅔ can (50 to 100 g) fish; 2 to 4 oz (50 to 100 g) meat, poultry or fish

## What About Foods That Don't Fit a Food Group?

Many foods and beverages are not part of the four food groups in Canada's Food Guide to Healthy Eating. These are called "other foods": fats (butter, margarine, oils and salad dressings); sugars (jam, honey, syrup, candies); snack foods that are high in fat and/or salt (chips, pretzels); beverages (water, tea, coffee, alcohol and soft drinks); and condiments (pickles, ketchup). We all include "other foods" in our diet because we like them. The main thing is to choose high-fat or high-calorie foods in moderation.

### WATER

When you are thirsty, choose water. Have water often, especially in hot weather or when you are very active.

### ALCOHOL

Moderate drinking means having no more than 1 drink a day and no more than 7 drinks a week. You can risk your health and safety if you have more than 4 drinks on one occasion, or more than 14 a week. (If you are pregnant avoid alcohol.)

> 1 drink = 1 bottle (or about 350 mL) beer
> 1 drink = 150 mL (about 5 oz) wine
> 1 drink = 50 mL (1½ oz) liquor

### CAFFEINE

You may use caffeine in moderation. It's found in coffee, tea or cola soft drinks, foods that contain cocoa and in some medications.

## How Does Canada's Food Guide Fit Into a Day's Menu?

Following Canada's Food Guide to Healthy Eating is easy. Consider the following day's menu, using this key:
G = Grain products serving; F = Fruit & Vegetable serving;
M = Milk products serving; MA = Meats & Alternatives serving;
O = Other foods

| BREAKFAST | DINNER |
|---|---|
| Orange juice (½ cup/125 mL) = 1F | Herbed Meat Loaf (page 128) = 1MA |
| Bran Flakes (¾ cup/175 mL) = 1G | Spanish Rice with Coriander (page 177) = |
| Plain yogurt, 1.5% b.f. (¾ cup/175 mL) = 1M | 1½G, 1F |
| Brown sugar (1 tbsp/15 mL) = O | Baked Squash (¼ acorn squash) = 1F |
| **LUNCH** |    Margarine or butter (1 tsp/5 mL) = O |
| 2 slices whole wheat bread = 2G | Green Beans (½ cup/125 mL) = 1F |
| Tuna, canned in water (½ cup/125 mL) = 1MA | Whole wheat bread (1 slice) = 1G |
| Light mayonnaise (2 tbsp/25 mL) = O |    Margarine or butter (1 tsp/5 mL) = O |
| Alfalfa sprouts (½ cup/125 mL) = ½F | Milk (1 cup/250 mL) = 1M |
| Fig bars (2) = ½F; ½G | Banana = 1F |

For one day, this adds up to: G=6, F=6, MA=2, M=2

Some people need to eat more. For example, growing teens, depending on their size, would add 1 to 4 more servings of either fruits and vegetables and 1 to 6 servings of grain products, 1 to 2 more servings of milk products and may choose another serving of meat and alternatives.

In my house, my university student sons would have double the portions of the rice, a peanut butter sandwich for a snack, another glass each of juice and of milk, then maybe start on cookies. This all fits into a healthy diet for growing, active students and follows Canada's Food Guide to Healthy Eating.

## Make More Lower-fat Choices

The Guide recommends making lower-fat choices more often. Adults should aim for not more than 30% of calories coming from fat.

It is amazing to see how seemingly minor changes in our meals can affect the amount of fat in our diet. For example, in the above day's menu, the total calories = 1680; grams of fat = 42; and % calories from fat = 23.

For example, in the above menu, a clinical, very low-fat diet would include some of these changes: skim milk and low-fat yogurt; yogurt instead of mayonnaise mixed with tuna; no margarine or butter on bread or on beans. Total calories = 1501; grams of fat = 21; % calories from fat = 12.*

If you're not careful, the fat can easily be too high, as you can see if you make these higher-fat choices: 4% b.f. yogurt; homo milk (3.5%); tuna canned in oil; regular mayonnaise, plus 1 tbsp (15 mL) butter (for sandwich); 2 tsp (10 mL) butter or margarine on bread and on beans. Total calories = 2125; grams of fat = 94; % calories from fat = 40.

When you add snacks, depending on your choices, the total amount of calories and fat increases but the % calories from fat could stay the same. Most of us would be better off choosing lower-fat snacks. For example, in the higher-fat menu above, you increase your calories and fat if you add snacks of 1 cola drink; 1 bag (55 g) potato chips; 1 sandwich of 2 slices whole wheat bread, 2 tbsp (25 mL) each peanut butter and jam; 4 chocolate chip cookies (boxed type). Total calories = 3157; grams of fat = 139; % calories from fat = 40.

---

* I'm not recommending this low a fat or calorie diet; this is just an example of how easy it can be to lower (or raise) the fat in our diet. Anyone on a low-fat diet should be under the care of a dietitian. The average woman aged 25 to 49 should have about 1900 calories a day.

# VEGETARIAN MEALS

I'm hearing from my friends more and more that their daughters are now vegetarians. In one family with six children, even the son has decided to give up meat. Mothers usually wonder if their kids are getting all the nutrients they need.

Whether you eat meat or not, it's still very important to follow the Food Guide. Have a variety of foods and include meat alternatives such as tofu, dried beans, peas and lentils and eggs. If one is eating dairy products daily, protein isn't usually a problem. If you are a strict vegetarian consult a dietitian. A vegan diet, which includes no animal products such as eggs, meat or dairy products, is a concern for teens and young children because it may not provide enough energy, vitamins $B_{12}$ and D and calcium.

I know you can get calcium from foods such as kidney beans, broccoli and most tofu. But you have to be careful to eat large amounts of these foods every day. If you are avoiding dairy products, you may need a vitamin D supplement.

---

### CALCIUM-RICH FOODS
Canned sardines (3 oz/90 g) ..........393 mg
Yogurt (¾ cup/175 mL) .................355 mg
Milk (1 cup/250 mL).......................315 mg
Cheddar cheese (1 oz/28 g) ...........216 mg
Salmon with bones (3 oz/90 g) ......183 mg
Scallops or shrimp (3 oz/90 g).......104 mg

**Vegetarian**
Cooked broccoli (1 cup/250 mL) ..187 mg
Tofu (4 oz/120 g) ...........................154 mg
Cooked spinach (½ cup/125 mL) .139 mg
Dried figs (4) ..................................108 mg
Cooked beans
(white, navy or pea beans)...............98 mg

- Teenaged girls need 700 to 1000 mg calcium daily.
- Taking calcium supplements at meals and drinking tea inhibit iron absorption.

### IRON-RICH FOODS
Calves liver (3 oz/90 g) .....................13 mg
Trout (3 oz/90 g).............................4.5 mg
Veal, pork or beef
(3 oz/90 g, cooked) .....................2 to 3 mg
Most fish (3 oz/90 g, cooked) .....1 to 2 mg

**Vegetarian**
Cooked enriched cream
of wheat (½ cup/125 mL) .................8 mg
Bran cereal (½ cup/125 mL) .............6 mg
Cooked spinach (½ cup/125 mL) ..3.5 mg
Cooked dried peas, beans
or lentils (½ cup/125 mL)...........2 to 4 mg
Broccoli, corn, carrots, peas
(1 cup/250 mL, cooked)..............1 to 3 mg

- Teenaged girls need 12 to 13 mg iron daily.
- Eating vitamin C-rich foods along with iron-rich plant foods helps maximize iron absorption.

---

*Hints for Cooking for Both Vegetarians and Non-vegetarians:*

**1.** Vegetarian pasta dishes often please everyone. If this isn't the case in your home, plan to have some leftover cooked meats to add to dinner plates.

**2.** In some dishes, such as the Chinese Vegetable Fried Rice, page 178 (do try it; everyone in my family loves it), the meat can be added after the vegetarians have been served.

**3.** Often vegetarian dishes are high in fat and cheese. The recipes in this book use part-skim milk or skim milk cheese and a minimum of fat.

**4.** Keep on hand lower-fat cheeses, eggs, tofu, canned chick-peas and kidney beans, peanuts or sunflower seeds to add to soups, salads, stir-frys or pasta dishes.

**5.** Canned pea or lentil soup or beans in tomato sauce, along with toasted whole wheat bread, are easy meal ideas.

**6.** When you serve meat, also include one of the substantial vegetarian dishes listed below. Include whole wheat bread, a vegetable or salad and milk; the vegetarians can choose not to have the meat and everyone should be happy.

**Appetizers**
Fresh Tomato Pizza *(page 45)*
Goat Cheese and Pesto Tortilla Pizzas *(page 47)*
Cheese and Tomato Quesadillas *(page 52)*

**Soups**
Three Grain Vegetable Soup *(page 65)*
Italian Chick-Pea and Pasta Soup *(page 67)*
Red Bean and Rice Soup *(page 66)*

**Salads**
Easy Couscous Vegetable Salad *(page 77)*
Mediterranean Lentil and Bean Salad *(page 75)*
Pasta Salad with Tomato Basil Dressing (omit ham) *(page 171)*
Spicy Noodle Salad *(page 169)*
Bulgur Salad with Cucumber and Feta *(page 76)*
Pasta Salad with Sun-Dried Tomatoes *(page 170)*

**Pastas**
Pasta with Chick-Peas, Tomato and Herbs *(page 154)*
Light Fettuccine Alfredo with Herbs *(page 158)*
Macaroni and Cheese *(page 157)*
Pasta Provençal with Tofu *(page 162)*
Pasta with Tomatoes, Cheese and Jalapeños *(page 155)*
Linguine with Mushrooms and Green Peppers *(page 159)*
Make-Ahead Party Thai Noodles *(page 165)*
Jiffy Chinese Noodles *(page 165)*
Singapore Noodles (omit pork) *(page 163)*

**Grains, Legumes and Meatless Main Dishes**
Potato, Bean and Tomato Stew *(page 187)*
Tomato, Eggplant and Zucchini Gratin *(page 193)*
Spinach Rice Casserole *(page 174)*
Indian Rice with Lentils *(page 176)*
Green Vegetable Risotto *(page 175)*
Chinese Vegetable Fried Rice (omit ham) *(page 178)*
Spanish Rice with Coriander *(page 177)*
Marinated Baked Tofu *(page 191)*
Spicy Vegetable Tofu Stir-Fry *(page 192)*
Bean Casserole (omit sausage) *(page 186)*
Winter Vegetable Curry with Couscous *(page 188)*
Crustless Vegetable Quiche *(page 190)*
Quinoa-Stuffed Peppers *(page 184)*
Barley and Corn Casserole *(page 185)*

# ALL ABOUT CHOLESTEROL AND FAT

## Cholesterol

Cholesterol is still very much in the news because high blood cholesterol levels are a major contributor to heart disease. Knowing the facts is important to help you keep your blood cholesterol levels in a healthy range.

First, it's important to know that we need cholesterol. It is a fat-like substance that is a component of body cells, and it's needed to produce hormones and vitamin D, and also bile acids (which help digest fat).

Part of the confusion surrounding cholesterol is because of the way people talk about the cholesterol you eat and the cholesterol in your blood. In fact, these are different things.

**Dietary cholesterol** is the cholesterol we get from eating foods of animal origin. Meat, fish, poultry, eggs and dairy products all contain cholesterol. Only foods of animal origin contain cholesterol.

**Blood cholesterol** exists as a natural component of our blood fats. The cholesterol in our blood comes from both our liver and from foods that we eat. About 80% of the cholesterol in our blood is produced by the liver, while the remaining 20% comes from what we eat.

Many people believe that the cholesterol from foods is the main cause of high blood cholesterol and heart disease. We now know that dietary cholesterol doesn't affect blood cholesterol nearly as much as dietary fat.

*The best dietary way to reduce the amount of cholesterol our body makes is to reduce the total amount of fat we eat—particularly saturated and partially hydrogenated fats—and to eat more foods containing carbohydrates and fibre.*

A word of warning: for people diagnosed with high blood cholesterol levels, limiting high-cholesterol foods may be important in addition to reducing total fat. Some high-cholesterol foods to limit include egg yolks, liver, kidney, shrimp and fish roe.

## Fat and Your Health

For most people, eating less fat is the most important dietary change they can make. That's because high-fat diets contribute to heart disease, cancer, high blood cholesterol levels and obesity. The following information will help you sort out the facts about fat.

### WHERE DOES THE FAT WE EAT COME FROM?

Many foods contain fat, including foods from each of the four food groups. The main sources of fat in our diet are fats (butter, margarine, lard), oils, higher-fat meats, poultry and dairy products, salad dressings, gravies, sauces, fried foods, muffins, croissants and other baked goods.

Some fats, such as the skin on poultry and the fat on meat and bacon, are quite visible. Other fats that you eat are hidden in foods such as peanut butter, dairy products, meat products, snack foods like chips, nuts and seeds, baked goods and rich desserts. Fat also gets into your diet when you add it to foods when preparing, serving or eating them. These fats include butter, margarine, oils, salad dressing and rich sauces, which should be your primary target for lowering your fat intake.

## THERE ARE DIFFERENT KINDS OF FAT

All fats are made up of a combination of fats. You may have heard about saturated, monounsaturated and polyunsaturated fats and trans fatty acids. All of these fats have different effects on your blood cholesterol levels.

**Saturated fats** have been shown to increase LDL* ("bad") cholesterol in blood. Saturated fats come from foods of animal origin including meats, dairy products (butter, cream, regular cheese, homo milk), egg yolks, lard, and some vegetable products such as coconut or palm kernel oil, shortening and hydrogenated vegetable oils.

**Monounsaturated fats** may help to lower harmful LDL cholesterol in blood. Olive, avocado, canola and peanut oils, some fish and some nut oils are included in this category. Olive oil has been found to contain some antioxidants which may protect against heart disease.

**Polyunsaturated fats** also tend to lower LDL cholesterol levels in the blood. Vegetable oils such as safflower, sunflower, corn and sesame are types of polyunsaturated fats.

**Trans fatty acids** tend to raise LDL cholesterol levels, but not as much as saturated fats do. The process of hydrogenation changes some unsaturated fatty acids to trans fatty acids that act like saturated fats. Some research shows that trans fatty acids may also lower HDL cholesterol. Most of the trans fatty acids that we eat come from partially hydrogenated vegetable oils, which are found in most margarines, shortenings, some packaged cookies, crackers, snack foods, pastries, muffins, breaded and fried chicken and fish, and other deep-fried foods. Check labels for the words partially hydrogenated.

## CONTROL TOTAL FAT

The bottom line here is to find ways to eat less of all types of fat. We should strive to keep our total fat intake to less than 30% of a day's calories.** This figure doesn't apply to each food or meal that you eat; it's meant as a guideline for your total fat allowance at the end of the day. That means sometimes you can have a higher-fat meal and balance it off with lower-fat choices for the rest of the day. It also means making choices. I have found it easiest to cut out butter or margarine by having cereal rather than toast some mornings, or by just using jam. I don't spread butter or margarine on bread when making a sandwich, but use either light mayonnaise or mustard, and I add sliced cucumber so it won't be dry. I eat both lower-fat and higher-fat cheeses.

---

*LDL and HDL: Cholesterol is transported in our blood by a fat and protein compound called lipoprotein. Too much low-density lipoprotein-cholesterol (LDL) in the blood is directly linked to clogged arteries or coronary artery disease. High-density lipoprotein-cholesterol (HDL) returns cholesterol back to the liver where it is removed from the blood. When you have your blood cholesterol checked, have it done for LDL and HDL as well as for total blood cholesterol. The higher the HDL the better, for it doesn't stay around and clog arteries.

**This guideline has some flexibility for growing children. Parents should not restrict the amount of fat that children under the age of two eat. Infants and children need fat in their diets to provide energy and nutrients for growth and development. Infants need fat to help form the nervous system. Because of this, skim, 1% and 2% milk are not recommended during the first two years of life. Children need to progress from a diet that contains about 50% of calories from fat (breast milk) to a lower-fat diet of an adult (30% of calories from fat).

## WHAT DOES 30% OF CALORIES FROM FAT REALLY MEAN?

An average woman, age 25 to 49, should keep her daily fat intake to about 65 grams of fat or less (based on 1900 calories). An average man, age 25 to 49, should keep his daily fat intake to about 90 grams of fat or less (based on 2700 calories).

| This means that if you have this many calories: | 1800 | 2000 | 2200 | 2400 | 2600 | 2800 |
|---|---|---|---|---|---|---|
| You should have not more than this many grams of fat daily: | 60 | 67 | 73 | 80 | 87 | 93 |

---

### COMPARE THE FAT

#### HIGHER-FAT MENU
(2374 calories, 50% calories from fat)

**BREAKFAST** *Fat (g)*

Orange juice ...............................................0
Croissant ..................................................12
   1 tbsp (15 mL) butter or margarine ..11
Milk 2% (8 oz/250 mL)..............................5
*Total* .......................................................**28**

**LUNCH**

Ham and cheese sandwich
   2 slices whole wheat bread ..................2
   1 oz (28 g) Cheddar cheese ................10
   1 oz (28 g) lean ham.............................2
   2 tsp (10 mL) butter or margarine .......8
   2 tsp (10 mL) mayonnaise....................8
Carrot cake (60 g) with
   cream cheese icing.............................13
*Total* .......................................................**43**

**DINNER**

1 chicken breast breaded
   and fried with skin (5 oz/140 g).........18
Baked potato ............................................0
   1 tsp (5 mL) butter or margarine.........4
   2 tbsp (25 mL) sour cream (14% b.f.) ..6
Carrots .....................................................0
   1 tsp (5 mL) butter or margarine.........4
Green salad...............................................0
   Oil and vinegar dressing
   (1 tbsp/15 mL ) ..................................11
Whole wheat bread (1 slice) .....................1
   2 tsp (10 mL) butter or margarine .......8
Vanilla ice cream (½ cup/125 mL) ........10
*Total* .......................................................**62**

**Daily total** .......................133 grams of fat

#### LOWER-FAT MENU
(1694 calories, 28% calories from fat)

**BREAKFAST** *Fat (g)*

Orange juice ...............................................0
2 slices whole wheat toast .........................2
   2 tsp (10 mL) butter or margarine.......8
   Jam .....................................................0
Milk 1% (8 oz/250 mL)...........................2.5
*Total* ....................................................**12.5**

**LUNCH**

Ham and cheese sandwich
   2 slices whole wheat bread ..................2
   1 oz (28 g) skim milk cheese
   (7% b.f.) ..............................................2
   1 oz (28 g) lean ham.............................2
   2 tsp (10 mL) light mayonnaise ..........4
2 oatmeal cookies with raisins.................4
1 banana ...................................................0
Milk 1% (8 oz/250 mL)...........................2.5
*Total* .......................................................**16.5**

**DINNER**

1 chicken breast, baked without skin ......3
1 baked potato ..........................................0
   2 tbsp (25 mL) light sour cream
   (5.5% b.f.) ...........................................2
Carrots .....................................................0
   1 tsp (5 mL) butter or margarine ........4
Green salad...............................................0
   1 tbsp (15 mL) lower-fat dressing........5
Whole wheat bread (1 slice) .....................1
   1 tsp (5 mL) butter or margarine ........4
Lime sorbet (½ cup/125 mL) ...................1
*Total* .......................................................**20**

**SNACKS**

1 bran muffin (small)................................4
1 apple ......................................................0

**Daily total** .......................53 grams of fat

## Tips to Cut Back on Fat

**1.** Use the recipes in this book because they are all lower in fat.

**2.** Have grain products like bread, cereal, pasta and rice at every meal. Use high-fat spreads, toppings or sauces in smaller amounts, or try lower-fat alternatives.

**3.** Eat lots of vegetables and fruit, but watch out for cream sauces, butter or margarine and deep-fat frying.

**4.** Choose lower-fat milk products such as milk and yogurt made with skim or 1% milk. Try a lower-fat cheese that contains less than 15% butterfat. Use milk in your coffee instead of cream.

**5.** Try lean cuts of meat, skinless poultry and lower-fat fish. Instead of frying, prepare these foods by broiling, baking, poaching or microwaving.

**6.** Use smaller amounts of regular salad dressing or mayonnaise or try a reduced fat type instead.

**7.** Prepare foods with herbs, spices, salsa, lemon juice, garlic and mustard for enjoyable flavors without extra fat.

**8.** Limit high-fat snack foods such as chips, chocolates, cookies and baked goods. Instead, choose unbuttered popcorn, pretzels, fruit, low-fat yogurt and fresh bread more often.

## How to Choose Your Fat Spreads

Butter and margarine both contain 70 calories and 8 g of fat per 2 tsp (10 mL). What you should be concerned about is the amount of saturated fat and hydrogenated or "trans" fat because these are linked with increased blood cholesterol levels. Butter is high in saturated fat. If you have high blood cholesterol levels, you should choose a soft tub or light margarine with the lowest amount of trans fat and saturated fats. To date, trans fats don't have to be declared on labels in Canada.

| BUTTER VS MARGARINE: HERE'S WHAT'S IN A 2 TSP (10 ML) SERVING | | | |
|---|---|---|---|
| | Saturated fat and/or trans fat (grams) | Total fat (grams) | Calories (kcal) |
| Butter | 5 | 8 | 70 |
| Margarine (hard) | 4 | 8 | 70 |
| Calorie-reduced or light butter | 2 to 3 | 4 | 35 |
| Soft tub margarine (healthier brand, see below) | 1 to 2 | 8 | 70 |
| Other soft tub margarines | 3 to 4 | 8 | 70 |
| Calorie-reduced or light soft tub margarine | 1 | 4 | 35 |

To make sure you are buying a healthier margarine, read the fat information listed on the nutrition information panel. If the margarine package doesn't have a nutrient label, don't buy it. Add the grams of polyunsaturated and monounsaturated fat only. The total of these two fats should equal 6 g of fat or more for regular margarine, or 3 g of fat or more for calorie-reduced or light margarine per 2 tsp (10 mL) serving.

## *Which Oil to Choose?*

Choose one that suits your taste but make sure that it's high in monounsaturated or polyunsaturated fat. I use safflower and canola oil for cooking and baking because they meet this criteria and are bland in flavor. In salad dressings and pasta sauces when I want good flavor, I often use extra-virgin olive oil. I also use a teaspoon or so of sesame oil for its strong nutty taste in stir-frys (add at the end of cooking), some pasta dishes and salad dressings.

# GETTING ENOUGH FIBRE FOODS

Eating more foods that are high in fibre is another positive healthy eating change. Besides helping to keep you regular, a high-fibre diet may help reduce blood cholesterol levels and reduce your risk for colon and other cancers.

Canadians generally have a diet that is relatively low in fibre. That's one of the reasons why Canada's Food Guide to Healthy Eating suggests that we increase the number of grain products, vegetables and fruit that we eat. Because most high-fibre foods are high in complex carbohydrates and vitamins and low in fat and calories, they play a very important part in a healthy eating pattern.

## *Where Does Fibre Come From?*

Fibre is found in foods of plant origin only. Grains, cereals, vegetables, fruit, beans, peas, lentils, nuts and seeds are all high in fibre.

## *Types of Fibre*

There are two main types of fibre, soluble and insoluble. Each has different health benefits. All plants provide both soluble and insoluble fibre; some sources have more of one than the other. In order to get a good combination of the different types of fibre, choose a variety of high-fibre foods.

**Insoluble fibre** is the type of fibre known to keep your digestive system working and help keep you regular. It may also play a preventive role, protecting against colon and rectal cancers. Insoluble fibre is found in wheat bran, bran cereals, bran muffins, whole grain products and some vegetables such as broccoli, carrots and peas and fruit skins.

**Soluble fibre** has been shown to help reduce blood cholesterol levels and to slow down the rate at which sugar is absorbed by the body. Dried peas, beans, lentils, oat bran, barley and some vegetables and fruit contain soluble fibre.

## *How Much Fibre Should You Eat?*

The average Canadian consumes around 15 g of fibre per day. The experts suggest that we need more, around 25 to 35 g of fibre per day. However, because sudden increases in fibre intake can cause abdominal discomfort, you should try to increase your fibre intake gradually.

## Tips to Increase Your Fibre Intake

**1.** Have 5 to 12 servings of whole grain- and bran-containing breads, cereals and other grain products every day. For instance, if you choose 4 slices of whole wheat bread instead of white, you add 4 g of fibre. If you sprinkle ¼ cup (50 mL) of All-Bran cereal over your favorite cereal, you add an extra 6 g of fibre.

**2.** Eat 5 to 10 servings of vegetables and fruit each day. Keep the skins on and choose vegetables and fruit more often than juice. For instance, if you add ½ cup (125 mL) cooked green peas to your serving of macaroni and cheese, you add an extra 4 g of fibre. If you have 1 cup (250 mL) of spinach salad instead of leaf lettuce, you add an extra 3 g of fibre.

**3.** Try meals made with dried peas, beans and lentils more often. If you add ½ cup (125 mL) cooked kidney beans to your serving of vegetable soup or green salad, you add 7 g of fibre.

**4.** Choose high-fibre snacks such as carrots, apples, berries, bran muffins and whole grain or rye bagels.

**5.** Add dried fruit to breakfast cereals, desserts, salads and casseroles.

**6.** Drink plenty of water and other fluids. They help your body use fibre properly.

### FIBRE CONTENT OF SOME COMMON FOODS

| Food Item | Calories (kcal) | Fibre(g) | Fat (g) |
|---|---|---|---|
| All-Bran–type cereal, ¾ cup (175 mL) | 105 | 16.1 | 0.8 |
| Baked beans, ¾ cup (175 mL) | 240 | 14.6 | 1.0 |
| Prunes, dried, uncooked (10) | 201 | 10.0 | tr |
| Lentils, cooked, 1 cup (250 mL) | 224 | 7.8 | 1.0 |
| Apricots, dried, ½ cup (125 mL) | 165 | 5.6 | tr |
| Raisin bran–type cereal, ¾ cup (175 mL) | 145 | 3.9 | 0.6 |
| Peas, green, boiled, ½ cup (125 mL) | 70 | 3.8 | tr |
| Bran flakes–type cereal, ¾ cup (175 mL) | 125 | 3.7 | 0.6 |
| Potato, baked with skin (1 medium) | 225 | 3.5 | tr |
| Apple, with skin (1 medium) | 80 | 3.5 | tr |
| Corn, boiled, ½ cup (125 mL) | 70 | 2.4 | 0.8 |
| Banana (1 large) | 105 | 2.4 | tr |
| Broccoli, boiled, ½ cup (125 mL) | 25 | 2.3 | tr |
| Carrot, raw (1 medium) | 30 | 2.2 | tr |
| Tomato, raw (1 medium) | 25 | 1.8 | tr |
| Bread, whole wheat (1 slice) | 60 | 1.4 | 0.8 |
| Peanut butter, smooth, 1 tbsp (15 mL) | 95 | 1.2 | 8.1 |
| Bread, white (1 slice) | 75 | 0.4 | 0.9 |
| Rice, white, long grain, ½ cup (125 mL) | 90 | 0.3 | 0.1 |
| Sole, baked without fat, 3 oz (90 g) | 85 | 0.0 | 1.0 |
| Beef, lean, inside round steak, broiled, 3 oz (100 g) | 163 | 0.0 | 3.9 |

# THE LATEST NEWS ON VITAMINS

There is a great deal of hype these days about the power of vitamins, especially vitamin C, beta carotene and vitamin E. New research shows that they may help fight heart disease, cancer and even boost the immune system of the elderly, but all the facts aren't in yet. There is also very important news about preconceptual and pregnant women's need for increased folate in order to prevent neural tube defects such as spina bifida.

## Antioxidants

Some scientists believe that antioxidant vitamins (C, E and beta carotene) can help lower your risk for cancer and heart disease by protecting you from free radicals. These antioxidants are thought to work by preventing the formation of, or destroying, disease causing compounds known as free radicals. Free radicals are unstable chemicals that form in our bodies at all times. If free radicals aren't inactivated or destroyed by an antioxidant, they can damage cells and contribute to blood vessel wall changes or start disease processes.

Certain nutrients can make free radicals harmless, particularly the antioxidant vitamins C and E and beta carotene (the plant form of vitamin A). Dark green and orange vegetables and orange fruit are good sources of these antioxidant vitamins as well as sources of other non-nutritive substances such as indoles, phenols, flavones and isothiocyantes which may have this protective effect.

The facts are not all in yet, but there are indications that these vitamins, along with other non-nutritive food substances found in fruits and vegetables, are natural antioxidants that help protect against cancer.

The following foods are good sources of antioxidant vitamins and other non-nutritive substances:

**VITAMIN C**
Grapefruit, oranges, papaya, kiwifruit, green peppers, fresh currants, canteloupe and broccoli

**VITAMIN E**
Sunflower seeds, wheat germ, fortified cereals, assorted nuts, olive oil, polyunsaturated vegetable oils such as sunflower or corn oil and dried apricots

**BETA CAROTENE**
Carrots, sweet potatoes, yellow squash, spinach, kale and cantaloupe

## Folate

New research indicates that folate, one of the B vitamins, is very important in the few months before pregnancy and for the first month after conception. Increased folate at these times greatly reduces the risk of neural tube birth defects such as spina bifida. While it's helpful to choose foods that are high in folate, most women who are considering becoming pregnant may need more than their diet can provide. These women are advised to speak to their dietitian or physician about a folic acid supplement.

Foods high in folate include dark green vegetables (broccoli, spinach, peas), corn, dried peas, beans and lentils, melons, oranges and orange juice.

## Should You Take Supplements?

Not necessarily. All the fibre supplements or pills in the world won't make up for a high-fat, high-salt diet that's lacking enough vegetables and fruit. Also they don't contain all the trace nutrients and fibre that your body needs to stay healthy or the non-nutritive substances found in high-fibre foods that may act as protective agents. Until we know for sure exactly what it is in these high-fibre foods that may act as protective agents, we should be eating the foods, not taking supplements.

While there's no harm for most of us in taking one multivitamin pill a day, there are potential toxic effects from taking some supplements in too large an amount (especially vitamin A and D). Also, until we have more proof that supplemental amounts of the antioxidant vitamins (beta carotene, vitamins C and E) or fibre supplements are beneficial, you should rely on food sources of these nutrients, such as vegetables and fruit.

Some supplements may benefit certain groups in the population such as preconceptual and pregnant women who have increased nutrient needs. Seniors who contract a lot of infections may need supplements to improve their nutritional status. There is some concern that people on a very low-fat diet may not get enough vitamin E. People who think they need supplements should check with their dietitian or physician for advice.

The best way to get all the vitamins you need is to follow Canada's Food Guide to Healthy Eating (see pages 246 to 247)—emphasizing vegetables, fruit and grain products and eating a variety of foods from each of the four food groups each day.

# DIETING — WHO NEEDS IT!

Dieting for many people is a short-term solution to help them lose weight, but it may cause long-term problems with weight gain. The reason— diets don't work. About 95% of people who lose weight regain it within 5 years and that weight gain is often higher than it was before. You don't need a special diet to help you attain or maintain a healthy weight. In fact, if you're dieting now, you should stop and take a new approach to eating and thinking about your weight.

Most often diets restrict caloric intake and offer only limited choices of foods. Because of that people get bored and feel deprived and return to their ususal way of eating. The key is to modify some of your usual food choices to a healthier eating pattern, make changes that you can follow for a lifetime and make physical activity part of your daily life.

## Body Mass Index (BMI)

Many people don't realize that they may already be at a healthy weight, and there really is no need for them to lose weight at all. Health experts now use the Body Mass Index (BMI) to determine healthy weights, but it is not intended to be used with children, pregnant and breast-feeding women, highly muscular people or people over the age of 65. To find out your BMI, follow these steps.

$$BMI = Body\ Weight\ (kg) \div Height\ (metres)^2$$
Example: For a person who is 140 lb and 5'6":

1. Find out your weight in kilograms (divide weight in pounds by 2.2).
   $140 \div 2.2 = 63.64$

2. Find out your height in metres (multiply height in inches by 0.025).
   $66 \times 0.025 = 1.65$

3. Multiply your height in metres by itself to square it.
   $1.65 \times 1.65 = 2.72$

4. Divide weight in kilograms by height in metres squared.
   $63.64 \div 2.72 = 23.39$

**HOW DOES YOUR BMI RATE?**

BMI 20: May contribute to health problems due to being underweight.

BMI 20 - 25: Good, this is a healthy weight range.

BMI 25 - 27: Caution. Watch your weight. A BMI like this may lead to health problems for some people.

BMI above 27: The higher your BMI goes above 27, the greater your risk of developing health problems such as heart disease, some cancers, diabetes and high blood pressure.

*Tips to Maintaining a Healthy Weight*

1. Follow Canada's Food Guide to Healthy Eating and pay special attention to the serving sizes it recommends. Part of healthy eating means choosing foods in appropriate amounts.

2. Follow the "Tips to Cut Back on Fat" on page 19.

3. Keep physically active. Participating in some form of physical activity every day can help you control your weight. It also benefits your heart, lungs and muscles. Choose activities that can become part of your regular day, such as walking, and those that you can do well into your later years, such as hiking, swimming and cycling.

By eating well, being active and feeling positive about who you are and how you look, you should be able to throw away the diet books forever.

# SHOPPING AND EATING OUT

Whether you are shopping for foods or eating out, it is important to make sure that your food choices follow healthy eating guidelines. Aim for foods that are lower in fat and sodium. Choose these foods more often:
   • whole grain and enriched products;
   • green and orange vegetables and orange fruit;
   • lower-fat milk products; and
   • leaner meats, poultry, fish, dried peas, beans and lentils.

## Shopping Means Reading Labels

Checking the information on a food label is the best way to find out what's inside. For example, labels can tell you if a food contains whole grain or enriched flour, provides hydrogenated or saturated fat, or if it is high in salt or sodium. Here's what you'll find on a food label:

### INGREDIENT LIST

Every packaged food must contain a list of the ingredients. They are listed in decreasing order by weight. If you are looking for a whole wheat bread, that means choosing one that has whole wheat flour listed first.

### CLAIMS (SUCH AS "LOW FAT," "HIGH FIBRE," "LOW SALT")

Nutrition claims are used on food packages to point out a key nutrition feature of the food. These claims are defined and regulated by the government. For example, foods labelled

- "low in fat" must contain less than 3 g of fat per serving;

- "high source of fibre" must contain at least 4 g of dietary fibre per serving;

- "source of/contains" (for a vitamin or mineral) must contain at least 5% of the recommended daily intake per serving.

Most claims can help you choose healthier foods, such as the ones that say low in fat or sodium. Other claims may be misleading and you should watch out for them. For example, potato chips may claim to contain no cholesterol, but the small print on the nutritional information panel tells you that they do contain fat.

When a claim is made, information will be given on how much of that nutrient is in a serving of that food.

### NUTRITION INFORMATION PANEL

The nutrition information panel is optional information on food labels. This panel tells you the nutrient content for a single serving of food. It can help you figure out how many grams of fat or how much sodium there is in a product. Check the serving size and compare to what you normally eat.

## Eating Out

Eating out can challenge your skill at maintaining a healthy eating pattern, but it can be done. If you eat out regularly:

- be sure to choose places that offer a variety of lower-fat, higher-fibre choices for a variety of foods;

- be sure to get enough vegetables and fruits—if eating lunches out every day you may have to bring some from home;

- avoid menu items that have been deep-fried, or are served with high-fat salad dressings or rich sauces;

- don't hesitate to ask for the lower-fat dressing (ie. buttermilk dressing), grilled rather than fried items and for a lower-fat sauce;

- remember moderation and balance are the keys to healthy eating. If you do have some high-fat foods, choose smaller amounts or balance them by making lower-fat choices at your other meals.

# WHERE TO GO FOR HELP

If you want more information on Canada's Food Guide to Healthy Eating, you can get it, and pamphlets called Using the Food Guide and Using Food Labels to Choose Foods for Healthy Eating free from your community health unit or by contacting Publications, Health Canada, Ottawa, K1A OK9. Excellent pamphlets on healthy eating are also available from your local Cancer Society or Heart and Stroke Foundation offices.

For more information on nutrition and healthy eating, or nutrition advice, contact the public health nutritionist or dietitian at your community public health unit (listed in the blue pages of your phone book). You can also contact your community hospital and ask to speak to the outpatient dietitian. Dietitians are the professional choice for nutritional advice.

## About the Nutritional Information on the Recipes

Unless otherwise stated, the recipes were tested and analyzed using 2% milk, 1.5% yogurt, 2% cottage cheese and 17% fat hard cheeses because these are the most commonly available. However, you can save even more on fat and calories by substituting lower-fat choices. Ground meat was assumed to be completely browned and thoroughly drained. Calculations of meat and poultry recipes, including those where fat or skin was not removed before cooking, assumed that only the lean portion was eaten. Calculations were based on the first ingredient listed where there was a choice and did not include optional ingredients. Unspecified amounts of salt (pinch or to taste) were not included in the analysis.

Nutrient values greater than 0.4 were rounded to the nearest whole number. Following criteria outlined in the *Guide for Food Manufacturers and Advertisers, Revised Edition 1988* (Consumer and Corporate Affairs), the recipes were also evaluated as sources of vitamins A and C, folate, iron and calcium. Other vitamins and minerals were not evaluated.

**Fibre:** It is recommended that we have 25 to 35 grams of fibre each day.
**Sodium:** Canadians consume too much sodium and lower levels of intake are recommended. Most of the recipes in this book are relatively low in sodium; where the levels are high, suggestions for reducing the sodium have been given to help those on sodium-restricted diets.
**Potassium:** Potassium is thought to have a positive effect on hypertension and strokes. A diet promoting foods high in potassium, emphasizing fruits and vegetables is recommended.

---

### DAILY TOTAL PROTEIN, FAT AND CARBOHYDRATE INTAKE
(based on 15% of calories from protein, 30% of calories from fat and 55% of calories from carbohydrate)
according to *Nutrition Recommendations for Adult Canadians*, Health and Welfare Canada, 1990.

| Calories /day | Protein (g) | Fat (g) | Carbohydrate (g) |
|---|---|---|---|
| 1800 | 68 | 60 | 248 |
| 2100 | 79 | 70 | 289 |
| 2300 | 86 | 77 | 316 |
| 2600 | 98 | 87 | 357 |
| 2900 | 109 | 97 | 399 |
| 3200 | 120 | 107 | 440 |

ANNE LINDSAY AND LYNN ROBLIN, DECEMBER, 1993

# MENUS

*Nutritional information is based on servings as follows: appetizers, 2 pieces; milk, 2%, 8 oz (250 mL); breads, 1 slice with 1 tsp (5 mL) butter or margarine; salads with 1 tbsp (15 mL) dressing; vegetables, plain, ½ cup (125 mL) with ½ tsp (2 mL) butter or margarine; dips, spreads and dessert sauces, 2 tbsp (25 mL); cookies and squares, 1 piece; fruit, ½ cup (125 mL) or 1 piece; ice cream, 5-7% b.f., ½ cup (125 mL); open-faced sandwiches, ½ of each type. See notes for children's and teens' parties on page 30.*

## Special Sunday Breakfast

Upside-Down Apple Pancake *(page 198)*

Apricot, Orange and Fig Compote *(page 235)*

Citrus Double Bran Muffin *(page 200)*

*Calories 501; Total Fat 13 g; % Calories from Fat 23*

---

## Fall or Winter Brunch

Hot Spiced Cider *(page 54)*

Crustless Vegetable Quiche *(page 190)*
Green Bean Salad with Buttermilk Dressing
*(page 79)*
Cherry tomatoes
Jalapeño Cornmeal Muffin *(page 201)*
OR Lemon Poppyseed Muffin *(page 202)*
Deep Dish Pear Pie with Apricots and Ginger
*(page 228)*

*Calories 730; Total Fat 23 g; % Calories from Fat 29*

---

## Spring Luncheon

White Sangria Punch *(page 56)*
Seafood Pasta Salad *(page 172)*
Asparagus and Mushroom Salad *(page 78)*
Muesli Soda Bread *(page 205)*
Easy Berry Flan *(page 222)*

*Calories 730; Total Fat 17 g; % Calories from Fat 22*

---

## Summer Weekend Lunch

Pasta and Ham Salad *(page 171)*
Sliced cucumbers
Toasted bagels/Herbed Cheese Spread
*(page 38)*

Gingerbread Cake *(page 212)*
Apple Cinnamon Cookies *(page 210)*
Fresh strawberries

*Calories 834; Total Fat 21 g; % Calories from Fat 23*

## Lunch Around the Pool

Fruit Spritzers *(page 55)*

Open-Faced Sandwiches *(page 50)*

Nectarine and Orange Compote *(page 234)*

Apricot Streusel Cake *(page 211)*

*Calories 863; Total Fat 18 g ; % Calories from Fat 18*

---

## Fall Luncheon

Fish 'n' Vegetable Chowder *(page 69)*

Open-Faced Sandwiches *(page 50)*

Fruit platter (grapes,melon wedges,
strawberries, pear wedges)

Apple Cinnamon Cookies *(page 210)*
Light Lemon Squares *(page 208)*

*Calories 1022; Total Fat 27 g; % Calories from Fat 24*

---

## Winter Holiday Family Lunch for 12

Cheese and Tomato Quesadillas *(page 52)*

Italian Chick-Pea and Pasta Soup *(page 67)*

Platter of celery, carrots, zucchini strips

Muesli Soda Bread *(page 205)*

Pumpkin Spice Cake *(page 213)*
Tangerines/ice cream

*Calories 980; Total Fat 27 g; % Calories from Fat 25*

---

## Spring Dinner Party

Oriental Noodle and Chicken Soup *(page 63)*

Baked Whole Salmon with Mushrooms
and Artichokes *(page 116)*

Asparagus

Lemon Parsley Rice Pilaf *(page 181)*
OR Green Vegetable Risotto *(page 175)*

Rhubarb Fool with Fresh Strawberries
*(page 232)*

*Calories 750; Total Fat 22 g; % Calories from Fat 26*

## Summer Barbecue Dinner

Chilled Cucumber Mint Soup *(page 58)*

Thai Barbecued Turkey Scaloppine *(page 108)*
Grilled sweet red peppers and yellow zucchini
Tiny new potatoes with fresh dill

Nectarines, blueberries and raspberries
with Vanilla Cream *(page 239)*

*Calories 485; Total Fat 12 g; % Calories from Fat 22*

---

## Easy Barbecue Suppers

*Each meal includes 1 slice fresh bread,
and milk*

Barbecue Salmon Fillets *(page 115)*
Baby beets and greens
Sliced tomatoes with basil
New potatoes with fresh dill
Strawberries

*Calories 725; Total Fat 26 g; % Calories from Fat 32*

Barbecue Trout with Light Tartar Sauce
*(page 114)*
Barbecue Potato Packets *(page 150)*
Ginger Stir-Fried Zucchini *(page 147)*
New carrots with fresh dill

*Calories 831; Total Fat 29 g; % Calories from Fat 31*

Grilled Chicken Breast Burger with
Sun-Dried Tomatoes *(page 91)*
on whole wheat bun
Easy Couscous Vegetable Salad *(page 77)*
on a bed of lettuces
Peaches

*Calories 706; Total Fat 17 g; % Calories from Fat 22*

Chinese Chicken Burgers *(page 90)*
Corn-on-the-cob
Tossed Green Salad with
Tomato Basil Dressing *(page 86)*

Ice Cream
Orange Hazelnut Biscotti *(page 209)*

*Calories 816; Total Fat 27 g; % Calories from Fat 30*

Barbecued Curried Chicken Breast *(page 100)*
Lemon Parsley Rice Pilaf *(page 181)*
Green beans
Sliced tomatoes

Apples
Cheese (1 oz/30 g 17% b.f.)

*Calories 701; Total Fat 22 g; % Calories from Fat 28*

## Easy Family Menus Following Canada's Food Guide

Chinese Chicken Burgers *(page 90)*
in hamburger bun
Purple Vegetable Slaw *(page 83)*
Sliced Tomato

Apple

Milk

*Calories 691; Total Fat 22 g; % Calories from Fat 28*

Potato, Bean and Tomato Stew *(page 187)*
Easy Couscous Vegetable Salad *(page 77)*
Whole wheat bread
Orange

Milk

*Calories 778; Total Fat 23 g; % Calories from Fat 26*

Thai Noodles with
Chicken and Broccoli *(page 167)*
Sesame Carrots *(page 142)*

Strawberries

Milk

*Calories 716; Total Fat 23 g; % Calories from Fat 29*

Lemon Tarragon Sole Fillets *(page 111)*
Bulgur with Red Onion and Pimiento
*(page 182)*
Spinach with Lemon and Nutmeg *(page 146)*
Tossed Salad Greens with
Mustard Garlic Vinaigrette *(page 88)*

Kiwifruit

Milk

*Calories 570; Total Fat 19 g; % Calories from Fat 30*

---

## Summer Make-Ahead Buffet For a Crowd

Chinese Chicken Balls
with Dipping Sauces *(page 41)*
Clam Dip with Herbs and Crudités *(page 35)*

Thai Pork Skewers *(page 49)* AND/OR
Garlic-Soy Marinated Beef Strips *(page 123)*
Grilled Salmon Ribbons with Sesame
and Coriander *(page 48)*
Spicy Noodle Salad *(page 169)*
Oriental Coleslaw *(page 82)*
Couscous, Tomato and Basil Salad *(page 77)*

Fresh Plum Flan *(page 223)*

*Calories 873; Total Fat 29 g; % Calories from Fat 30*

## Make-Your-Own Summer Pizza Party

White Sangria Punch *(page 56)*

Goat Cheese and Pesto Tortilla Pizzas *(page 47)*

Easy Berry Flan *(page 222)*

*Calories 513; Total Fat 17 g; % Calories from Fat 29*

---

## End-of-Summer Dinner

Chilled Purée of Tomato Soup
with Basil *(page 59)*

Herb and Buttermilk Barbecued Chicken
*(page 93)*
Portobello Mushrooms
with Sweet Peppers *(page 148)*
Barley and Corn Casserole *(page 185)*

Amaretto Custard Sauce *(page 238)*
over sliced peaches

*Calories 492; Total Fat 15 g; % Calories from Fat 27*

---

## Summer/Fall Vegetarian Dinner

Fresh Tomato Pizza *(page 45)*

Marinated Baked Tofu *(page 191)* served on
Purple Vegetable Slaw *(page 83)*
Jiffy Chinese Noodles *(page 164)*

Fresh Plum Flan *(page 223)*

*Calories 1012; Total Fat 31 g; % Calories from Fat 27*

---

## Fall Dinner Party Menu

Thai Shrimp Salad in Pita (4 each) *(page 43)*
Hot and Sour Soup *(page 62)*

Honey-Garlic Roast Pork *(page 135)*
Rice with Black Beans and Ginger *(page 180)*
Sherried Green Beans with Sweet Peppers
*(page 144)*

Apple-Pecan Phyllo Crisps *(page 225)*

*Calories 831; Total Fat 28 g; % Calories from Fat 30*

---

## Make-Ahead Winter Dinner Party

Leek and Mushroom Soup *(page 61)*

Moroccan Rabbit Tagine *(page 140)*
Quick and Easy Spiced Couscous *(page 189)*

Lemon Mousse with Raspberry Sauce *(page 221)*

*Calories 1019; Total Fat 27 g; % Calories from Fat 24*

---

## Winter Sunday Dinner

Chicken and Vegetable Stew with
Parsley Dumplings *(page 101)*
Buttermilk Mashed Potatoes *(page 151)*

Baked Pear Bread Pudding with
Honey Almond Sauce *(page 224)*

*Calories 1040; Total Fat 18 g; % Calories from Fat 16*

---

## Winter Vegetarian Dinner Party

Cheese and Tomato Quesadillas *(page 52)*

Winter Vegetable Curry with Couscous
*(page 188)*
Tossed Green Salad with
Yogurt Herb Dressing *(page 87)*

Chocolate Marbled Cheesecake *(page 219)*

*Calories 840; Total Fat 25 g; % Calories from Fat 26*

---

## Make-Ahead Winter Buffet

Clam Dip with Herbs *(page 35)* and crudités

Shrimp and Chicken Jambalaya *(page 118)*

Salad Greens with Mustard Garlic Vinaigrette
*(page 88)*

Whole wheat rolls

Deep Dish Pear Pie with Apricots and Ginger
*(page 228)*

*Calories 941; Total Fat 21 g; % Calories from Fat 20*

---

## Ski Chalet Dinner with Teens

Carrot and Corn Chowder *(page 68)*

Chalupas *(page 132)*

Chocolate Mocha Ice Cream Pie
*(page 218)*

*Calories 1050; Total Fat 22 g; % Calories from Fat 19*

---

## After-Bridge Supper

Salmon Salad Fajitas *(page 120)*

Elizabeth Baird's Chocolate Angel Food Cake
*(page 214)*

*Calories 494; Total Fat 16 g; % Calories from Fat 30*

## Cookbook Cover Photo Dinner

Hoisin Sesame Chicken Platter *(page 96)*

Chinese Vegetable Fried Rice (omit ham)
*(page 198)*

French bread

Easy Berry Flan *(page 222)* and
Nectarine and Orange Compote *(page 234)*

*Calories 988; Total Fat 21 g; % Calories from Fat 19*

---

## Easy But Different Dinner Party

Hot and Sour Soup *(page 62)*

Asian Chicken *(page 98)*

Light Lemon Squares *(page 208)*
Nectarine and Orange Compote *(page 234)*

*Calories 759; Total Fat 13 g; % Calories from Fat 15*

---

## Children's or Teens' Party[1]

Jiffy Salsa Dip *(page 34)* with raw veggies

Chicken Fingers *(page 40)* with
Apricot Dipping Sauce *(page 41)*

Herbed Cheese Spread *(page 38)*
on Crostini *(page 39)*

Tortilla Pizza Triangles *(page 46)*

Candied Corn *(page 53)*
Make-Your-Own Ice Cream Sundaes
with Three Sauces
Chocolate Sauce *(page 217)*,
Butterscotch Sauce *(page 240)*,
Raspberry Sauce *(page 221)*

*Calories 985; Total Fat 28 g; % Calories from Fat 25*

---

## Teenagers' Buffet Birthday Dinner[2]

Garlic-Soy Marinated Beef Strips *(page 123)*

Spicy Noodle Salad *(page 169)*
OR Jiffy Chinese Noodles *(page 164)*

Caesar salad

Hot herb bread or buns

Orange Chocolate Refrigerator Cake *(page 220)*

*Calories 897; Total Fat 31 g; % Calories from Fat 31*

---

## Special Birthday Dinner

Seafood Vegetable Chowder *(page 69)*

Beef Filet with Mustard Peppercorn Crust
*(page 129)*
Asparagus or green beans
Portobello Mushrooms with
Sweet Red Peppers *(page 148)*
Quick and Easy Spiced Couscous *(page 189)*
OR new potatoes with dill

Elizabeth Baird's Chocolate Angel Food Cake
*(page 214)*
with Vanilla Cream *(page 239)* and strawberries

*Calories 1036; Total Fat 25 g; % Calories from Fat 22*

---

## Buffet Dinner for 24

Sun-Dried Tomato and Onion Toasts
*(page 44)*
Roasted Eggplant Dip *(page 37)* with crudités
Lemon Grass Marinated Leg of Lamb
*(page 137)*
Make-Ahead Party Thai Noodles
*(page 165)*
Snow Peas with Mushrooms *(page 143)*
Tossed Green Salad with Asian Vinaigrette
*(page 85)*
Meringues with Lemon Cream *(page 230)*

*Calories 800; Total Fat 21 g; % Calories from Fat 24*

---

## Cocktail Party

Thai Shrimp Salad in Mini Pitas *(page 43)*
Chinese Chicken Balls with Dipping Sauces
*(page 41)*
Mushrooms AND/OR cherry tomatoes stuffed
with Herbed Cheese Spread *(page 38)*
Sun-Dried Tomato and Onion Toasts
*(page 44)*
Goat Cheese and Pesto Tortilla Pizza Triangles
*(page 47)*
Roasted Red Pepper and Basil Dip *(page 36)*
with crudités
Smoked Turkey-Wrapped Melon Balls
*(page 42)*

*Calories 411; Total Fat 15 g; % Calories from Fat 32*

---

[1] *Nutritional information based on: 8 pieces of chicken; 8 pieces pizza triangles; 1 cup (250 mL) candied corn; ¾ cup (175 mL) ice cream; 1 tbsp (15 mL) each sauce.*

[2] *Nutritional information based on: 2 servings beef strips; light dressing on Caesar salad.*

## Easy Friday Night Dinner

Miso Soup with Tofu *(page 64)*

Linguine with Scallops and Leeks *(page 161)*
OR Summer Shrimp and Tomato Pasta
*(page 160)*

Whole wheat French bread

Berries with Orange Cream *(page 236)*

*Calories 978; Total Fat 20 g; % Calories from Fat 19*

---

## Holiday Family Reunion Dinner

Jiffy Salsa Dip *(page 34)* with vegetables

Chutney-Glazed Ham *(page 136)*
Rosemary Garlic Roasted Potatoes *(page 150)*
Sesame Broccoli and Carrots *(page 142)*
Tossed Salad with Yogurt Herb Dressing
*(page 87)*

Gingerbread Cake *(page 212)* with fresh fruit
and Vanilla Cream *(page 239)* or frozen yogurt

*Calories 682; Total Fat 19 g; % Calories from Fat 24*

---

## New Year's Eve Dinner Party

Warm Scallop Salad *(page 73)*

Sherry Chicken Breasts Stuffed with
Zucchini and Carrots *(page 94)*
Spinach with Lemon and Nutmeg *(page 146)*
Sweet Potato and Apple Purée *(page 152)*

Chocolate Crêpes with Banana Cream Filling
and Chocolate Sauce *(page 216)*

*Calories 889; Total Fat 26 g; % Calories from Fat 27*

## Thanksgiving or Christmas Dinner

Cranberry Lime Punch *(page 56)*

Crudités and Clam Dip with Herbs
*(page 35)*

Thai Shrimp Salad in Pita Pockets *(page 43)*

Roast Turkey with Giblet Gravy *(page 104)*
Sausage Apple and Herb Stuffing
*(page 105)*
Buttermilk Mashed Potatoes *(page 151)*
Sweet Potato and Apple Purée *(page 152)*
Green Beans with Herbs and Pine Nuts
*(page 145)*

Pumpkin Pie with Orange Yogurt Cream
*(page 226)*
OR Winter Berry Trifle *(page 229)*

*Calories 1062; Total Fat 27 g; % Calories from Fat 23*

---

## Christmas Eve Dinner

Herbed Cheese Spread *(page 38)* with
melba toasts (top with slice of smoked salmon)

Pork Tenderloin Teriyaki *(page 130)*
OR Honey-Garlic Roast Pork *(page 135)*

Bulgur with Red Onion and Pimiento
*(page 182)*
OR Barley and Corn Casserole *(page 185)*
OR Make-Ahead Party Thai Noodles
*(page 165)*

Broccoli or Green Beans or Snow Peas with
Mushrooms *(page 143)*

Chocolate Mocha Ice Cream Pie *(page 218)*

*Calories 806; Total Fat 23 g; % Calories from Fat 26*

# INFORMATION ON INGREDIENTS

### CHILI PASTE OR SAUCE
Used in Asian cooking, red in color and made from chili peppers, salt and often garlic, this adds hotness to dishes. I use the Indonesian chili paste called *sambal oelek*; Chinese chili sauce or Thai chili paste are others to use.

### CHILI PEPPERS
Canadians are enjoying chili peppers— fresh, canned and bottled—on everything from pizza to pasta and Mexican to Thai cooking. Start with green chili, the mildest, work your way up to jalapeño and serrano. When your mouth can stand it and you want some punishment, try Scotch Bonnet, the hottest.

### CILANTRO OR CORIANDER
Cilantro is the leaf part of the coriander plant. Often called Chinese parsley or fresh coriander, it has a distinct, pungent flavor that most people either love or hate. It is available in many supermarkets and most greengrocers. The dry leaf cilantro is not a good substitute.

### FISH SAUCE
This staple in Thai and Vietnamese cooking has a salty taste and awful smell but adds wonderful flavor to sauces. You'll find it, bottled, in Oriental and specialty food stores and in some supermarkets.

### GARLIC
Because garlic cloves vary so much in size, I give a measure in teaspoons of chopped garlic rather than the number of cloves if I use more than one clove in a recipe. I do not suggest that you use bottled chopped garlic; fresh chopped garlic is much superior. If you would rather not measure, just estimate one medium-large clove per teaspoon (5 mL) of chopped garlic.

### GINGER
Fresh gingerroot adds wonderful flavor to vegetables, salads, sauces, stir-frys and marinades. Buy smooth, shiny, firm gingerroot; not shrivelled or mouldy. Peel the ginger with a vegetable peeler or paring knife. Dried powdered ginger is a poor substitute.

### HOISIN SAUCE
Made from soybeans, vinegar, sugar and spices, this thick brown sauce adds flavor and a touch of sweetness to dishes. It is available bottled or canned.

### LEMON GRASS
This contributes a wonderful lemon flavor to dishes and is becoming more easily available at greengrocers and Asian markets in Canada's bigger cities. Fresh lemon grass has pale green straw-textured stalks about the size of green onions. The top two-thirds and outer leaves are discarded. Dried lemon grass is sold in bags at some markets; soak in hot water for 15 minutes before using.

### OYSTER SAUCE
Made from oysters and soy sauce but without a fishy taste, this thick brown sauce is used in Chinese dishes. It is sold bottled in Chinese grocery stores and some supermarkets.

### SESAME OIL
A dark, strong-flavored oil made from roasted sesame seeds, this is used in small amounts to add wonderful flavor to stir-fries, vegetable dishes, salad dressings and marinades. Don't buy the light sesame oil as it is light in flavor, not in fat; instead buy ones from Asia.

*Goat Cheese and Pesto Tortilla Pizza (page 47)*

# APPETIZERS, SNACKS AND BEVERAGES

Jiffy Salsa Dip

Clam Dip with Herbs

Roasted Red Pepper and Fresh Basil Dip

Roasted Eggplant Dip

Herbed Cheese Spread

Crostini

Chicken Fingers

Chinese Chicken Balls with Dipping Sauces

Smoked Turkey-Wrapped Melon Balls

Thai Shrimp Salad in Mini Pita Pockets

Sun-Dried Tomato and Onion Toasts

Fresh Tomato Pizza

Tortilla Pizza Triangles

Goat Cheese and Pesto Tortilla Pizzas

Grilled Salmon Ribbons with Sesame and Coriander

Thai Pork Skewers

Open-Faced Sandwiches

Cheese and Tomato Quesadillas

Spicy Popcorn

Candied Corn

Tofu Blender Drink

Hot Spiced Cider

Fruit Spritzers

White Sangria Punch

Cranberry Lime Christmas Eve Punch

Salmon Salad Fajitas (page 120)

# Jiffy Salsa Dip

*This easy-to-make dip is one-quarter the fat and calories of a cream cheese (or sour cream) and packaged onion soup mix combination.*

## Salsa

Sometimes I chop a tomato, some cucumber and fresh cilantro (coriander leaves) and add to bought salsa.

When I have time I make my own:

Finely chop and combine: 1 large tomato, 1 cup (250 mL) cucumber, 1 green (mild) or jalapeño (hot) pepper, 2 tbsp (25 mL) onion, 1 tbsp (15 mL) wine vinegar, chopped fresh coriander leaves to taste and one small clove garlic. Makes 2 cups (500 mL).

| ½ cup | salsa | 125 mL |
| ½ cup | light sour cream | 125 mL |
| ¼ cup | chopped fresh coriander | 50 mL |

**1.** In small bowl, stir together salsa, sour cream and coriander. **Makes about 1 cup (250 mL).**

**MAKE AHEAD:** Dip can be covered and refrigerated for up to two days.

## Low-Fat Dips

Check out your local stores for low-fat dips to keep on hand: look for tzatziki (yogurt, cucumber and garlic), salsa or puréed sweet red peppers.

*PER SERVING (1 TBSP/15 ML):*

11 calories

1 g protein

1 g total fat
    0 g saturated fat
    2 mg cholesterol

1 g carbohydrate
    0 g dietary fibre

51 mg sodium

44 mg potassium

| DIP BASES | | |
|---|---|---|
| **Compare 1 cup (250 mL):** | **Fat (g)** | **Calories** |
| Yogurt (1.5% b.f.) | 4 | 154 |
| Cottage cheese (1.5%) | 4 | 202 |
| Sour cream (1%) | 3 | 253 |
| Light sour cream (7%) | 16 | 277 |
| Regular sour cream (14%) | 32 | 351 |
| Light cream cheese (23%) | 53 | 572 |
| Cream cheese (35%) | 81 | 809 |
| Light mayonnaise | 73 | 726 |
| Mayonnaise | 176 | 1604 |

# Clam Dip with Herbs

*This lightened-up version of an old favorite is much lower in fat and calories than a dip made with cream cheese, sour cream or mayonnaise — yet is just as good. Serve with vegetables for dipping.*

| 1 cup | low-fat cottage cheese* | 250 mL |
|---|---|---|
| 1 | can (142 g) clams | 1 |
| ¼ cup | chopped fresh parsley | 50 mL |
| 3 tbsp | low-fat yogurt* | 50 mL |
| 2 tbsp | coarsely chopped fresh basil or dill (or 1 tsp/5 mL dried basil or dillweed) | 25 mL |
| 1 tbsp | minced onion | 15 mL |
| 1 tbsp | lemon juice | 15 mL |
| Dash | hot pepper sauce | Dash |

**1.** In blender or food processor, blend cottage cheese until smooth.

**2.** Drain clams, reserving 1 tbsp (15 mL) liquid.

**3.** In bowl, combine cottage cheese, clams, parsley, yogurt, basil, onion, lemon juice, reserved clam juice and hot pepper sauce.

**4.** Cover and refrigerate for at least 1 hour. **Makes about 2 cups (500 mL).**

* Nutrient information is based on cottage cheese and yogurt with 2% b.f. (butterfat).

**MAKE AHEAD:** Dip can be refrigerated for up to two days.

*PER SERVING (1 TBSP/15 ML):*

11 calories
2 g protein
0.2 g total fat
    0.1 g saturated fat
    2 mg cholesterol
1 g carbohydrate
    0 g dietary fibre
33 mg sodium
28 mg potassium

# Roasted Red Pepper and Fresh Basil Dip

*Serve this delicious dip in the fall when red peppers are plentiful and fresh basil is easy to find.*

| 2 | sweet red peppers | 2 |
|---|---|---|
| ⅓ cup | light ricotta cheese | 75 mL |
| ⅓ cup | soft goat cheese (chèvre) | 75 mL |
| ⅓ cup | chopped fresh basil* | 75 mL |
| Pinch | cayenne pepper | Pinch |
| | Salt and pepper | |

**1.** On baking sheet, bake red peppers in 400°F (200°C) oven for 30 minutes, turning once or twice, or until peppers are blackened and blistered. (Or barbecue until blistered.) Let cool and scrape off skin; discard seeds. Purée in food processor until smooth to make almost ¾ cup (175 mL).

**2.** Add ricotta cheese, goat cheese, basil and cayenne pepper; process until well blended. Season with salt and pepper to taste. **Makes 1½ cups (375 mL).**

\* If you can't find fresh basil, substitute ⅓ cup (75 mL) chopped fresh parsley, and ½ tsp (2 mL) dried basil or more to taste.

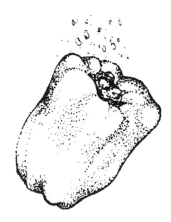

## Stuffed Mushrooms

Prepare dip recipe. Wash mushrooms quickly in small amount of water; dry on towels. Remove stems and spoon about 1 tsp (5 mL) dip into each cavity. Cover and refrigerate for up to 4 hours. Makes 72 pieces.

*PER SERVING (1 TBSP/15 mL):*

19 calories
1 g protein
1 g total fat
   1 g saturated fat
   4 mg cholesterol
1 g carbohydrate
   0.2 g dietary fibre
24 mg sodium
23 mg potassium

**MAKE AHEAD:** Dip can be covered and refrigerated for up to two days.

# Roasted Eggplant Dip

*For the best flavor, barbecue the eggplant. Eggplant can be baked in the oven, but don't microwave it for this recipe. Garnish with sprigs of parsley and serve with small pita rounds or raw vegetables for dippers.*

| | | |
|---|---|---:|
| ½ cup | low-fat yogurt (no gelatin) (or ¼ cup/50 mL light sour cream) | 125 mL |
| 2 | medium eggplants (each 1 lb/500 g) | 2 |
| ¼ cup | chopped fresh parsley | 50 mL |
| 3 tbsp | lemon juice | 50 mL |
| 2 | green onions, minced | 2 |
| 1 | clove garlic, minced | 1 |
| 1 tsp | sesame oil or olive oil | 5 mL |
| ½ tsp | each ground cumin and salt | 2 mL |
| | Pepper | |

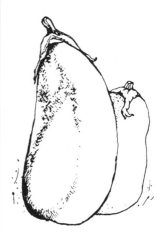

**1.** In cheesecloth-lined sieve set over bowl, drain yogurt in refrigerator for 4 hours or until yogurt is ¼ cup (50 mL). Discard liquid. (Do not drain light sour cream or extra-thick yogurt.)

**2.** Prick eggplants with fork. Grill over high heat for 1 hour or until black and blistered. (Or bake on baking sheet in 400°F/200°C oven for 40 to 45 minutes or until softened, turning once during baking.) Cut in half and drain; scoop out flesh. Purée in food processor or mash until smooth to make about 1½ cups (375 mL).

**3.** Stir in yogurt, parsley, lemon juice, onions, garlic, sesame oil, cumin, salt, and pepper to taste. Transfer to serving dish. **Makes 2 cups (500 mL).**

**MAKE AHEAD:** Dip can be covered and refrigerated for up to two days.

*PER SERVING (1 TBSP/15 ML):*

10 calories
0.4 g protein
0.3 g total fat
    0.1 g saturated fat
    0 mg cholesterol
2 g carbohydrate
    1 g dietary fibre
39 mg sodium
67 mg potassium

# Herbed Cheese Spread

### Herbed Cheese Mushrooms

Remove stems from mushrooms. Spoon Herbed Cheese Spread into caps. Garnish with a strip of smoked salmon, tiny shrimp or a sprig of fresh herb. Makes about 50 pieces.

### Yogurt Herbed Cheese Spread

Instead of quark, use 1 cup (250 mL) extra-thick or pressed yogurt or 2 cups (500 mL) low-fat yogurt and 1 cup (250 mL) low-fat cottage cheese. Drain regular yogurt in cheesecloth-lined sieve set over bowl in refrigerator for 4 hours or until 1 cup (250 mL). Discard liquid. Press cottage cheese through sieve into bowl. Stir in 1 tbsp (15 mL) lemon juice, drained yogurt and fresh herbs and garlic as in recipe.

*PER SERVING*
*(1 TBSP/15 ML):*

19 calories
2 g protein
1 g total fat
   1 g saturated fat
   4 mg cholesterol
1 g carbohydrate
   0 g dietary fibre
36 mg sodium
5 mg potassium

*Quark, a low-fat soft cheese, is an ideal base for this herbed spread. If it's unavailable, use the yogurt variation described in the margin. Spread this on Crostini (page 39) or melba toast rounds and garnish with a thin strip of red pepper and a sprig of fresh basil or dill. Or spoon it into cherry tomatoes or endive spears.*

| | | |
|---|---|---|
| 2 cups | plain quark (7% b.f.) | 500 mL |
| ¼ cup | chopped fresh parsley | 50 mL |
| ¼ cup | chopped fresh dill or basil | 50 mL |
| 2 | small cloves garlic, minced | 2 |
| 2 tbsp | chopped chives or green onions | 25 mL |
| ½ tsp | salt | 2 mL |
| | Pepper | |

**1.** In bowl, combine quark, parsley, dill, garlic, chives, salt, and pepper to taste; mix well. **Makes 2 cups (500 mL).**

**MAKE AHEAD:** Spread can be covered and refrigerated for up to two days.

---

**ABOUT QUARK**

Quark is a creamy, smooth, unripened soft cheese. It is a fresh cultured product that, depending on how it is made and packaged, can have a shelf life in the refrigerator of up to 6 months. It can be used in dips, spreads and baked desserts. It ranges in fat content from 7% or higher to less than 1%. The lower-fat variety can sometimes have a slightly bitter taste. Quark is available at some supermarkets, cheese stores, delicatessens and dairies. Use the plain, not the flavored, variety in recipes.

# Crostini

*Crostini are Italian-style toasted bread rounds and are a nice change from crackers to top with your favorite spread. They vary slightly from one area of Italy to another. For a fat-restricted diet, omit oil and simply rub toasted bread rounds with cut clove of garlic.*

| | | |
|---|---|---|
| 1 tbsp | olive oil | 15 mL |
| 1 | small clove garlic, minced | 1 |
| 1 | baguette (French bread stick) | 1 |

**1.** Combine oil and garlic; set aside.

**2.** Cut bread into ½-inch (1 cm) thick slices (if large, cut slices in half); place on baking sheet.

**3.** Brush with oil and toast in 350°F (180°C) oven for 5 to 8 minutes or until crisp. **Makes about 36 slices**.

**MAKE AHEAD:** Crostini can be covered and stored at room temperature for up to three days.

---

### USE LEANER SPREADS ON YOUR BREAD

Compare the calories and fat in these spreads with those in butter.

| 1 tbsp (15 mL): | Calories | Fat (g) | Protein (g) |
|---|---|---|---|
| 1% b.f. cottage cheese | 12 | trace | 2 |
| Skim-milk process cheese spread | 30 | 1 | 4 |
| Light cream cheese | 36 | 3 | 1 |
| Cheddar process cheese spread | 46 | 3 | 3 |
| Cream cheese | 51 | 5 | 1 |
| Jelly or jam | 54 | 0 | 0 |
| Peanut butter | 93 | 8 | 4 |
| Butter or margarine | 101 | 11 | trace |

---

### *Eating Out: Best Nutritional Bets for Fast Food*

*At fast food chains*
- Chili
- Burger (keep it regular-size and skip the cheese, "special sauce" and bacon)
- Broiled or grilled chicken sandwich
- Pizza with vegetable toppings and small amount of cheese
- Submarine sandwich with lean turkey or ham (not salami), lower-fat dressing, all the vegetables you want but no spread
- Burrito or tostada with vegetables (skip the sour cream, avocado and guacamole)
- Frozen yogurt, milk

*At salad bars*
- Spinach, vegetables, chick-peas, bean salad, light dressing
- Fresh fruit salad

*At delis*
- Sandwiches: sliced turkey, chicken, beef, on whole wheat with tomato, cucumber or sprouts (skip the butter and mayo)
- Soups

PER SERVING (1 SLICE):
- 31 calories
- 1 g protein
- 1 g total fat
  - 0.1 g saturated fat
  - 0 mg cholesterol
- 5 g carbohydrate
  - 0.2 g dietary fibre
- 55 mg sodium
- 9 mg potassium

# Chicken Fingers

*This is a hit with my teenagers and their friends for snacks or a meal.*

| | | |
|---|---|---|
| ½ lb | boneless skinless chicken breasts | 250 g |
| 1 | small clove garlic, minced | 1 |
| ¼ cup | fine dry bread crumbs | 50 mL |
| 1 tbsp | freshly grated Parmesan cheese | 15 mL |
| 1 tbsp | finely chopped fresh parsley | 15 mL |
| ½ tsp | paprika | 2 mL |
| ¼ tsp | dried oregano | 1 mL |
| | Pepper | |
| ¼ cup | low-fat milk | 50 mL |

**1.** Cut chicken into 2½- x ½-inch (6 x 1 cm) strips.

**2.** Combine garlic, bread crumbs, cheese, parsley, paprika, oregano, and pepper to taste. Dip chicken into milk; roll in crumbs. Place in single layer on lightly greased baking sheet.

**3.** Bake in 425°F (220°C) oven for 5 minutes; turn and bake for 2 minutes longer or until chicken is no longer pink inside. Serve hot. **Makes 16 pieces.**

## Cajun Chicken Fingers

Follow recipe for Chicken Fingers but omit bread crumb mixture. Instead, use ¼ cup (50 mL) fine dry bread crumbs, ½ tsp (2 mL) each dried basil, oregano, thyme, pepper and dried parsley flakes, ¼ tsp (1 mL) each salt and onion and garlic powders.

*PER PIECE:*

27 calories

4 g protein

0.5 g total fat
    0.2 g saturated fat
    9 mg cholesterol

2 g carbohydrate
    0.1 g dietary fibre

31 mg sodium

50 mg potassium

**MAKE AHEAD:** Through step 2, covered and refrigerated for up to two hours. Best when prepared and eaten hot from the oven.

# Chinese Chicken Balls with Dipping Sauces

*Meatballs are always a favorite, and these juicy ones will be particularly liked, especially with the dipping sauces.*

| | | |
|---|---|---|
| 1 | recipe Chinese Chicken Burgers (page 90) | 1 |
| | Minted Coriander Dipping Sauce | |
| | Spicy Apricot or Plum Sauce | |

**1.** Mix ingredients for chicken burger recipe; shape mixture into twenty-four 1-inch (2.5 cm) balls. Place on baking sheet.

**2.** Broil for 6 to 8 minutes or until browned and no longer pink inside. Serve with dipping sauces. **Makes 24 pieces.**

**MAKE AHEAD:** Chicken balls can be covered and refrigerated for up to one day.

## Minted Coriander Dipping Sauce

| | | |
|---|---|---|
| ½ cup | low-fat yogurt | 125 mL |
| 2 tbsp | each chopped fresh coriander and mint | 25 mL |
| | Salt and pepper | |

**1.** Combine yogurt, coriander and mint; stir in salt and pepper to taste. **Makes ½ cup (125 mL).**

## Spicy Apricot or Plum Sauce

| | | |
|---|---|---|
| ½ cup | apricot or plum jam | 125 mL |
| 2 tbsp | lemon juice | 25 mL |
| ¼ tsp | crushed red pepper flakes or hot chili paste to taste | 1 mL |

**1.** Combine jam, lemon juice and red pepper flakes; mix well. **Makes ⅔ cup (150 mL).**

**MAKE AHEAD:** Coriander Sauce can be covered and refrigerated for up to one week; Apricot Sauce for one month.

*PER SERVING (1 BALL):*
32 calories
4 g protein
2 g total fat
    0.4 g saturated fat
    21 mg cholesterol
1 g carbohydrate
    0 g dietary fibre
35 mg sodium
41 mg potassium

*PER SERVING (½ TEASPOON / 2 ML):*
2 calories
0.1 g protein
0 g total fat
    0 g saturated fat
    0 mg cholesterol
0.2 g carbohydrate
    0 g dietary fibre
2 mg sodium
7 mg potassium

*PER SERVING (½ TEASPOON / 2 ML):*
7 calories
0 g protein
0 g total fat
    0 g saturated fat
    0 mg cholesterol
2 g carbohydrate
    0 g dietary fibre
0 mg sodium
3 mg potassium

# Smoked Turkey-Wrapped Melon Balls

*These juicy snacks make a nice addition to an hors d'oeuvres platter. They are delicious on their own or with Minted Coriander Dipping Sauce (page 41). Prosciutto or thinly sliced ham can be used instead of turkey.*

| 1 | large cantaloupe | 1 |
|------|-------------------|-------|
| 8 oz | thinly sliced smoked turkey | 250 g |

**1.** Cut melon in half; scoop out seeds. Using melon baller, scoop out melon rounds.

**2.** Cut turkey into strips about 1 inch (2.5 cm) wide and 5 inches (12 cm) long. Wrap each strip around melon ball; fasten with toothpick. Makes about 48 pieces.

**MAKE AHEAD:** Melon balls can be covered and refrigerated for up to six hours.

---

### Tips to Avoid Overeating at Parties

- Just as you shouldn't go grocery shopping when you're hungry, don't go to parties on an empty stomach. Rather than starve all day then gorge at the party, have a glass of milk and a light snack before you go out. This way you'll have the willpower to eat reasonably.

- Go easy on pastry-based appetizers, chips and deep-fried foods; instead, choose items such as marinated vegetables, shrimp and salsa dip. Skip the butter on the rolls. And ask for small servings, especially for dessert.

- Don't skip meals; when you know you will have a special lunch, plan for light suppers and vice versa.

- On occasions where you eat more than usual, try to get a little extra exercise.

*PER PIECE:*

10 calories
1 g protein
0.4 g total fat
   0.1 g saturated fat
   3 mg cholesterol
1 g carbohydrate
   0.1 g dietary fibre
35 mg sodium
25 mg potassium

# Thai Shrimp Salad in Mini Pita Pockets

*Perfect for a cocktail party menu or with drinks before dinner, these easy-to-make hors-d'oeuvres are one of my new favorites, mainly because of the fabulous flavor combination of fresh mint and fresh coriander. Instead of mini pitas, you can use Crostini (page 39) or cucumber cups (hollowed-out cucumber rounds).*

| | | |
|---|---|---|
| 2 tbsp | light mayonnaise | 25 mL |
| 1 tbsp | lemon juice | 15 mL |
| 1 tsp | minced gingerroot | 5 mL |
| Dash | hot pepper sauce | Dash |
| 1 cup | cooked salad shrimp | 250 mL |
| 1 cup | bean sprouts | 250 mL |
| ½ cup | grated carrot | 125 mL |
| ¼ cup | coarsely chopped fresh mint | 50 mL |
| ¼ cup | chopped fresh coriander | 50 mL |
| 14 | whole wheat mini pitas, halved | 14 |

**1.** In bowl, whisk together mayonnaise, lemon juice, gingerroot and hot pepper sauce.

**2.** Add shrimp, bean sprouts, carrot, mint and coriander; mix gently.

**3.** Spoon shrimp mixture into pita halves. **Makes 28 pieces.**

**MAKE AHEAD:** Through step 2, covered and refrigerated early in the day. Through step 3 for up to two hours.

### Shrimp

Shrimp is very low in fat but high in cholesterol. This recipe combines the shrimp with other ingredients so the total cholesterol is low and fits into a healthy diet.

*PER PIECE:*

24 calories
2 g protein
1 g total fat
    0.1 g saturated fat
    10 mg cholesterol
3 g carbohydrate
    0.4 g dietary fibre
41 mg sodium
28 mg potassium

# Sun-Dried Tomato and Onion Toasts

*Tender-sweet onions, full-flavored dried tomatoes and balsamic vinegar make a delightful flavor combo. To save time, slice the onions in a food processor.*

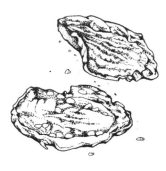

### Sun-Dried Tomatoes

Sun-dried tomatoes are available at supermarkets and specialty food stores. They come packed in oil or dry packed. To keep fat at a minimum, buy the dry ones and soak them in hot water for ten minutes to soften before using as a pizza topping (Goat Cheese and Pesto Tortilla Pizzas, page 47) or in a salad such as the pasta salad on page 170.

Soaking isn't necessary when cooking in liquid as in this recipe.

| | | |
|---|---|---|
| 5 cups | thinly sliced cooking onions (1 lb/500 g) | 1.25 L |
| 1 cup | chicken stock | 250 mL |
| ¼ cup | chopped dry-packed sun-dried tomatoes | 50 mL |
| 2 tsp | granulated sugar | 10 mL |
| ¼ cup | chopped fresh parsley | 50 mL |
| ⅓ cup | freshly grated Parmesan cheese | 75 mL |
| 4 tsp | balsamic vinegar | 20 mL |
| | Salt and pepper | |
| 1 | baguette (French bread stick) | 1 |
| 2 | cloves garlic, halved | 2 |

**1.** In skillet, bring onions, chicken stock, tomatoes and sugar to boil; reduce heat to low and simmer, uncovered, for 45 minutes or until onions are tender and only 1 tbsp (15 mL) liquid remains.

**2.** Stir in parsley, half of the Parmesan, vinegar, and salt and pepper to taste.

**3.** Meanwhile, slice bread into ½-inch (1 cm) thick rounds. Toast in 350°F (180°C) oven for 5 minutes. Rub one side of each round with cut side of garlic.

**4.** Spread each round with about 1 tsp (5 mL) onion mixture. Sprinkle with remaining cheese. Arrange on baking sheet.

**5.** Broil for 2 to 3 minutes or until hot. **Makes about 36 pieces**.

**MAKE AHEAD:** Through step 3 (except omit parsley), covered and refrigerated for up to two days. Through step 4, adding parsley, up to three hours ahead.

*PER PIECE:*

43 calories
2 g protein
1 g total fat
    0.3 g saturated fat
    1 mg cholesterol
8 g carbohydrate
    1 g dietary fibre
103 mg sodium
65 mg potassium

# Fresh Tomato Pizza

*Using Armenian or Italian-style flatbread, or a ready-made pizza base, means easy homemade pizza. This one has far less fat than the pepperoni-and-cheese variety. Frozen pizza crusts don't need to be thawed before using. To serve as an appetizer, cut into bite-size squares.*

| | | |
|---|---|---|
| 1 | 12-inch (30 cm) pizza crust or flatbread round | 1 |
| 1 cup | shredded part-skim mozzarella cheese | 250 mL |
| ½ cup | very thinly sliced onion (preferably Spanish or sweet) | 125 mL |
| 2 tbsp | chopped fresh basil (or 1 tsp/5 mL dried) | 25 mL |
| ½ tsp | dried oregano | 2 mL |
| 2 | large tomatoes, thinly sliced | 2 |
| 2 tbsp | freshly grated Parmesan cheese | 25 mL |

**1.** On baking sheet, sprinkle pizza crust with mozzarella cheese, onion and half of the basil and oregano.

**2.** Arrange tomato slices over top; sprinkle with Parmesan, remaining basil and oregano.

**3.** Bake in 450°F (230°C) oven for 15 minutes or until cheese is bubbly. **Makes 4 servings**.

**MAKE AHEAD:** Through step 2, covered and set aside at room temperature for up to one hour or refrigerated for up to three hours.

### Pizza Toppers

There's a wide choice of delicious low-fat, low-calorie pizza toppings. On top of the tomatoes, sprinkle one or two of the following:
- chopped jalapeño peppers
- chopped sweet peppers
- shrimp
- slivers of barbecued chicken or meats
- artichokes
- lightly cooked asparagus or broccoli
- goat cheese
- wild or button mushrooms

### Frozen Store-Bought Pizza

Compare the serving size and nutrient information on the label, then choose ones that are lower in fat. If the information is not on the label, look for an 800 telephone number on the label and call to request the information.

*PER SERVING:*

386 calories
20 g protein
10 g total fat
    4 g saturated fat
    18 mg cholesterol
55 g carbohydrate
    3 g dietary fibre
801 mg sodium
331 mg potassium

GOOD: Vitamin A; Calcium

# Tortilla Pizza Triangles

*You can make these cocktail tidbits in a jiffy using your favorite pizza toppings.*

## Tortilla Chips

Using scissors, cut tortillas into chip-size pieces. Arrange in single layer on baking sheet. Sprinkle with grated Parmesan cheese (optional). Bake in 375° F (190° C) oven for 3 minutes or until crisp.

## Tortillas

Soft flour tortillas are available, refrigerated, in most supermarkets. They make a delicious, crisp pizza base.

| | | |
|---|---|---|
| 2 | soft 9-inch (23 cm) flour tortillas | 2 |
| ½ cup | tomato sauce | 125 mL |
| ½ tsp | dried oregano | 2 mL |
| ½ tsp | dried basil | 2 mL |
| ½ cup | shredded part-skim mozzarella cheese or crumbled goat cheese | 125 mL |
| 2 | mushrooms, sliced | 2 |
| 4 | black olives, cut in strips | 4 |
| Quarter | sweet green pepper, cut in thin strips | Quarter |

**1.** Using scissors or knife, cut tortillas into 2-inch (5 cm) triangles; place on baking sheet.

**2.** Combine tomato sauce, oregano and basil; spread about 1 tsp (5 mL) over each triangle.

**3.** Sprinkle with cheese, mushrooms, olives and green pepper.

**4.** Bake in 400°F (200°C) oven for 3 to 5 minutes or until cheese melts. Serve hot. **Makes about 32 pieces**.

*PER PIECE:*

17 calories

1 g protein

1 g total fat
    0.3 g saturated fat
    1 mg cholesterol

2 g carbohydrate
    0.2 g dietary fibre

54 mg sodium

24 mg potassium

**MAKE AHEAD:** Through step 3 for up to three hours.

# Goat Cheese and Pesto Tortilla Pizzas

*I first had these fabulous crisp thin-crust pizzas at a barbecue at my friend Marilyn Short's house in Toronto. In the summer, I put out the toppings in small bowls, then let guests make their own pizzas and cook them on the barbecue. (Pictured opposite page 32.)*

| | | |
|---|---|---|
| 8 | soft 6-inch (15 cm) flour tortillas | 8 |
| 1 tsp | olive oil | 5 mL |
| 1 cup | sliced mushrooms (portobello or regular) | 250 mL |
| ⅓ cup | dry-packed sun-dried tomatoes (about 8) | 75 mL |
| 8 | medium asparagus spears | 8 |
| ¼ cup | pesto sauce | 50 mL |
| 1 cup | shredded part-skim mozzarella cheese (4 oz/125 g) | 250 mL |
| 2 oz | goat cheese (chèvre), diced | 50 g |
| 1 | roasted sweet red pepper (homemade or bottled), cut in thin strips | 1 |
| 1 tbsp | sesame seeds | 15 mL |

**1.** Place tortillas on ungreased baking sheet. Bake in 350°F (180°C) oven for 5 minutes. Set aside.

**2.** In nonstick skillet, heat oil over medium-high heat; cook mushrooms for 5 to 8 minutes or until tender, stirring often. In bowl, pour boiling water over tomatoes; let stand for 5 minutes. Drain well; cut into strips.

**3.** Steam or boil asparagus for 3 minutes or until tender-crisp; drain. Cool under cold water; drain. Cut in 2-inch (5 cm) lengths.

**4.** Spread a little pesto sauce on each tortilla round; sprinkle with mushrooms, tomatoes, asparagus, mozzarella cheese, goat cheese, red pepper and sesame seeds.

**5.** Barbecue over medium-high heat, covered, for 5 minutes or until cheese melts. Or, bake on baking sheet in 400°F/200°C oven for 8 minutes. **Makes 8 servings**.

**MAKE AHEAD:** Through step 3 for up to six hours; refrigerate mushrooms and asparagus.

---

## Goat Cheese and Pesto Tortilla Hors d'Oeuvres

Prepare and bake as for pizza but cut into quarters after baking.

## Roasted Peppers

Buy bottled roasted red peppers or roast your own: Place peppers on barbecue grill or in 400°F (200°C) oven for 20 to 30 minutes (turning when one side is blackened) or until skins are blistered and peppers are soft. Let cool. Scrape skin from peppers; discard seeds.

### Portobello Mushrooms

See sidebar, page 148, for details on this meaty mushroom.

*PER SERVING:*

223 calories
11 g protein
10 g total fat
   3 g saturated fat
   11 mg cholesterol
24 g carbohydrate
   3 g dietary fibre
355 mg sodium
297 mg potassium

GOOD: Calcium; Iron
EXCELLENT: Vitamin C; Folate

# Grilled Salmon Ribbons with Sesame and Coriander

*Serve these as an appetizer or main course. Easy to eat without cutlery, they are great for a buffet. (Pictured after page 128.)*

| | | |
|---|---|---|
| 1 lb | skinless salmon fillet (1-inch/2.5 cm thick) | 500 g |
| 3 tbsp | lemon juice | 50 mL |
| 1 tbsp | dark sesame oil | 15 mL |
| 2 tbsp | chopped fresh coriander | 25 mL |
| 1 tbsp | sesame seeds | 15 mL |

**1.** Soak 16 wooden skewers in water to cover for at least 10 minutes to prevent scorching. Cut salmon into ¼-inch (5 mm) thick slices to make sixteen 6- x 1-inch (15 x 2.5 cm) strips. Thread salmon onto skewers. Place in single layer in shallow dish.

**2.** Combine lemon juice and sesame oil; pour over salmon. Sprinkle with coriander. Let marinate for 15 minutes.

**3.** Arrange salmon on lightly greased broiling pan or grill; sprinkle with sesame seeds. Broil or grill 6 inches (15 cm) from heat for 3 to 5 minutes or until opaque. **Makes 4 main-course servings, or 16 appetizer pieces.**

PER SERVING AS APPETIZER (AS MAIN COURSE):

43 (173) calories
6 (23) g protein
2 (8) g total fat
    0.3 (1) g saturated fat
    16 (62) mg cholesterol
0.1 (0.3) g carbohydrate
    0 (0) g dietary fibre
13 (51) mg sodium
141 (564) mg potassium

**MAKE AHEAD:** Through step 2, covered and refrigerated for up to four hours.

# Thai Pork Skewers

*These strips of spicy meat are wonderful for cocktail snacks or buffets when you want something that's easy to eat without using a knife. For a dinner party appetizer, serve with peanut sauce (see sidebar, page 123). Fresh coriander adds wonderful flavor; if it's unavailable, substitute parsley and 1 tsp (5 mL) dried cilantro leaves (another name for coriander). (Pictured after page 128.)*

| | | |
|---|---|---|
| 1 lb | thinly sliced pork | 500 g |
| 3 tbsp | chopped fresh coriander | 50 mL |
| 2 tbsp | dry sherry or lime juice | 25 mL |
| 1 tbsp | wine vinegar | 15 mL |
| 1 tbsp | fish sauce or hoisin sauce | 15 mL |
| 1 tbsp | dark sesame oil | 15 mL |
| 1 tbsp | honey | 15 mL |
| 1 tbsp | sodium-reduced soy sauce | 15 mL |
| 1 tbsp | minced gingerroot | 15 mL |
| 1 | large clove garlic, minced | 1 |
| Pinch | crushed red pepper flakes | Pinch |

**1.** Trim fat from pork; slice pork into thin strips (short pieces if for cocktail snacks; 6-inch/15 cm long pieces if for buffet or first course).

**2.** In bowl, combine coriander, sherry, vinegar, fish sauce, sesame oil, honey, soy sauce, gingerroot, garlic and red pepper flakes. Add pork, stirring to coat. Cover and marinate in refrigerator for at least 2 or up to 24 hours.

**3.** Soak wooden skewers or toothpicks in water for 15 minutes. Thread pork strips onto skewers.

**4.** Broil on broiler pan in single layer for 3 to 5 minutes or until browned. **Makes about 30 pieces on skewers, 48 on toothpicks**.

**MAKE AHEAD:** Through step 2 for up to one day. Through step 3 (pour remaining marinade over), covered and refrigerated for up to four hours.

## Beef, Chicken or Turkey Skewers

Substitute 1 lb (500 g) of beef, chicken or turkey for pork.

## Buying Pork

Buy pork either very thinly sliced or 1-inch (2.5 cm) thick and cut crosswise. Cut strips to fit length of skewer or toothpick. For a barbecue main course, use longer pieces of meat. For ease-of-eating with cocktails, you might want one-bite-size lengths.

*PER SERVING ON SKEWER (ON TOOTHPICK):*

27 (17) calories
3 (2) g protein
1 (1) g total fat
   0.2 (0.1) g saturated fat
   8 (5) mg cholesterol
1 (1) g carbohydrate
   0 g dietary fibre
36 (22) mg sodium
53 (33) mg potassium

# Open-Faced Sandwiches

*A large platter of colorful open-faced sandwiches is an easy, make-ahead, no-fuss way to entertain. Each type of sandwich makes four pieces and when you assemble the whole platter, you'll have enough for eight people.*

## Bruschetta

| | | |
|---|---|---|
| 4 | thick slices Italian bread | 4 |
| ½ cup | soft mild goat cheese (chèvre) or light cream cheese | 125 mL |
| 1 cup | diced tomato | 250 mL |
| | Salt and pepper | |
| | Chopped fresh basil | |

**1.** Toast bread; spread one side with cheese. Cover with tomato. Sprinkle with salt and pepper to taste. Just before serving, sprinkle basil over top. **Makes 4 pieces.**

## Greek Salad

| | | |
|---|---|---|
| | Focaccia bread* | |
| 2 tsp | olive oil | 10 mL |
| 1 | small clove garlic, crushed | 1 |
| 2 | tomatoes, sliced | 2 |
| 1 | small red onion, thinly sliced | 1 |
| ½ cup | crumbled feta cheese | 125 mL |
| 2 | drained canned or marinated artichoke hearts, sliced | 2 |
| 12 | black Greek-style olives, pitted | 12 |
| | Salt and pepper | |
| | Chopped fresh or dried oregano | |

**1.** Cut bread into four 5- x 3-inch (12 x 8 cm) portions. Combine olive oil and garlic; brush over bread.

**2.** Cover each with 2 or 3 overlapping slices of tomato, then 3 red onion rings. Top each with feta cheese, artichoke slices and 3 olives. Sprinkle with salt, pepper and oregano to taste. **Makes 4 pieces.**

* Use prepared pizza crust-type bread if focaccia is unavailable

---

*PER PIECE (BRUSCHETTA):*

193 calories
9 g protein
9 g total fat
    6 g saturated fat
    28 mg cholesterol
19 g carbohydrate
    1 g dietary fibre
359 mg sodium
122 mg potassium

---

### Bridge Party Lunch
- Open-Faced Sandwiches
- Raw Vegetables with Clam Dip with Herbs (page 35)
- Apricot Streusel Cake (page 211)

---

*PER PIECE (GREEK SALAD):*

333 calories
10 g protein
12 g total fat
    4 g saturated fat
    16 mg cholesterol
48 g carbohydrate
    4 g dietary fibre
1022 mg sodium
484 mg potassium

GOOD: Vitamin C; Calcium; Iron
EXCELLENT: Folate

## Smoked Turkey with Asparagus

| | | |
|---|---|---|
| 12 | asparagus spears | 12 |
| 2 tbsp | light mayonnaise | 25 mL |
| 1 tbsp | Dijon mustard | 15 mL |
| 4 | slices pumpernickel bread | 4 |
| 6 oz | thinly sliced smoked turkey | 175 g |
| 1 tsp | low-fat milk | 5 mL |

**1.** Cook asparagus in boiling water until tender-crisp, 3 to 5 minutes. Refresh under cold water; drain and pat dry. Mix mayonnaise with mustard; spread some of the mixture over bread. Cover with turkey. Top with asparagus.

**2.** Just before serving, mix milk into remaining mayonnaise mixture; drizzle over each sandwich. **Makes 4 pieces**.

*PER PIECE*
*(SMOKED TURKEY):*

214 calories
17 g protein
7 g total fat
   1 g saturated fat
   32 mg cholesterol
26 g carbohydrate
   5 g dietary fibre
615 mg sodium
440 mg potassium

GOOD: Vitamin C; Iron
EXCELLENT: Folate

## Grilled Chicken Breast with Mango Salsa

| | | |
|---|---|---|
| 2 | boneless skinless chicken breasts | 2 |
| | Salt and pepper | |
| 2 | hamburger buns, halved or 4 French bread slices | 2 |
| 4 tsp | light mayonnaise | 20 mL |

*Mango Salsa*

| | | |
|---|---|---|
| 1 | chopped peeled mango or 2 peaches | 1 |
| Half | sweet red pepper, chopped | Half |
| 2 tbsp | chopped fresh coriander | 25 mL |
| 2 tbsp | lime juice | 25 mL |

**1.** Mango Salsa: In bowl, combine mango, red pepper, coriander and lime juice.

**2.** Grill chicken until no longer pink inside, 5 to 8 minutes on each side. Sprinkle with salt and pepper to taste; let cool. Cut into $\frac{1}{3}$-inch (8 mm) thick slices.

**3.** Spread buns with mayonnaise. Cover with chicken and top with salsa. **Makes 4 pieces**.

*PER PIECE*
*(GRILLED CHICKEN):*

215 calories
16 g protein
5 g total fat
   1 g saturated fat
   37 mg cholesterol
27 g carbohydrate
   2 g dietary fibre
219 mg sodium
262 mg potassium

EXCELLENT: Vitamin A;
Vitamin C

**MAKE AHEAD:** All sandwiches can be covered and refrigerated for up to three hours; remove from refrigerator 20 minutes before serving.

# Cheese and Tomato Quesadillas

## Quesadillas

Quesadillas are folded tortillas filled with melted cheese and usually chili peppers. Any cooked meats or chopped vegetables can also be added.

## Grilled (Barbecued) Quesadillas

Grill over medium heat or coals for 2 to 3 minutes on each side or until golden and cheese melts.

## Oven-Baked Quesadillas

Bake on baking sheet in 400°F (200°C) oven for 10 minutes or until golden and cheese melts.

*PER PIECE:*

75 calories

4 g protein

3 g total fat
   1 g saturated fat
   6 mg cholesterol

9 g carbohydrate
   1 g dietary fibre

118 mg sodium

55 mg potassium

*I keep a jar of pickled jalapeño peppers in the refrigerator to use in this zesty recipe.*

| | | |
|---|---|---:|
| 4 | soft 9-inch (23 cm) flour tortillas | 4 |
| ¾ cup | shredded Danbo or part-skim mozzarella cheese | 175 mL |
| 1 oz | soft mild goat cheese (chèvre), diced | 28 g |
| 1 | medium tomato, diced | 1 |
| 1 | green onion, chopped | 1 |
| 2 tsp | chopped pickled jalapeño pepper | 10 mL |
| ¼ cup | chopped fresh coriander | 50 mL |

**1.** Sprinkle half of each tortilla with Danbo and goat cheeses, tomato, green onion, jalapeño pepper and coriander. Fold uncovered half over filling and press edges together.

**2.** Heat ungreased skillet over medium heat; cook quesadillas for 3 to 4 minutes on each side or until golden and cheese melts. To serve, cut each into 3 wedges. **Makes 12 pieces**.

**MAKE AHEAD:** Through step 1, covered and refrigerated for up to three hours.

---

### SNACKS

Choose snacks that are lower in fat. All fruits and vegetables (except avocados) are good choices. This chart will help.

| | Fat (g) |
|---|---:|
| Peanuts (½ cup/125 mL) | 36 |
| Potato chips (55 g bag) | 20 |
| Popcorn with cheese (35 g bag) | 12 |
| Popcorn, microwave natural flavor (3 cups/750mL; 24 g) | 8 |
| Popcorn (plain) air-popped (3 cups/750 mL) | 0 |
| Pretzels (5 sticks or 3 rings) | trace |
| Cookie (1)   Small chocolate chip | 3 |
|              Sandwich-type with cream | 3 |
|              Oatmeal or chocolate marshmallow | 2 |
|              Fig/Gingersnap | 1 |
|              Social Tea/Arrowroot | 1 |

# Spicy Popcorn

*When it comes to healthy eating, my downfall isn't dessert, but salty, chiplike snacks. Popcorn is usually my solution.*

| | | |
|---|---|---|
| 3 cups | popped corn | 750 mL |
| 2 tsp | soft margarine or butter, melted | 10 mL |
| ½ tsp | chili powder | 2 mL |
| ¼ tsp | each ground cumin and salt | 1 mL |

**1.** Place popcorn in plastic bag. In small dish, stir together margarine, chili powder, cumin and salt; pour over popcorn and shake to mix. **Makes 3 cups (750 mL).**

PER SERVING (1 CUP):

65 calories

1 g protein

3 g total fat
  0.4 g saturated fat
  0 mg cholesterol

8 g carbohydrate
  1 g dietary fibre

230 mg sodium

39 mg potassium

# Candied Corn

*This is really tasty and uses only a minimum of sugar and fat. For variation, add ¼ tsp (1 mL) cinnamon to the sugar mixture.*

| | | |
|---|---|---|
| 2 tbsp | packed brown sugar | 25 mL |
| 1 tbsp | soft margarine or butter | 15 mL |
| 1 tbsp | corn syrup | 15 mL |
| 4 cups | popped corn | 1 L |

**1.** In microwaveable custard cup or small dish, combine sugar, margarine and corn syrup. Microwave on Medium power (50%) for 20 seconds; stir. Microwave on Medium for another 30 seconds; stir.

**2.** Pour over popcorn and toss to mix. Spread on baking sheet. Bake in 275°F (140°C) oven for 20 minutes, stirring every 5 minutes. **Makes 4 cups (1 L).**

PER SERVING (1 CUP):

106 calories

1 g protein

3 g total fat
  1 g saturated fat
  0 mg cholesterol

18 g carbohydrate
  1 g dietary fibre

44 mg sodium

52 mg potassium

**MAKE AHEAD:** Popcorn can be kept in airtight container up to one day.

# Tofu Blender Drink

The recipe for this creamy-tasting orange drink is from Vancouver vegetarian dietitian and author Vasanto Crawford. I think it's one of the best-tasting and easiest ways to use tofu, which is a good source of protein, calcium, iron, phosphorous and some B vitamins. This is great for breakfast or a snack.

| | | |
|---|---|---|
| 10 oz | tofu (about 1 pkg), drained | 300 g |
| 1 cup | frozen orange juice concentrate | 250 mL |
| 1½ cups | water | 375 mL |
| 1 | ripe banana | 1 |

**1.** In blender or food processor, combine tofu, orange juice, water and banana; blend until smooth. **Makes 4 servings**.

**MAKE AHEAD:** Drink can be covered and refrigerated for up to one day; stir before serving.

# Hot Spiced Cider

This old-fashioned favorite provides all the warmth you'll need on a wintry day. If children are part of the gathering, leave out the brandy; the cider is still as heartwarming.

| | | |
|---|---|---|
| 8 cups | apple cider or apple juice | 2 L |
| 1 | lemon, thinly sliced | 1 |
| 6 | whole cloves | 6 |
| 4 | whole allspice | 4 |
| 4 | sticks cinnamon | 4 |
| 1 cup | Calvados or brandy (optional) | 250 mL |

**1.** In large saucepan, combine cider, lemon, cloves, allspice and cinnamon sticks. Cover and simmer for 15 to 30 minutes or until hot and fragrant.

**2.** Just before serving, strain. Stir in Calvados (if using). **Makes 16 servings, ½ cup (125 mL) each**.

**MAKE AHEAD:** Through step 1 for up to one day.

**Party Quantities**

For 32 servings, double the recipe. For 64 servings, use 32 cups (8 L) cider, 2 lemons, 12 whole cloves, 8 whole allspice, 8 sticks cinnamon, and 1 bottle (700 mL) Calvados (if using). When making large quantities, tie spices in cheesecloth bag; remove before serving.

# Fruit Spritzers

*You won't miss the wine in these refreshing drinks. However, you could add an ounce of dry white wine and still be drinking much less alcohol than in a glass of wine or a regular spritzer.*

| | | |
|---|---|---|
| 2 tbsp | peach, pear or blackcurrent nectar concentrate | 25 mL |
| 1 tbsp | lemon juice | 15 mL |
| ¼ cup | soda water | 50 mL |
| | Crushed ice | |

**1.** In wine glass, combine peach nectar concentrate and lemon juice; stir to mix.

**2.** Add soda water and ice. **Makes 1 drink**.

**MAKE AHEAD:** Through step 1 for up to three hours.

---

## For a Party

Combine 1 cup (250 mL) nectar concentrate and ½ cup (125 mL) lemon juice up to 24 hours in advance. At serving time, pour 1½ ounces (3 tbsp/45 mL) into wine glass; top with crushed ice and soda. Makes 8 drinks.

## Non-Alcoholic Drinks

- Fruit Spritzer variations: mix fruit juices such as apple, pineapple, grapefruit, passion fruit or fruit nectars with soda water, adding a slice of fruit or twist of citrus peel and ice.
- Virgin Bloody Mary; Virgin Bloody Caesar; frozen daiquiri mix made without the alcohol.
- Soda water with a dash of angostura bitters and slice of lemon or lime.

---

## JUICES

### Fruit juice versus fruit drinks
When buying juice, be label-smart. Look for the word *juice* rather than *drink*, *cocktail*, *punch* or *blend*. Packaged fruit-flavored drinks, or ones made from crystals, might contain Vitamin C but not the potassium, folate and other nutrients that real fruit juice provides. *Note:* Both fresh and processed juices provide similar nutrients.

### Too much of a good thing
For children, too much fruit juice can contribute to tooth decay, lack of appetite at mealtimes and, in some cases, diarrhea.

### The real thing or its juice?
While juices and their nutrients are often a concentrated source of vitamins and part of a healthy diet, whole fruits and vegetables are higher in fibre and some nutrients than the juice alone. Variety in our diet means we should have both.

*PER DRINK:*

90 calories
0.1 g protein
0 g total fat
   0 g saturated fat
   0 mg cholesterol
24 g carbohydrate
   0 g dietary fibre
16 mg sodium
17 mg potassium

# White Sangria Punch

*Make this light punch with white grape juice, white wine or a de-alcoholized white wine.*

| | | |
|---|---|---|
| 4 cups | white grape juice (or 1 bottle/750 mL white wine) | 1 L |
| | Juice of 1 lemon and 1 lime | |
| 1 | lime, sliced | 1 |
| 1 | bottle (750 mL) soda water, chilled | 1 |

**1.** In large pitcher, combine grape juice, lemon and lime juice and sliced lime. Refrigerate until chilled.

**2.** Just before serving, add soda water. **Makes 12 servings, each ¾ cup (175 mL).**

**MAKE AHEAD:** Through step 1 for up to three hours.

# Cranberry Lime Christmas Eve Punch

*We often have this punch that both children and adults enjoy. If ginger beer is unavailable, substitute ginger ale.*

| | | |
|---|---|---|
| 1 | bottle (64 oz/1.8 L) Cranberry Cocktail | 1 |
| 2 cups | frozen limeade concentrate | 500 mL |
| 2 cups | pineapple juice | 500 mL |
| 3 | bottles (300 mL each) ginger beer, chilled | 3 |
| 2 | bottles (750 mL each) soda water, chilled | 2 |
| | Ice | |

**1.** In punch bowl, combine Cranberry Cocktail, limeade concentrate, pineapple juice and ginger beer.

**2.** Just before serving, add soda water and ice. **Makes 28 servings, each ¾ cup (175 mL).**

**MAKE AHEAD:** Through step 1 for up to two hours.

### Garnish

Garnish with sliced lime.

### Variation

For an alcohol version, add either rum or wine to taste.

# SOUPS

Curried Cauliflower Soup

Chilled Cucumber Mint Soup

Purée of Tomato Soup with Fresh Basil

Broccoli Soup

Leek and Mushroom Soup with Fresh Basil

Hot and Sour Soup

Oriental Noodle and Chicken Soup

Miso Soup with Tofu

Three-Grain Vegetable Soup

Red Bean and Rice Soup

Italian Chick-Pea and Pasta Soup

Carrot and Corn Chowder

Fish 'n' Vegetable Chowder

Hearty Scotch Broth

# Curried Cauliflower Soup

*Cool and creamy, this is a wonderful soup for a warm day.*

| Half | cauliflower, cut in chunks (about 6 cups/1.5 L) | Half |
|---|---|---|
| 1 cup | sliced peeled potato | 250 mL |
| 3½ cups | 2% milk | 875 mL |
| 1 tbsp | soft margarine or butter | 15 mL |
| 1 tsp | each salt, curry powder and ground cumin | 5 mL |
| 2 tbsp | chopped fresh chives or green onion | 25 mL |

**1.** In saucepan, combine cauliflower, potato and milk; bring to boil. Reduce heat; cover and simmer for 20 minutes or until tender. Purée in food processor or blender.

**2.** Stir in margarine, salt, curry powder and cumin.

**3.** Cover and refrigerate for 2 hours or until cold. If desired, thin with additional milk. Garnish with chives. **Makes 6 servings, about ¾ cup (175 mL) each**.

# Chilled Cucumber Mint Soup

*Refreshing and easy to make, this soup is a nice way to start a summer meal.*

| 1 | English cucumber, seeded | 1 |
|---|---|---|
| ¼ cup | chopped green onion | 50 mL |
| ¼ cup | chopped fresh mint | 50 mL |
| 2 tbsp | chopped fresh coriander or parsley | 25 mL |
| 1½ cups | 2% milk | 375 mL |
| ½ cup | light sour cream | 125 mL |
| ½ cup | low-fat yogurt | 125 mL |

**1.** In food processor, purée cucumber, onion, mint and coriander; add milk and sour cream and process to mix.

**2.** Stir in yogurt. Season with salt and pepper to taste. Refrigerate for at least 1 hour. **Makes 6 servings, about ¾ cup (175 mL) each**.

**MAKE AHEAD:** Both soups can be covered and refrigerated for up to two days.

## Cucumbers

English, or greenhouse, cucumbers can grow up to 24 inches (60 cm) long and are usually seedless.

For this soup, peel the cucumber only if the skin is waxed or very thick.

# Purée of Tomato Soup
# with Fresh Basil

*This is one of my husband's favorite soups; he likes it cold and says it's better than gazpacho. Make it in the summer when garden tomatoes and basil are at their best.*

| | | |
|---|---|---|
| 2 lb | ripe tomatoes (about 5) | 1 kg |
| 1 tbsp | olive oil | 15 mL |
| Half | Spanish onion, thinly sliced | Half |
| 2 tsp | chopped fresh garlic | 10 mL |
| 2 tbsp | chopped fresh basil | 25 mL |
| ¼ tsp | salt | 1 mL |
| | Pepper | |
| 2 tbsp | light sour cream (optional) | 25 mL |
| 2 tbsp | chopped fresh chives | 25 mL |

**1.** Peel tomatoes by blanching in boiling water for 1 minute; peel off skins. Cut in half, then squeeze or scoop out seeds.

**2.** In skillet, heat oil over medium heat; cook onion and garlic until tender, about 5 minutes.

**3.** In food processor or blender, purée tomatoes and onion mixture until smooth; stir in basil, salt, and pepper to taste; reheat but don't boil. Or cover and refrigerate for at least 30 minutes.

**4.** Garnish each bowlful with sour cream (if using) and chives. **Makes 6 servings, about ½ cup (125 mL) each.**

***Best Flavor Tomatoes***
For the most flavor, don't refrigerate tomatoes; store at room temperature or in a cool place, but not as cold as the refrigerator.

**MAKE AHEAD:** Through step 3, covered and refrigerated for up to two days.

*PER SERVING:*
56 calories
2 g protein
3 g total fat
    1 g saturated fat
    1 mg cholesterol
7 g carbohydrate
    2 g dietary fibre
111 mg sodium
293 mg potassium

GOOD: Vitamin C

# Broccoli Soup

*This is one of the easiest and most nutritious ways to make soup — throw everything into the pot and cook until tender. This method keeps all the nutrients rather than draining them away in the cooking water; it doesn't use any fat to first cook the onions, and it thickens with a potato rather than with a flour-and-butter mixture. Since there isn't any other fat, I like to use 2% milk.*

**Broccoli**

Broccoli is packed with nutrients: it has many vitamins, including folate, Vitamin C and beta carotene; it has minerals, including calcium and iron; it even has some protein and is a high source of fibre.

| | | |
|---|---|---|
| 1 | bunch broccoli | 1 |
| 1 | onion, chopped | 1 |
| 2 cups | diced peeled potatoes | 500 mL |
| 1 | clove garlic, minced | 1 |
| 1½ cups | vegetable stock or water | 375 mL |
| ½ tsp | dried thyme | 2 mL |
| ¼ tsp | pepper | 1 mL |
| Pinch | nutmeg | Pinch |
| 1½ cups | milk | 375 mL |
| | Salt | |

**1.** Peel broccoli stems; chop coarsely. Separate florets to make 2 cups (500 mL); set aside. Coarsely chop remaining florets.

**2.** In saucepan, combine chopped stems and florets, onion, potatoes, garlic, stock, thyme, pepper and nutmeg; bring to boil. Reduce heat, cover and simmer for 10 minutes or until potatoes are very tender.

**3.** Meanwhile, steam reserved florets for 5 minutes or until tender-crisp; set aside.

**4.** In blender or food processor, purée soup in batches until smooth; return to pan. Add milk; heat through but do not boil. Season with salt to taste.

**5.** Divide broccoli florets among 5 soup bowls; pour soup into bowls. **Makes 5 servings, about 1 cup (250 mL) each.**

**MAKE AHEAD:** Through step 4, covered and refrigerated for up to two days. Reheat gently.

PER SERVING:

118 calories

6 g protein

2 g total fat
  1 g saturated fat
  5 mg cholesterol

21 g carbohydrate
  3 g dietary fibre

66 mg sodium

591 mg potassium

GOOD: Vitamin A
EXCELLENT: Vitamin C;
Folate

# Leek and Mushroom Soup with Fresh Basil

*Fresh basil adds wonderful flavor to the mild tastes of mushrooms and leeks. This soup is nice for a first course at dinner or for lunch. Use the white of leek and just a little of the tender green part.*

| | | |
|---|---|---|
| 1 tbsp | olive oil | 15 mL |
| 5 cups | chopped white of leeks (5 medium) | 1.25 L |
| 5 cups | coarsely chopped mushrooms (10 oz/300 g) | 1.25 L |
| 1 | potato, peeled and chopped | 1 |
| 2 cups | water or chicken or vegetable stock | 500 mL |
| 2½ cups | milk (2% or whole) | 625 mL |
| ¼ cup | packed chopped fresh basil* | 50 mL |
| ½ tsp | salt | 2 mL |
| ¼ tsp | pepper | 1 mL |

**1.** In large saucepan, heat oil over medium heat; cook leeks for 5 minutes, stirring occasionally. Add mushrooms and potato; cook for 2 minutes, stirring often.

**2.** Add water and bring to boil; reduce heat, cover and simmer for 15 minutes or until vegetables are tender. Purée in blender or food processor; return to pan. Add milk, basil, salt and pepper; heat until hot. **Makes 6 servings, about 1 cup (250 mL) each.**

\* If fresh basil is not available, substitute chopped fresh parsley plus ½ tsp (2 mL) dried basil or more to taste, or chopped fresh dill.

**MAKE AHEAD:** Through step 2, except omit basil; covered and refrigerated for up to two days, or freeze for up to one month. Reheat, adding basil just before serving.

### Washing Leeks
Trim off root ends of leeks and most of dark green. Split leeks lengthwise and hold under running water to remove any grit.

*PER SERVING (USING 2% MILK):*

117 calories
5 g protein
5 g total fat
    2 g saturated fat
    8 mg cholesterol
15 g carbohydrate
    2 g dietary fibre
251 mg sodium
425 mg potassium

# Hot and Sour Soup

*As its name implies, this soup tastes hot (chili paste) and sour (vinegar). The sharpness of ginger and saltiness of soy sauce also contribute to the soup's wonderful flavor. If you like a fiery hot soup, you will want to add more chili paste to taste.*

| | | |
|---|---|---|
| 6 | dried Chinese mushrooms | 6 |
| 6 cups | chicken stock | 1.5 L |
| ¼ lb | lean boneless pork, cut in thin 1 inch (2.5 cm) long strips | 125 g |
| 1 tbsp | grated gingerroot | 15 mL |
| ½ cup | julienned bamboo shoots | 125 mL |
| 1⅓ cups | diced firm tofu (8 oz/250 g) | 325 mL |
| 3 tbsp | rice vinegar | 50 mL |
| 2 tbsp | sodium-reduced soy sauce | 25 mL |
| 1 tbsp | dark sesame oil | 15 mL |
| 1 tsp | chili paste* | 5 mL |
| 2 tbsp | cornstarch | 25 mL |
| ½ tsp | granulated sugar | 2 mL |
| 2 | green onions, thinly sliced | 2 |

**1.** Soak dried mushrooms in enough warm water to cover for 15 minutes or until softened. Drain. Remove and discard stems; cut mushrooms into thin strips.

**2.** In large saucepan, bring stock to boil. Add mushrooms, pork and ginger; simmer, covered, for 10 minutes. Add bamboo shoots and tofu.

**3.** In small bowl, combine vinegar, soy sauce, oil and chili paste; stir in cornstarch and sugar until smooth. Stir into soup; bring to boil. Reduce heat and simmer, stirring, for 2 minutes.

**4.** Sprinkle each serving with green onions. **Makes 8 servings, about ¾ cup (175 mL) each.**

*See Information on Ingredients, page 32.

**MAKE AHEAD:** Through step 3, cooled, covered and refrigerated for up to two days.

### Adding an Egg

Usually an egg is swirled into this soup, which adds body but can make the soup cloudy. I omit the egg because I usually serve the soup as an appetizer and I prefer a clear one. If you want to add an egg, gradually stir in one beaten egg after step 3.

*PER SERVING:*

129 calories
12 g protein
6 g total fat
  1 g saturated fat
  8 mg cholesterol
8 g carbohydrate
  1 g dietary fibre
718 mg sodium
349 mg potassium

GOOD: Calcium
EXCELLENT: Iron

# Oriental Noodle and Chicken Soup

*This light soup is a combination of Vietnamese and Thai cooking and is a nice way to start a dinner party, especially if some of the other dishes are Oriental. Make most of the soup a day or two in advance, then it's easy to assemble just before serving.*

| | | |
|---|---|---|
| 6 | stalks fresh lemon grass* | 6 |
| 1½ lb | chicken necks, backs, wings | 750 g |
| ⅓ cup | chopped gingerroot | 75 mL |
| 8 cups | water | 2 L |
| 5 oz | rice vermicelli or rice stick noodles | 150 g |
| ¼ cup | bottled Thai fish sauce* | 50 mL |
| 2 tbsp | lime juice | 25 mL |
| | Pepper | |
| ½ cup | fresh coriander leaves* | 125 mL |
| 3 | green onions, chopped | 3 |

**1.** Remove and discard top half of lemon grass stalk. Trim off outside leaves and roots; cut remaining stalk into ½-inch (1 cm) thick slices.

**2.** In large pot, simmer chicken, ginger, lemon grass and water, covered, for 45 minutes. Remove chicken from broth and let cool; remove meat from bones and shred. Strain broth and return to pot. Skim any fat from surface.

**3.** Cut rice vermicelli into about 3-inch (8 cm) pieces.

**4.** Bring broth to simmer and add fish sauce and lime juice; simmer for 2 minutes. Add rice vermicelli, chicken, and pepper to taste; simmer for 1 minute.

**5.** Ladle into soup bowls; top each with coriander and onions. **Makes 8 servings, about ¾ cup (175 mL) each.**

* See Information on Ingredients, page 32.

**MAKE AHEAD:** Through step 3, covered and refrigerated for up to two days. Remove any fat from top of broth.

## Buying Chicken

When you buy a whole chicken and want only the legs and breasts, freeze the rest to use in this recipe.

## Lemon Grass

Instead of stalks of fresh lemon grass, you can use 3 tbsp (50 mL) dried lemon grass, or zest (grated rind) of 1 lemon.

THAI FISH SAUCE

*PER SERVING:*

    145 calories
    10 g protein
    4 g total fat
        1 g saturated fat
        31 mg cholesterol
    17 g carbohydrate
        1 g dietary fibre
    280 mg sodium
    128 mg potassium

# Miso Soup with Tofu

*This Japanese light soup is from Heather Epp, a recipe tester at* Canadian Living *magazine. Miso is delicious as a soup base paste, and is available at health food stores in a wide variety of flavors. Heather prefers a barley or brown rice miso for this soup. I used a brown soybean miso, and my family liked it.*

| | | |
|---|---|---|
| 1 tsp | sesame oil | 5 mL |
| Half | onion, chopped | Half |
| 1 | large carrot, thinly sliced | 1 |
| 3 cups | water | 750 mL |
| 2 tbsp | miso | 25 mL |
| 1 tbsp | sodium-reduced soy sauce | 15 mL |
| 3 | green onions, diagonally sliced | 3 |
| ½ cup | diced firm tofu (3 oz/85 g) | 125 mL |

**1.** In saucepan, heat oil over medium heat; cook onion and carrot, stirring occasionally, for 5 to 7 minutes or until tender.

**2.** Add water and bring to boil; reduce heat and simmer for 3 minutes.

**3.** Remove from heat; stir in miso until dissolved. Add soy sauce, green onions and tofu. Serve hot. **Makes 4 servings, about ¾ cup (175 mL) each.**

### Soy Sauce

Make your own sodium-reduced soy sauce by mixing regular naturally brewed soy sauce with an equal amount of water. It has just as much flavor if not more than the bottled sodium-reduced soy sauce, and it's half the cost.

### Miso

Miso, packed with protein and taste, is a staple in Japanese cooking. It is made from soybeans and wheat, barley or rice. It will keep refrigerated for up to a year.

*PER SERVING:*

78 calories
5 g protein
4 g total fat
   1 g saturated fat
   0 mg cholesterol
8 g carbohydrate
   2 g dietary fibre
458 mg sodium
163 mg potassium

GOOD: Calcium; Iron
EXCELLENT: Vitamin A

**MAKE AHEAD:** Soup can be covered and refrigerated for up to two days; reheat over medium heat but don't boil.

Baked Buttermilk Herb Chicken (sidebar, page 93)
Bulgur with Red Onion and Pimiento (page 182)
Snow Peas with Mushrooms (page 145)

# Three-Grain Vegetable Soup

*This easy soup is economical, low calorie and packed with nutrients. You can use this recipe as a base and add a ham bone or a chicken carcass or other vegetables. I use whatever vegetables I have on hand, but always like to include rutabaga, for it adds a great deal of flavor. I like to use a combination of grains and legumes, but you can use one or two to make a total of ½ cup (125 mL). Sometimes I add fresh herbs, such as basil, rosemary or dill, or sprinkle each serving with grated Parmesan cheese.*

| | | |
|---|---|---|
| 1 tbsp | soft margarine or butter | 15 mL |
| 1 | large onion, chopped | 1 |
| 1 tbsp | minced fresh garlic | 15 mL |
| 6 cups | chicken or vegetable stock | 1.5 L |
| 2 tbsp | each barley, bulgur, whole grain rice and green lentils | 25 mL |
| 2 | carrots, diced | 2 |
| 2 cups | diced peeled rutabaga | 500 mL |
| 2 cups | thinly sliced cabbage | 500 mL |
| 2 tsp | dried basil | 10 mL |
| ¼ cup | chopped fresh parsley | 50 mL |
| | Salt and pepper | |

**1.** In large saucepan, melt margarine over medium heat; cook onion until tender, about 5 minutes.

**2.** Add garlic, stock, barley, bulgur, rice, lentils, carrots and rutabaga; bring to boil. Reduce heat, cover and simmer for 30 minutes.

**3.** Add cabbage and basil; simmer for 10 to 15 minutes or until vegetables and grains are tender.

**4.** Add parsley, and salt and pepper to taste. **Makes 6 servings, about 1 cup (250 mL) each.**

**MAKE AHEAD:** Soup can be covered and refrigerated for up to two days; add parsley when reheating.

### Rutabaga or Turnip?

Rutabagas are yellow, and are larger and stronger in flavor than turnips. Turnips are white with purple tops, and are smaller than rutabagas.

### What's in a Rice?

Brown and/or whole grain rice are the best choice nutritionally in terms of B vitamins, iron and fibre. In Canada, plain white rice cannot be enriched, although instant white rice can. Parboiled, or converted, rice undergoes processing before the milling (which removes the bran layer), which forces the nutrients in the outer bran layer to the centre of the grain. They are a more nutritious choice than plain white rice.

It's a different story if you use packaged rice mixes: they are often extremely high in sodium and call for added fats when cooking.

PER SERVING:

152 calories
8 g protein
4 g total fat
   1 g saturated fat
   0 mg cholesterol
22 g carbohydrate
   5 g dietary fibre
833 mg sodium
567 mg potassium

GOOD: Vitamin C; Folate
EXCELLENT: Vitamin A

Chicken and Vegetable Stew with Parsley Dumplings (page 101)

# Red Bean and Rice Soup

*This thick and warming soup will ward off any winter chills.*

| | | |
|---|---|---|
| 1 tbsp | vegetable oil | 15 mL |
| 1 | onion, chopped | 1 |
| 2 | stalks celery, chopped | 2 |
| 1 | clove garlic, minced | 1 |
| 2 tbsp | all-purpose flour | 25 mL |
| 2 cups | water | 500 mL |
| 1½ cups | chicken or vegetable stock | 375 mL |
| 1 cup | chopped tomatoes (fresh or canned) | 250 mL |
| ¼ cup | long grain rice | 50 mL |
| 2 tsp | chili powder | 10 mL |
| ¼ tsp | salt | 1 mL |
| 2 cups | cooked kidney beans (19 oz/540 mL can, drained) | 500 mL |
| 1 tbsp | lemon juice | 15 mL |

**1.** In large saucepan, heat oil over medium heat; cook onion, celery and garlic for 5 minutes or until softened. Sprinkle with flour; cook, stirring, for 1 minute.

**2.** Stir in water, stock, tomatoes, rice, chili powder and salt; bring to boil. Reduce heat, cover and simmer for 20 minutes.

**3.** Stir in beans and lemon juice; heat through. **Makes 6 servings, about 1 cup (250 mL) each.**

### Nutritional Note

The combination of rice and kidney beans provides a good source of protein.

### Sodium-Restricted Diets

Nutrient analyses of recipes in this book are based on canned stock or stock made from a cube, because most people don't have time to make stocks. However, these products are high in sodium.

Even the canned chicken broth with a label claim of "less than 1% salt" has 763 mg sodium per cup (250 mL), when reconstituted with an equal amount of water.

To reduce sodium, make your own meat or vegetable stock but don't add any salt. Flavor with bay leaves, parsley, thyme, peppercorns, celery, onion and carrots.

*Per Serving:*

162 calories
8 g protein
3 g total fat
    0.3 g saturated fat
    0 mg cholesterol
26 g carbohydrate
    7 g dietary fibre
522 mg sodium
376 mg potassium

Good: Folate

**Make Ahead:** Soup can be covered and refrigerated for up to two days.

# Italian Chick-Pea and Pasta Soup

*Any kind of cooked beans can be used instead of chick-peas in this filling soup. For a thicker soup, purée 1 cup (250 mL) of the soup and stir back into soup.*

| | | |
|---|---|---|
| 1 tsp | olive oil | 5 mL |
| 1 | onion, chopped | 1 |
| 1 tbsp | minced fresh garlic | 15 mL |
| 1 | tomato, chopped | 1 |
| 1 tbsp | tomato paste | 15 mL |
| 1 cup | cooked or canned chick-peas | 250 mL |
| 3 cups | chicken or vegetable stock | 750 mL |
| ¾ cup | small pasta (elbow macaroni or orzo) | 175 mL |
| 1½ tsp | dried basil | 7 mL |
| ½ tsp | dried rosemary | 2 mL |
| ¼ cup | chopped fresh parsley | 50 mL |
| | Salt and pepper | |
| ¼ cup | freshly grated Parmesan cheese | 50 mL |

**1.** In large saucepan, heat oil over medium heat; cook onion and garlic until softened. Stir in tomato and tomato paste; cook for 1 minute.

**2.** Add chick-peas and stock; bring to boil. Add pasta, basil and rosemary; reduce heat and simmer, uncovered, for 10 to 15 minutes or until pasta is tender yet firm.

**3.** Add parsley, and salt and pepper to taste. Sprinkle each bowlful with Parmesan. **Makes 4 servings, about 1¼ cups (300 mL) each.**

**MAKE AHEAD:** Soup can be refrigerated for up to two days.

***Nutritional Note***

For someone on a sodium-restricted diet, use either water or homemade stock without salt, not canned stock or a bouillon cube. Sodium would then be 224 g per serving

***Fresh Herbs***

Instead of dried herbs in this soup, use 2 tbsp (25 mL) chopped fresh basil and 2 tsp (10 mL) fresh rosemary.

*PER SERVING:*

233 calories

13 g protein

6 g total fat
  2 g saturated fat
  5 mg cholesterol

33 g carbohydrate
  2 g dietary fibre

806 mg sodium

478 mg potassium

GOOD: Iron
EXCELLENT: Folate

# Carrot and Corn Chowder

*Hannah's Kitchen in Toronto is a favorite lunch spot for surrounding office staff. Here is one of their delicious soup recipes from co-owner Susan Hughes.*

| | | |
|---|---|---|
| 1 tsp | olive oil | 5 mL |
| 1 | onion, chopped | 1 |
| 1 | leek (white part only), thinly sliced | 1 |
| 1½ cups | water or vegetable stock | 375 mL |
| 1 | potato, peeled and diced | 1 |
| 3 | medium carrots, peeled and diced | 3 |
| 1 | sweet potato, peeled and diced | 1 |
| ½ cup | coarsely chopped fresh parsley | 125 mL |
| 2 tbsp | all-purpose flour | 25 mL |
| 1½ cups | low-fat milk | 375 mL |
| 1½ cups | corn niblets | 375 mL |
| | Salt and pepper | |
| 1 tbsp | fresh thyme (or 1 tsp/5 mL dried) | 15 mL |

**1.** In large nonstick saucepan, heat oil over medium heat; cook onion and leek, stirring occasionally, for 5 to 10 minutes or until onions are tender. Add a little of the water if necessary to prevent sticking.

**2.** Add 1¼ cups (300 mL) of the water, potato, carrots, sweet potato and half of the parsley; cover and simmer until vegetables are tender, about 15 minutes.

**3.** Mix flour with remaining ¼ cup (50 mL) water; stir into soup.

**4.** Add milk; bring to simmer, stirring. Add corn, and salt and pepper to taste.

**5.** Add thyme and remaining parsley; simmer for 1 minute. **Makes 6 servings, about ¾ cup (175 mL) each**.

*PER SERVING:*

143 calories
5 g protein
2 g total fat
   1 g saturated fat
   5 mg cholesterol
28 g carbohydrate
   3 g dietary fibre
67 mg sodium
405 mg potassium

GOOD: Folate
EXCELLENT: Vitamin A

**MAKE AHEAD:** Through step 4, covered and refrigerated for up to two days. Add thyme and parsley when reheating.

# Fish 'n' Vegetable Chowder

*This is an easy recipe to vary depending on what is in your refrigerator. The potatoes are necessary because they thicken the soup. However, the other vegetables add flavor and color and can be added to or omitted; add sweet peppers, green beans, or other vegetables you have on hand.*

| | | |
|---|---|---|
| 1 tsp | olive oil | 5 mL |
| 1 | onion, chopped | 1 |
| 2 | carrots, sliced | 2 |
| 1 | stalk celery, sliced | 1 |
| 2 | cloves garlic, minced | 2 |
| 3 | potatoes, peeled and cubed | 3 |
| 1½ cups | water or fish stock | 375 mL |
| 1 | small zucchini, cubed | 1 |
| 1 cup | sliced mushrooms | 250 mL |
| 1 lb | sole, cod or haddock fillets (frozen or thawed), cut in chunks | 500 g |
| 1 cup | corn niblets or frozen peas | 250 mL |
| 2 cups | 2% milk | 500 mL |
| ½ tsp | dried basil or dillweed (or 3 tbsp/50 mL chopped fresh) | 2 mL |
| | Salt and pepper | |

**1.** In heavy saucepan, heat oil over medium heat; cook onion for 5 minutes or until softened.

**2.** Add carrots, celery, garlic, potatoes and water; bring to boil. Reduce heat, cover and simmer for 10 minutes. Add zucchini, mushrooms, fish and corn; bring to simmer. Cook, covered, for 3 minutes, or until fish is opaque.

**3.** Add milk and basil; bring to a simmer over medium-low heat. Season with salt and pepper to taste. **Makes 4 servings, about 1¾ cups (425 mL) each.**

**MAKE AHEAD:** Soup can be covered and refrigerated for up to two days; reheat gently.

## Seafood Vegetable Chowder

Follow recipe for Fish 'n' Vegetable Chowder, but instead of 1 lb (500 g) fish fillets, substitute ½ lb (250 g) fish fillets and ¼ lb (125 g) each shucked clams and shelled chopped medium or small shrimp or scallops. Use any liquid from clams plus water to make 1½ cups (375 mL). Garnish with chopped fresh dill or parsley.

*PER SERVING:*

330 calories
30 g protein
5 g total fat
    2 g saturated fat
    64 mg cholesterol
43 g carbohydrate
    5 g dietary fibre
197 mg sodium
1255 mg potassium

GOOD: Folate; Calcium
EXCELLENT: Vitamin A

# Hearty Scotch Broth

*In the winter, I like to serve this hearty soup for supper along with some fresh bread and a salad. It's very handy to have in the refrigerator for those rushed weekday dinners. It's best to make the soup in advance — not only does the flavor improve but when it is cool, you can remove any fat that hardens on top.*

| | | |
|---|---|---|
| 2 cups | chopped cooked lamb or 1½ lb (750 g) lamb shanks | 500 mL |
| 8 cups | water | 2 L |
| 1 | bay leaf | 1 |
| 2 | medium onions, chopped | 2 |
| 2 | stalks celery, diced | 2 |
| 2 | medium potatoes, peeled and diced | 2 |
| ¼ cup | barley | 50 mL |
| 1½ cups | diced peeled rutabaga | 375 mL |
| 2 cups | chopped cabbage | 500 mL |
| 2 | medium carrots, grated | 2 |
| ½ cup | chopped fresh parsley | 125 mL |
| ¼ tsp | each salt and pepper | 1 mL |

**1.** In large pot, combine lamb, water, bay leaf and onions; bring to boil. Cover, reduce heat and simmer for 1 hour. (If using cooked meat, simmer until onion is tender.) Skim fat from top.

**2.** Add celery, potatoes, barley and rutabaga; simmer for 15 minutes.

**3.** Add cabbage and carrots; simmer until vegetables are tender, about 10 minutes.

**4.** Remove lamb shank; cut meat from bones and return to soup. Discard bay leaf. Add parsley, salt and pepper. **Makes 8 servings, about 1 cup (250 mL) each.**

## Lamb

Because lamb has a stronger flavor than beef or poultry, it is particularly good for soups — a little meat will add a lot of flavor. You can use any cut of lamb, however you might as well use less expensive cuts such as shank or shoulder. If using shoulder, use about 1 lb (500 g) as there will be much less bone than in shank.

For fat-restricted diets, make the broth first: bring lamb shank, water, bay leaf and 1 chopped onion to boil; simmer for 1 hour. Remove lamb and cut meat from bone; reserve. Refrigerate broth for 4 hours or overnight; skim all fat from top. Reheat broth; add remaining onion and continue as in recipe.

**MAKE AHEAD:** Soup can be covered and refrigerated for up to two days; skim off any fat; add parsley when reheating.

# SALADS

Light Tuna Salad in Tomatoes

Warm Scallop Salad

Chick-Pea, Sweet Pepper and
Fresh Basil Salad

Mediterranean Lentil and Bean Salad

Bulgur Salad with Cucumber and Feta

Easy Couscous Vegetable Salad

Asparagus and Mushroom Salad

Green Bean Salad with
Buttermilk Dressing

Salade Composée

Thai Cucumber Salad

Oriental Coleslaw

Purple Vegetable Slaw

Warm Potato and Tuna Salad

Tossed Green Salad with
Asian Vinaigrette

Tomato Basil Dressing

Yogurt Herb Dressing

Mustard Garlic Vinaigrette

# Light Tuna Salad in Tomatoes

*This is a lightened-up version of something my mother used to make in the summer for lunch or as part of a salad plate at supper. It's very handy when the refrigerator is bare but the cupboard has a can of tuna on the shelf. Coarsely chopped olives or capers are also good in this. Be sure to buy tuna packed in water. You might also want to try the low-sodium canned tuna.*

## Tuna Salad Plate

On individual plates, arrange leaf lettuce, grated carrot, sliced cucumber, and drained canned chick-peas tossed with lemon juice, parsley and pepper. Place a Light Tuna Salad in Tomato in centre of plate.

| | | |
|---|---|---|
| 1 | can (6½ oz/184 g) water-packed tuna, drained | 1 |
| 2 | green onions, chopped | 2 |
| 1 | stalk celery, diced | 1 |
| ½ cup | corn niblets | 125 mL |
| 2 tbsp | light mayonnaise | 25 mL |
| 2 tbsp | low-fat yogurt | 25 mL |
| 2 tbsp | each chopped fresh coriander and parsley | 25 mL |
| 2 tsp | lemon juice | 10 mL |
| | Pepper | |
| 3 | tomatoes | 3 |

**1.** Combine tuna, onions, celery, corn, mayonnaise, yogurt, coriander, parsley, lemon juice, and pepper to taste; mix well.

**2.** Quarter tomatoes, cutting almost but not completely through to bottom. Spoon tuna mixture into centre. **Makes 3 servings**.

 **MAKE AHEAD:** Through step 1, covered and refrigerated for up to 24 hours.

| TUNA TYPES | | | |
|---|---|---|---|
| Compare ½ cup (125 mL) tuna: | Calories | Fat (g) | Sodium (mg) |
| Packed in oil, drained | 157 | 7 | 334 |
| Packed in water, drained | 115 | 2 | 331 |
| Low-sodium | 115 | 2 | 42 |

# Warm Scallop Salad

*My friend Donna Osler serves this fabulous salad as a first course at dinner parties. It's a good choice: not only does it taste delicious but it serves as both a fish course and a salad.*

| | | |
|---|---|---|
| 1 | bunch arugula | 1 |
| 8 cups | torn mixed greens | 2 L |
| 2 tsp | vegetable oil | 10 mL |
| 1 tbsp | grated gingerroot | 15 mL |
| 1 | clove garlic, minced | 1 |
| ¼ cup | diced sweet red pepper | 50 mL |
| 1 lb | large scallops | 500 g |
| ¼ cup | dry sherry | 50 mL |
| ¼ cup | chopped fresh coriander | 50 mL |

### Vinaigrette

| | | |
|---|---|---|
| 2 tbsp | sesame oil | 25 mL |
| 1 | clove garlic, minced | 1 |
| 1 tbsp | lemon juice | 15 mL |
| 1 tsp | sodium-reduced soy sauce | 5 mL |
| ¼ tsp | granulated sugar | 1 mL |

1. Vinaigrette: In large bowl, mix oil, garlic, lemon juice, soy sauce and sugar; add arugula and greens and toss well. Divide among plates.

2. In skillet, heat oil over medium heat; cook ginger, garlic and red pepper, stirring, for 2 minutes.

3. Add scallops, sherry and coriander; cover and cook for 3 minutes or until scallops are opaque through to centre, turning once. Using slotted spoon, divide scallops among plates.

4. Increase heat to high and cook until pan liquid is reduced slightly; drizzle over salads. **Makes 6 appetizer or 3 main-course servings.**

**MAKE AHEAD:** Prepare vinaigrette. Measure out all ingredients up to one day in advance.

### *Arugula*

Arugula is an oak-leaf-shaped salad green with a delicious nutty, peppery taste. If unavailable substitute watercress in this recipe.

### *Tip*

If using frozen scallops, be sure they are completely thawed before using in this recipe.

*PER SERVING (APPETIZER):*

153 calories
15 g protein
7 g total fat
    1 g saturated fat
    25 mg cholesterol
6 g carbohydrate
    1 g dietary fibre
178 mg sodium
617 mg potassium

GOOD: Vitamin C
EXCELLENT: Vitamin A;
Folate

# Chick-Pea, Sweet Pepper and Fresh Basil Salad

### Dried Chick-Peas or Garbanzo Beans

For the best texture, flavor and lowest cost, cook your own chick-peas: Soak dried chick-peas overnight or for a minimum of 4 hours. Or quick-soak chick-peas by covering with water and bringing to a boil; boil 2 minutes. Remove from heat, cover and let stand for 1 hour; drain.

To cook soaked chick-peas, cover with water and bring to a boil; reduce heat, partially cover and simmer for 2 to 2½ hours or until tender. Add more water if necessary. Do not add salt until beans are tender or they will take even longer to cook.

- 1 cup (250 mL) dried = 2 to 2½ cups (500 to 625 mL) cooked.
- 1 can (19 oz/540 mL) chick-peas = 2 cups (500 mL) cooked.

*Per Serving:*

88 calories

4 g protein

3 g total fat
   0.3 g saturated fat
   0 mg cholesterol

13 g carbohydrate
   2 g dietary fibre

105 mg sodium

138 mg potassium

Good: Folate
Excellent: Vitamin C

*This salad tastes best if made a few hours (or even a day) in advance to allow the flavors to develop and blend. If you don't have time to roast the red pepper, you can use a raw sweet red pepper or a canned red pepper. White kidney beans instead of chick-peas makes a tasty variation.*

| | | |
|---|---|---|
| 1 | sweet red pepper | 1 |
| 1 | can (19 oz/540 mL) chick-peas, drained | 1 |
| 1 cup | diced cucumber | 250 mL |
| ¼ cup | minced red onion | 50 mL |
| ¼ cup | packed chopped fresh parsley | 50 mL |
| ¼ cup | packed chopped fresh basil | 50 mL |
| ¼ cup | lemon juice | 50 mL |
| 1 tbsp | olive oil | 15 mL |
| 1 | clove garlic, minced | 1 |
| | Salt and pepper | |

**1.** Roast red pepper over grill or gas flame for 15 minutes, turning often, or in 400°F (200°C) oven for 40 minutes, or until blackened and soft. Peel and seed pepper; chop coarsely.

**2.** In bowl, combine red pepper, chick-peas, cucumber, onion, parsley and basil.

**3.** In small dish, whisk together lemon juice, olive oil, garlic and salt and pepper to taste; pour over salad and toss lightly. Cover and refrigerate for at least 15 minutes or up to 1 day. **Makes 8 servings**.

**Make Ahead:** Salad can be covered and refrigerated for up to one day.

# Mediterranean Lentil and Bean Salad

*Grill extra red peppers when barbecuing one night to use in this recipe. In the winter, use canned or bottled sweet (not hot) red peppers, however, they won't have the smoky flavor of home-roasted ones. Use canned white kidney beans or navy (pea) beans.*

| | | |
|---|---|---|
| 3 | sweet red peppers | 3 |
| 1 | can (19 oz/540 mL) white beans | 1 |
| 1 | can (19 oz/540 mL) lentils | 1 |
| ½ cup | diced celery | 125 mL |
| ¼ cup | each chopped fresh basil and parsley | 50 mL |
| ¼ cup | balsamic vinegar | 50 mL |
| | Salt and pepper | |

**1.** Roast red peppers over grill or gas flame for 15 minutes, turning often, or in 400°F (200°C) oven for 40 minutes, or until peppers are soft and blackened. Peel and seed peppers; cut into strips.

**2.** Drain and rinse beans and lentils.

**3.** In bowl, combine red peppers, beans, lentils, celery, basil and parsley; toss with vinegar. Season with salt and pepper to taste. **Makes 8 servings**.

**MAKE AHEAD:** Salad can be covered and refrigerated for up to three days.

## Summer Salad Plate

Arrange Mediterranean Lentil and Bean Salad, sliced cucumbers, melon wedges and lean ham slices on each plate.

### Balsamic Vinegar

Balsamic vinegar has a mellow, sweet taste. If unavailable, substitute 3 tbsp (45 mL) red wine vinegar mixed with 1 tsp (5 mL) granulated sugar in this Mediterranean Salad.

*PER SERVING:*

138 calories
9 g protein
1 g total fat
    0.1 g saturated fat
    0 mg cholesterol
26 g carbohydrate
    7 g dietary fibre
224 mg sodium
438 mg potassium

GOOD: Vitamin A; Iron
EXCELLENT: Vitamin C; Folate

# Bulgur Salad with Cucumber and Feta

*This salad is good any time of year for packed lunches, a buffet or with barbecued chicken, meat or fish.*

| 1 cup | bulgur* | 250 mL |
|---|---|---|
| 2 cups | diced cucumber | 500 mL |
| 1 cup | chopped fresh parsley | 250 mL |
| ½ cup | finely chopped red onion | 125 mL |
| ½ cup | crumbled feta cheese | 125 mL |

**Dressing**

| 2 | cloves garlic, minced | 2 |
|---|---|---|
| ¼ cup | lemon juice | 50 mL |
| ½ tsp | salt | 2 mL |
| ¼ cup | olive oil | 50 mL |
| | Pepper | |

**1.** Soak bulgur in 6 cups (1.5 L) hot water for 1 hour; drain.

**2.** In bowl, combine bulgur, cucumber, parsley, onion and feta.

**3.** Dressing: In small bowl, combine garlic, lemon juice and salt; gradually whisk in oil. Season with pepper to taste.

**4.** Pour over salad; stir to mix. **Makes 12 servings**.

\* If you cannot find bulgur and want to use cracked wheat instead, follow package instructions for cooking cracked wheat.

## Tomatoes Stuffed with Bulgur Salad

Serve for lunch or as part of a salad plate: Cut tomatoes in half; scoop out seeds and some pulp. Fill hollow with Bulgur Salad.

## Buying Bulgur

Bulgur comes in coarse, medium or fine grind. Medium is best for salads and mixed vegetable dishes. Coarse is often used in pilafs, and fine grind is used in breads.

*Per Serving:*

101 calories
3 g protein
6 g total fat
   1 g saturated fat
   5 mg cholesterol
11 g carbohydrate
   3 g dietary fibre
159 mg sodium
106 mg potassium

**MAKE AHEAD:** Salad can be covered and refrigerated for up to two days.

# Easy Couscous Vegetable Salad

*Couscous is fast to prepare and much cheaper bought in bulk than by the box. For an appetizing summer salad plate, serve with leafy greens, sliced tomato and a piece of low-fat cheese or lean meat or hard-cooked egg. (Salad pictured after page 128.)*

| ¾ cup | water | 175 mL |
|---|---|---|
| ½ cup | couscous | 125 mL |
| 1 | stalk celery, chopped | 1 |
| 1 | green onion, chopped | 1 |
| 1 | medium carrot, shredded | 1 |
| ¾ cup | diced cucumber | 175 mL |
| ¼ cup | chopped fresh parsley | 50 mL |
| 2 tbsp | sunflower seeds | 25 mL |

**Lemon Cumin Vinaigrette**

| 2 tbsp | lemon juice | 25 mL |
|---|---|---|
| 1 tbsp | each olive oil and water | 15 mL |
| ¼ tsp | ground cumin | 1 mL |
| | Salt and pepper | |

**1.** In saucepan, bring water to boil; add couscous, cover and remove from heat. Let stand for 5 minutes; fluff with fork.

**2.** In salad bowl, combine couscous, celery, green onion, carrot, cucumber, parsley and sunflower seeds.

**3.** Lemon Cumin Vinaigrette: Whisk together lemon juice, oil, water, cumin, and salt and pepper to taste; pour over salad and toss. **Makes 4 servings**.

 **MAKE AHEAD:** Salad can be covered and refrigerated for up to two days.

## Rice Vegetable Salad

Follow recipe for Easy Couscous Vegetable Salad except cook ½ cup (125 mL) rice in 1 cup (250 mL) boiling water for 20 minutes or according to package directions. If using left-over cooked rice, use about 2 cups (500 mL).

## Couscous, Tomato and Basil Salad

Follow recipe for Easy Couscous Vegetable Salad, omitting carrot, sunflower seeds and cumin.

Add 1 chopped large tomato and ¼ cup (50 mL) or more to taste of chopped fresh basil.

*PER SERVING:*

159 calories
5 g protein
6 g total fat
    1 g saturated fat
    0 mg cholesterol
23 g carbohydrate
    3 g dietary fibre
25 mg sodium
239 mg potassium

GOOD: Folate
EXCELLENT: Vitamin A

# Asparagus and Mushroom Salad

*I like this salad for summer barbecues, buffets and to take to potlucks, because it goes with anything, tastes delicious and is easy to make. (Pictured after page 128.)*

| | | |
|---|---|---|
| 1 lb | asparagus | 500 g |
| 3 | mushrooms, diced | 3 |

**Sesame Vinaigrette**

| | | |
|---|---|---|
| 1 tbsp | rice vinegar or white wine vinegar | 15 mL |
| 1 tbsp | sodium-reduced soy sauce | 15 mL |
| 1 tbsp | sesame oil | 15 mL |
| ¼ tsp | granulated sugar | 1 mL |
| | Salt and pepper | |
| 1 tbsp | toasted sesame seeds* | 15 mL |

**1.** Cut or break off tough stem ends of asparagus. Peel stalks if large. In large pot of boiling water, cook asparagus until tender-crisp, about 4 minutes; drain. Cool under cold water; drain. Dry on paper towels.

**2.** Sesame Vinaigrette: Whisk together vinegar, soy sauce, sesame oil and sugar.

**3.** Arrange asparagus on platter; pour vinaigrette over. Add salt and pepper to taste; roll to coat. Sprinkle with sesame seeds and mushrooms. **Makes 6 servings.**

\* Toast sesame seeds in nonstick skillet over medium heat for 3 minutes or until golden.

### Green Bean and Mushroom Salad

Substitute green beans for asparagus.

**MAKE AHEAD:** Through step 2 for up to 24 hours. Cover asparagus with damp paper towel or plastic wrap and refrigerate. Through step 3 up to one hour before serving.

*PER SERVING:*

51 calories

3 g protein

3 g total fat
  1 g saturated fat
  0 mg cholesterol

4 g carbohydrate
  1 g dietary fibre

89 mg sodium

159 mg potassium

EXCELLENT: Folate

# Green Bean Salad with Buttermilk Dressing

*The idea for this salad came from Babette's Feast, a unique catering group in Toronto.*

| | | |
|---|---|---|
| 1 lb | green beans, trimmed | 500 g |
| 1 cup | coarsely chopped fresh parsley | 250 mL |
| ⅓ cup | thinly sliced red onion | 75 mL |
| 1 | sweet yellow pepper, thinly sliced | 1 |
| 3 | slices bacon, cooked and crumbled | 3 |
| ½ cup | Buttermilk Dill Dressing (sidebar, page 87) | 125 mL |

**1.** In large pot of boiling water, cook beans for 1 minute; drain and rinse under cold water. Drain and pat dry.

**2.** In salad bowl, toss together beans, parsley, onion, yellow pepper and bacon.

**3.** Add dressing and toss. **Makes 6 servings**.

**MAKE AHEAD:** Through step 2, covered and refrigerated for up to 24 hours; add dressing up to one hour before serving.

*Per Serving:*

78 calories
3 g protein
4 g total fat
    1 g saturated fat
    3 mg cholesterol
9 g carbohydrate
    3 g dietary fibre
172 mg sodium
343 mg potassium

Good: Folate
Excellent: Vitamin C

# Salade Composée

*This salad reminds me of our bicycling holidays in France because it is on every French summer menu and was my favorite lunch. I try to cook extra beets and potatoes to have on hand for this easy meal. Grated celery root (celeriac), sliced cucumber and any cold meat or fish can be added to this salad plate.*

### To Cook Beets

Trim stems 1-inch (2.5 cm) from bulb. Cook in saucepan of boiling water for about 40 minutes or until fork-tender. Drain; rinse under cold running water and slip off skins.

### To Cook Potatoes

Cook whole potatoes in saucepan of boiling water for 20 minutes or until fork-tender; drain. Shake pan over medium heat for about 1 minute to dry potatoes.

|  | Lettuce leaves |  |
|---|---|---|
| 4 | medium beets, cooked and sliced (about ¾ lb/375 g) | 4 |
| ½ cup | Mustard Garlic Vinaigrette (page 88) | 125 mL |
| 8 | small new red potatoes (unpeeled), cooked and sliced | 8 |
| 4 | medium carrots, peeled and grated (about 1½ cups/375 mL) | 4 |
| 1 cup | cooked or canned corn niblets | 250 mL |
| 1 | can (19 oz/540 mL) chick-peas, drained | 1 |
| ¼ cup | chopped fresh parsley | 50 mL |
| 2 tsp | ground cumin | 10 mL |
| 2 tbsp | balsamic vinegar | 25 mL |
| 4 | slices smoked turkey (4 oz/125 g) | 4 |

**1.** Line 4 plates with lettuce.

**2.** In small bowl, toss beets with 2 tbsp (25 mL) of the dressing; divide among plates. Repeat with potatoes, carrots and corn, arranging attractively on plates.

**3.** Toss chick-peas with parsley, cumin and vinegar; divide among plates.

**4.** Roll turkey and divide among plates. **Makes 4 servings**.

PER SERVING:

382 calories

17 g protein

13 g total fat
  2 g saturated fat
  21 mg cholesterol

53 g carbohydrate
  8 g dietary fibre

503 mg sodium

788 mg potassium

GOOD: Vitamin C
EXCELLENT: Vitamin A; Folate; Iron

**MAKE AHEAD:** Salad can be covered and refrigerated for up to 30 minutes.

# Thai Cucumber Salad

*This light, tangy salad, from my friend and cookbook author Rose Murray, is perfect with grilled meats, poultry, fish or as part of an Oriental meal. For a special meal, garnish with tiny salad shrimp.*

| | | |
|---|---|---|
| 1 | English cucumber | 1 |
| ¼ cup | chopped fresh coriander | 50 mL |
| ¼ cup | lime juice | 50 mL |
| 2 tbsp | minced red onion | 25 mL |
| 2 tbsp | rice vinegar or cider vinegar | 25 mL |
| 1 tsp | granulated sugar | 5 mL |
| ¼ tsp | red pepper flakes* | 1 mL |
| | Boston lettuce leaves (optional) | |
| | Chopped peanuts (optional) | |

**1.** Cut cucumber in half lengthwise. By hand or in food processor, cut into thin slices.

**2.** In bowl, combine coriander, lime juice, onion, vinegar, sugar and red pepper flakes, stirring to dissolve sugar.

**3.** Add cucumber and toss gently. Cover and refrigerate for 4 hours.

**4.** Line individual salad plates or platter with lettuce leaves (if using). Spoon cucumber mixture in centre; sprinkle with peanuts (if using). **Makes 6 servings.**

\* You could use 1 small fresh hot pepper, such as a jalapeño or serrano chili, seeded and cut into thin strips, or Thai chili paste instead of red pepper flakes.

**MAKE AHEAD:** Through step 3, covered and refrigerated for up to one day.

***Nutritional Note***
This is one of the few salads with no oil in the dressing, so it is very low in fat.

*PER SERVING:*

16 calories
1 g protein
0.1 g total fat
    0 g saturated fat
    0 mg cholesterol
4 g carbohydrate
    1 g dietary fibre
2 mg sodium
129 mg potassium

# Oriental Coleslaw

*My sister-in-law Linda Elliott made this salad for a family dinner in Vancouver using a combination of red and green cabbage. I sometimes use Napa or Chinese cabbage instead.*

| | | |
|---|---|---|
| ¼ cup | sliced almonds | 50 mL |
| ¼ cup | sunflower seeds | 50 mL |
| 2 tbsp | sesame seeds | 25 mL |
| 6 cups | thinly sliced cabbage (green, red or Napa) | 1.5 L |
| 3 cups | bean sprouts | 750 mL |
| ½ cup | chopped green onions | 125 mL |
| 1 | pkg (85 g) dried Oriental soup noodles, crushed* | 1 |

**Dressing**

| | | |
|---|---|---|
| ¼ cup | cider vinegar or rice vinegar | 50 mL |
| 2 tbsp | granulated sugar | 25 mL |
| 2 tbsp | sodium-reduced soy sauce | 25 mL |
| 2 tbsp | sesame oil | 25 mL |
| | Pepper | |

**1.** Spread almonds, sunflower and sesame seeds on baking sheet; bake in 350°F (180°C) oven for 5 minutes. Let cool.

**2.** In bowl, combine cabbage, bean sprouts, onions and noodles.

**3.** Dressing: In small bowl, combine vinegar, sugar and soy sauce; whisk in oil. Add pepper to taste.

**4.** Toss toasted nuts and dressing with cabbage mixture. Cover and refrigerate for at least 1 hour. **Makes 12 servings.**

*If soup noodles are unavailable, add about 1 cup (250 mL) cooked chow mein or other thin noodles, cut in 2-inch (5 cm) pieces.

*Per Serving:*

114 calories
4 g protein
6 g total fat
    1 g saturated fat
    7 mg cholesterol
12 g carbohydrate
    2 g dietary fibre
92 mg sodium
206 mg potassium

Good: Vitamin C; Folate

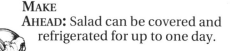

**MAKE AHEAD:** Salad can be covered and refrigerated for up to one day.

# Purple Vegetable Slaw

*This salad (pictured opposite page 160) is fabulous to serve with any grilled meats or with Marinated Baked Tofu (page 191), or with soup for a light meal.*

| | | |
|---|---|---|
| 2 cups | finely shredded red cabbage | 500 mL |
| | Salt | |
| ½ cup | red kidney beans, drained and rinsed | 125 mL |
| ½ cup | corn niblets | 125 mL |
| ⅓ cup | chopped fresh coriander | 75 mL |
| 1 | tomato, diced | 1 |
| 1 | green onion, chopped | 1 |
| 2 tbsp | balsamic or red wine vinegar | 25 mL |
| 1 tbsp | sesame oil | 15 mL |
| ¼ tsp | red pepper flakes | 1 mL |
| 1 | clove garlic, minced | 1 |
| | Pepper | |

**1.** Sprinkle cabbage with ¼ tsp (1 mL) salt; set aside.

**2.** In bowl, combine kidney beans, corn, coriander, tomato, green onion, vinegar, oil, red pepper flakes and garlic; mix well.

**3.** Add cabbage, and salt and pepper to taste. **Makes 4 servings**.

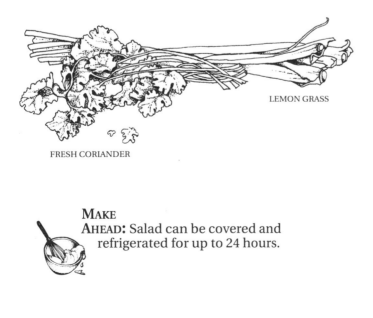

LEMON GRASS

FRESH CORIANDER

**MAKE AHEAD:** Salad can be covered and refrigerated for up to 24 hours.

### Coriander

Fresh coriander, or cilantro, has a wonderful, distinct flavor. Don't confuse it with coriander seeds or ground coriander, which are totally different. If you can't find fresh coriander leaves, substitute ⅓ cup (75 mL) chopped fresh parsley and 1 tsp (5 mL) dried cilantro.

*PER SERVING:*

92 calories

3 g protein

4 g total fat
  1 g saturated fat
  0 mg cholesterol

13 g carbohydrate
  4 g dietary fibre

223 mg sodium

299 mg potassium

GOOD: Vitamin C; Folate

# Warm Potato and Tuna Salad

## Warm Potato Salad

For a side-dish potato salad, omit tuna; green beans and red pepper are optional.

### Cooking Tips

Don't peel the potatoes; the red skins are attractive and contain fibre and nutrients. To save time, cut the potatoes into ¾-inch (2 cm) pieces so they will cook faster.

To refrigerate salad for up to 24 hours, cook green beans separately; remove from refrigerator 30 minutes before serving and add green beans.

### Nutritional Note

To reduce sodium in this salad, use low-sodium canned tuna or fresh cooked tuna and omit anchovy paste.

PER SERVING:

291 calories
17 g protein
6 g total fat
    1 g saturated fat
    9 mg cholesterol
45 g carbohydrate
    5 g dietary fibre
321 mg sodium
1152 mg potassium

EXCELLENT: Vitamin C; Folate; Iron

*This salad is a meal in itself to serve on lettuce leaves with fresh bread and sliced tomatoes or perhaps a bowl of soup.*

| | | |
|---|---|---|
| 2 lb | new red potatoes, cut into chunks | 1 kg |
| ½ lb | green beans, halved | 250 g |
| 4 | green onions, chopped | 4 |
| 2 | stalks celery, chopped | 2 |
| 1 | sweet red pepper, chopped (optional) | 1 |
| ¼ cup | coarsely chopped fresh parsley | 50 mL |
| 1 | can (6½ oz/184 g) water-packed tuna, drained and broken into chunks | 1 |
| | Salt | |

### Dressing

| | | |
|---|---|---|
| 3 tbsp | tarragon or cider vinegar | 50 mL |
| 2 tbsp | water | 25 mL |
| 1 tbsp | Dijon mustard | 15 mL |
| 1 tbsp | anchovy paste | 15 mL |
| 4 tsp | olive oil | 20 mL |
| 1 | clove garlic, minced | 1 |
| | Pepper | |

**1.** In saucepan, cover potatoes with water; bring to boil. Reduce heat and simmer until nearly tender, about 5 minutes. Add green beans; cook for 3 to 5 minutes or until tender-crisp; drain.

**2.** Dressing: Whisk together vinegar, water, mustard, anchovy paste, oil, garlic, and pepper to taste; toss ¼ cup (50 mL) with hot potato mixture.

**3.** Add green onions, celery, red pepper (if using) and parsley. Add remaining dressing and toss.

**4.** Gently stir in tuna, without breaking up chunks. Add salt and pepper to taste. **Makes 4 main-course servings**.

**MAKE AHEAD:** Salad can be covered and refrigerated for up to four hours.

# Tossed Green Salad with Asian Vinaigrette

*Use any combination of colorful seasonal greens in this tossed salad; here is just a suggestion.*

| 3 cups | each torn Boston lettuce, radicchio, watercress and spinach | 750 mL |
|---|---|---|

### Asian Vinaigrette

| ¼ cup | rice vinegar | 50 mL |
|---|---|---|
| 2 tbsp | water | 25 mL |
| 2 tbsp | sesame oil | 25 mL |
| 2 tbsp | sodium-reduced soy sauce | 25 mL |
| ½ tsp | granulated sugar | 2 mL |
| 1 | clove garlic, minced | 1 |
| 1 | green onion, minced | 1 |

**1.** In large salad bowl, combine Boston lettuce, radicchio, watercress and spinach.

**2.** Asian Vinaigrette: Whisk together vinegar, water, sesame oil, soy sauce, sugar, garlic and onion. Pour half over salad; toss to mix. Add more dressing if desired. **Makes 8 servings.**

**MAKE AHEAD:** Prepare greens; wrap in towels, place in plastic bag and refrigerate for up to eight hours. Vinaigrette will keep, covered and refrigerated, for up to three days.

## Light Salads

Be careful: salads aren't light if they're drowned in high-fat dressings.

There's a good selection of calorie-reduced or fat-free dressings available — I counted 26 in one supermarket. Be sure to read the nutrition information on the labels: choose the salad dressings with 3 g of fat or less per 1 tbsp (15 mL).

Better yet, mix your own flavorful low-fat salad dressings. They take only minutes to make, taste fresher and are about one-third of the cost of store-bought ones. The secret is adding extra herbs, mustard, garlic or other seasonings for flavor and replacing some of the oil in a traditional dressing with water, buttermilk, low-fat yogurt or juicy tomatoes.

*PER SERVING:*

30 calories
2 g protein
2 g total fat
   0.3 g saturated fat
   0 mg cholesterol
3 g carbohydrate
   1 g dietary fibre
87 mg sodium
268 mg potassium

GOOD: Vitamin A
EXCELLENT: Folate

# Tomato Basil Dressing

*For a starter salad, spoon this dressing over a mixture of lettuces arranged on individual plates. Or toss with a pasta salad.*

| | | |
|---|---|---|
| 1 cup | finely chopped tomatoes | 250 mL |
| ¼ cup | chopped fresh basil | 50 mL |
| 1 | clove garlic, minced | 1 |
| 2 tbsp | chopped green onion | 25 mL |
| 2 tbsp | olive oil | 25 mL |
| 2 tbsp | lemon juice or balsamic vinegar | 25 mL |
| ½ tsp | granulated sugar | 2 mL |
| ¼ tsp | each salt and pepper | 1 mL |

**1.** In small bowl, combine tomatoes, basil, garlic, onion, oil, lemon juice, sugar, salt and pepper. Let stand for at least 15 minutes. **Makes 1 cup (250 mL).**

## Basil

Basil is one of the easiest herbs to grow. I plant some in the garden and more in a pot. I take a pot when I go to the cottage (my husband groans at another thing to pack into an already filled car). In the fall, I bring the pots indoors and have fresh basil for another few months.

**MAKE AHEAD:** Dressing can be covered and refrigerated for up to one day.

PER SERVING
(1 TBSP/15 ML):

19 calories
0.1 g protein
2 g total fat
    0.2 g saturated fat
    0 mg cholesterol
1 g carbohydrate
    0.2 g dietary fibre
37 mg sodium
34 mg potassium

# Yogurt Herb Dressing

*Use this creamy dressing for pasta salads, green salads and potato salad.*

| | | |
|---|---|---|
| 1 cup | low-fat yogurt | 250 mL |
| ½ cup | light mayonnaise | 125 mL |
| ⅓ cup | chopped fresh parsley | 75 mL |
| ⅓ cup | chopped fresh dill* | 75 mL |
| 1 | clove garlic, minced | 1 |
| 1 tbsp | lemon juice | 15 mL |
| 1 tsp | Dijon mustard | 5 mL |
| ½ tsp | salt | 2 mL |
| | Pepper | |

**1.** In bowl or large measuring cup, combine yogurt, mayonnaise, parsley, dill, garlic, lemon juice, mustard, salt, and pepper to taste. Using whisk or fork, mix well. **Makes 1⅔ cups (400 mL).**

* If fresh dill isn't available, substitute ½ tsp (2 mL) dried dillweed.

**MAKE AHEAD:** Dressing can be covered and refrigerated for up to one week.

## Potato Salad with Yogurt Herb Dressing

Lightly mix 2 cups (500 mL) cooked cubed potatoes with ¼ cup (50 mL) Yogurt Herb Dressing. Add sliced radishes to taste.

## Buttermilk Dill Dressing

Prepare Yogurt Herb Dressing except substitute 1 cup (250 mL) buttermilk for the yogurt.

*PER SERVING (1 TBSP/15 mL):*

20 calories
1 g protein
2 g total fat
    0.2 g saturated fat
    1 mg cholesterol
1 g carbohydrate
    0 g dietary fibre
82 mg sodium
30 mg potassium

# Mustard Garlic Vinaigrette

*This is a good all-purpose vinaigrette.*

| | | |
|---|---|---|
| 2 tbsp | cider vinegar or white wine vinegar | 25 mL |
| 1 tbsp | Dijon mustard | 15 mL |
| ½ tsp | granulated sugar | 2 mL |
| 1 | clove garlic, minced | 1 |
| ⅓ cup | water | 75 mL |
| ⅓ cup | olive oil | 75 mL |
| 2 tsp | freshly grated Parmesan cheese | 10 mL |
| | Salt and pepper | |

**1.** In small bowl, mix together vinegar, mustard, sugar, garlic and water; gradually whisk in oil. Stir in Parmesan.

**2.** Season with salt and pepper to taste. **Makes about 1 cup (250 mL).**

***Pasta Salads***

For pasta salads, see pages 168 to 172.

*PER SERVING*
*(1 TBSP/15 ML):*

43 calories
0.2 g protein
5 g total fat
   1 g saturated fat
   0 mg cholesterol
0.4 g carbohydrate
   0 g dietary fibre
18 mg sodium
4 mg potassium

**MAKE AHEAD:** Vinaigrette can be covered and refrigerated for up to one week.

# POULTRY

Chinese Chicken Burgers

Grilled Chicken Breast Burgers with
Sautéed Onions and Sun-Dried Tomatoes

Jamaican Jerk Chicken

Herb and Buttermilk Barbecued Chicken

Sherry Chicken Breasts Stuffed with
Zucchini and Carrots

Hoisin Sesame Chicken Platter

Chicken and Snow Peas in
Black Bean Sauce

Asian Chicken

Asian Sauce

Barbecued Curried Chicken Breasts

Chicken and Vegetable Stew with
Parsley Dumplings

Turkey Vegetable Casserole

Roast Turkey with Sausage, Apple
and Herb Stuffing

Sausage, Apple and Herb Stuffing

Giblet Gravy

Lemon Pepper Turkey Loaf

Thai Barbecued Turkey Scaloppine

# Chinese Chicken Burgers

*Serve these juicy, delicious burgers in a bun with sliced tomato and lettuce, or as patties along with stir-fried bok choy and rice or Oven-Baked Fries (page 151).*

| | | |
|---|---|---|
| 1 lb | lean ground chicken | 500 g |
| 1 | egg (or 2 egg whites) | 1 |
| 2 | green onions, chopped | 2 |
| 1 tbsp | sodium-reduced soy sauce | 15 mL |
| 1 tbsp | cornstarch | 15 mL |
| 2 tsp | minced gingerroot | 10 mL |
| 2 | cloves garlic, minced | 2 |
| 1 tbsp | chopped fresh coriander or parsley | 15 mL |
| | Pepper | |

**1.** In bowl, combine chicken, egg, onions, soy sauce, cornstarch, ginger, garlic, coriander, and pepper to taste; mix gently.

**2.** Form into 4 patties (mixture will be moist) about ½-inch (1 cm) thick.

**3.** Broil on greased broiler pan or baking sheet for 6 minutes or until browned on top; turn and broil for 2 to 3 minutes or until no longer pink inside. **Makes 4 servings**.

*PER SERVING:*

191 calories
23 g protein
9 g total fat
   2 g saturated fat
   125 mg cholesterol
4 g carbohydrate
   0.3 g dietary fibre
210 mg sodium
245 mg potassium

**MAKE AHEAD:** Through step 2, covered and refrigerated for up to four hours.

# Grilled Chicken Breast Burgers with Sautéed Onions and Sun-Dried Tomatoes

*The idea for this came from Browne's Bistro in Toronto, where they serve the most wonderful grilled chicken sandwich with a sun-dried tomato pesto and sautéed onions. Serve with coleslaw or a tossed salad.*

| | | |
|---|---|---|
| 1 tbsp | soft margarine or butter | 15 mL |
| 4 cups | sliced Spanish onions | 1 L |
| ¼ cup | chopped dry-packed sun-dried tomatoes | 50 mL |
| 1 | large clove garlic, minced | 1 |
| | Water | |
| 4 | boneless skinless chicken breasts (about 1 lb/500 g) | 4 |
| 4 | whole wheat buns or Kaiser rolls | 4 |

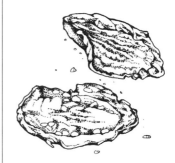

SUN-DRIED TOMATOES

**1.** In large nonstick skillet, melt margarine over medium heat; cook onions, stirring occasionally, for 10 minutes or until tender.

**2.** Add tomatoes, garlic and 1 tbsp (15 mL) water; cook for 5 minutes, adding another tablespoon (15 mL) water if needed to prevent sticking.

**3.** Meanwhile, place chicken on greased grill over medium heat; grill for about 4 minutes on each side or until no longer pink inside.

**4.** Toast buns. Spoon some of the onion mixture over bottom halves. Top with chicken, then remaining onion mixture and bun tops. **Makes 4 servings**.

**MAKE AHEAD:** Through step 2, covered and refrigerated for up to one day; reheat to serve.

*PER SERVING:*

378 calories
35 g protein
6 g total fat
   1 g saturated fat
   73 mg cholesterol
48 g carbohydrate
   6 g dietary fibre
527 mg sodium
762 mg potassium

GOOD: Iron
EXCELLENT: Folate

# Jamaican Jerk Chicken

*This fabulous spicy sauce is traditionally cooked with dried meats in a large pot over an open fire. It is absolutely delicious with chicken or a roast of pork. I prefer to use a jalapeño pepper instead of the traditional Scotch bonnet pepper because the jalapeño is not as hot.*

## Jerk

The term jerk refers to a traditional method of preserving meats: cutting them into strips and drying them in the sun. I use regular chicken in this recipe.

## Low Sodium

For a sodium-restricted diet, omit soy sauce and salt. Sodium will then be 122 mg/serving.

| | | |
|---|---|---|
| 1 | onion, quartered | 1 |
| 1 | Scotch bonnet* or hot pepper, halved | 1 |
| 3 | cloves garlic, halved | 3 |
| 4 | green onions, coarsely chopped | 4 |
| ¼ cup | orange juice | 50 mL |
| ¼ cup | sodium-reduced soy sauce | 50 mL |
| 1 tbsp | vegetable oil | 15 mL |
| 1 tbsp | wine vinegar | 15 mL |
| 1 tsp | each dried thyme and ground allspice | 5 mL |
| ¼ tsp | each cinnamon, curry powder, salt and pepper | 1 mL |
| 2 lb | skinless chicken pieces | 1 kg |

**1.** In food processor, purée onion, hot pepper, garlic and green onions. Add orange juice, soy sauce, oil, vinegar, thyme, allspice, cinnamon, curry powder, salt and pepper; process to mix.

**2.** Pour marinade over chicken pieces; cover and refrigerate for 2 hours, turning occasionally.

**3.** Grill over high heat for about 20 minutes on each side, or bake in 325°F (160°C) oven for 40 minutes, or until no longer pink inside. **Makes 4 servings**.

\* A Scotch bonnet pepper is fiery hot. You can substitute jalapeño, serrano or banana pepper and wear rubber gloves when handling. I discard the seeds because they are so hot.

PER SERVING:

256 calories

32 g protein

8 g total fat
  1 g saturated fat
  95 mg cholesterol

15 g carbohydrate
  3 g dietary fibre

750 mg sodium

713 mg potassium

EXCELLENT: Vitamin C; Folate; Iron

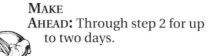

**MAKE AHEAD:** Through step 2 for up to two days.

# Herb and Buttermilk Barbecued Chicken

*This delicious chicken recipe is from* Canadian Living *food writer and test kitchen assistant, Vicki Burns. Buttermilk is low in fat yet thick and creamy, perfect for marinating. If it's not available, substitute 2% evaporated milk.*

| 3 lb | chicken parts, skinned | 1.5 kg |
|---|---|---|

**Buttermilk Marinade**

| ¾ cup | buttermilk | 175 mL |
|---|---|---|
| 2 tbsp | Dijon mustard | 25 mL |
| 2 | cloves garlic, minced | 2 |
| 2 tsp | each dried oregano, basil, thyme and rosemary | 10 mL |
| ¼ tsp | each salt and pepper | 1 mL |

**1.** Buttermilk Marinade: In large bowl, combine buttermilk, mustard, garlic, oregano, basil, thyme, rosemary, salt and pepper.

**2.** Add chicken, turning pieces to coat. Cover and refrigerate for 3 hours, turning occasionally.

**3.** Place chicken on greased grill over medium heat; grill, turning occasionally, for 30 to 40 minutes or until juices run clear when chicken is pierced. **Makes 6 servings**.

 **MAKE AHEAD:** Through step 2 for up to 24 hours.

---

### BARBECUING SAFELY

Recent research shows that whenever fat drips onto a heat source, chemicals form on the outside of the meat, fish or poultry that might increase the risks of some types of cancer. The Canadian Cancer Society suggests you barbecue in moderation. Also:

• For meat or poultry that requires a long cooking time, microwave first, then discard juices, and grill; or wrap in foil, then grill.

• Prevent flare-ups: raise rack if necessary and keep the water spray bottle handy for dousing. Use a drip can to catch fat, or cover the grill with foil and poke holes in it to let fat drip through.

• Cook meat until medium well done: if too rare, it will be higher in fat and may contain harmful bacteria; if too well done or charred, it will be higher in chemicals.

• Use a **clean** platter for the cooked meat. Don't eat charred parts.

---

*Very Good*

### Baked Buttermilk Herb Chicken

Follow recipe for Herb and Buttermilk Barbecued Chicken through step 2. Spread ¾ cup (175 mL) cornmeal on plate. Remove chicken from marinade; coat each piece all over with cornmeal. Bake on baking sheet in 350°F (180°C) oven for 45 minutes or until juices run clear when chicken is pierced with fork. (Pictured opposite page 64.)

*else ½ flour for breading*

### Buttermilk

Despite its name, buttermilk is not high in fat and is wonderful to use in lower-fat cooking and baking.

The dilemma everyone faces is what to do with the rest of the buttermilk in the carton. See index for other recipes using buttermilk.

*PER SERVING:*
- 152 calories
- 25 g protein
- 4 g total fat
  - 1 g saturated fat
  - 78 mg cholesterol
- 3 g carbohydrate
  - 0.1 g dietary fibre
- 264 mg sodium
- 271 mg potassium

# Sherry Chicken Breasts Stuffed with Zucchini and Carrots

*Light yet full of flavor, these make-ahead chicken breasts are perfect for a dinner party.*

| | | |
|---|---|---|
| 6 | boneless skinless chicken breasts (1½ lb/750 g) | 6 |
| 1 tsp | soft margarine or butter | 5 mL |
| ½ cup | sherry | 125 mL |
| 12 | large spinach leaves | 12 |

**Stuffing**

| | | |
|---|---|---|
| 1 tbsp | soft margarine or butter | 15 mL |
| 1 | onion, chopped | 1 |
| 2 | cloves garlic, minced | 2 |
| 1 cup | coarsely grated zucchini | 250 mL |
| ½ cup | coarsely grated carrot | 125 mL |
| ½ tsp | dried thyme | 2 mL |
| ½ cup | fresh bread crumbs | 125 mL |
| 2 tbsp | chopped fresh parsley | 25 mL |
| 1 | egg white | 1 |
| ¼ tsp | each salt and pepper | 1 mL |

## Chicken Breasts Stuffed with Mushrooms and Leeks

Omit onion, zucchini and carrot from stuffing. Substitute 1½ cups (375 mL) finely chopped mushrooms and ¾ cup (175 mL) chopped white of leek.

**1.** Between sheets of waxed paper, pound chicken to ¼-inch (5 mm) thickness.

**2.** Remove tough stems from spinach; rinse spinach. With just the water clinging to leaves, cook spinach for 1 minute or just until wilted; drain and set aside.

**3.** Stuffing: In nonstick skillet, melt margarine over medium heat; cook onion and garlic for 3 minutes. Stir in zucchini, carrot and thyme; cook, stirring often, for 5 minutes or until tender. Remove from heat. Add crumbs, parsley, egg white, salt and pepper; mix well.

**4.** Cover top of each chicken breast with 2 spinach leaves; spread stuffing evenly over spinach. Carefully roll up each breast and tie each end with cotton string.

**5.** In large nonstick skillet, melt margarine over medium heat; cook stuffed breasts for 5 minutes, turning often.

**6.** Pour in sherry; reduce heat to medium-low and cook, covered, for 10 to 12 minutes or until chicken is no longer pink inside, turning to coat in sauce for last 2 minutes.

**7.** Let stand for 5 minutes. Untie each roll and slice diagonally into 3 or 4 slices. **Makes 6 servings**.

Make Ahead: Through step 4, covered and refrigerated for up to eight hours.

---

### BUYING GROUND MEAT OR POULTRY

If you're making that late-afternoon dash to the supermarket, quick-cooking ground meat is a good choice for a fast, family-pleasing dinner. But when you're sorting through the labels for lower-fat grinds, percentages of fat and terms like *regular*, *lean* and *extra lean* may break your stride.

Beef is the only ground meat that must meet government regulations for fat content: by weight, regular grinds contain no more than 30 per cent fat; medium, 23 per cent; and lean, 17 per cent. Some retailers use the term *extra lean* for ground beef with less than 10 per cent fat.

To date, there are guidelines, but no enforced regulations, for fat content labelling of ground turkey, chicken, pork, lamb or veal. Along with the lean ground poultry, both the skin and fat are often included in the grinder. To ensure that you are getting lower-fat ground poultry, choose packages labelled not with just the word lean, but with the actual percentage of fat—10 per cent or lower is your best choice. Or, buy larger pieces of poultry or meat, remove the fat, bones and skin (if any) and grind it yourself.

Do keep in mind that the percentage of fat on the label is measured by weight and doesn't reflect the percentage of calories from fat. For example, a quarter-pound beef patty made from lean meat, which has 17 per cent fat by weight, actually contains 12 grams of fat when broiled—and that means that 54 per cent of the calories come from fat.

---

*Elegant Dinner For Six*
- Warm Scallop Salad (page 73)
- Sherry Chicken Breasts Stuffed with Zucchini and Carrots
- Snow Peas with Mushrooms (page 143)
- Sweet Potato and Apple Purée (page 152)
- Lemon Mousse with Raspberry Sauce (page 221)

*Per Serving:*
197 calories
29 g protein
4 g total fat
  1 g saturated fat
  69 mg cholesterol
7 g carbohydrate
  1 g dietary fibre
251 mg sodium
482 mg potassium

---

Excellent: Vitamin A

# Hoisin Sesame Chicken Platter

*Serve this tasty dish (pictured on front cover) with crusty bread, and/or Lemon Parsley Rice Pilaf (page 181).*

### Oven-Baked Chicken

Instead of grilling chicken, place on baking sheet and bake in 375° F (190° C) oven for 20 to 30 minutes for boneless or 45 minutes with bones or until no longer pink inside.

### Easy Entertaining

I got the idea for this dish at an after-tennis dinner at my friend Marg Churchill's. The colorful platter of tossed greens topped with hoisin chicken combines two courses into one dish—perfect for elegant yet casual entertaining.

| | | |
|---|---|---|
| ½ cup | Asian Sauce (page 99) | 125 mL |
| 6 | skinless chicken breasts or 3 lb (1.5 kg) skinless chicken parts | 6 |
| 1 tbsp | dark sesame oil | 15 mL |
| 1 tbsp | rice vinegar | 15 mL |
| Dash | hot pepper sauce | Dash |
| 8 cups | torn mixed lettuces | 2 L |
| | Salt and pepper | |
| 2 cups | cherry tomatoes | 500 mL |
| 6 | black olives | 6 |

**1.** Spread Asian Sauce over chicken; cover and refrigerate for 4 hours.

**2.** Grill chicken over high heat for 15 to 20 minutes on each side or until no longer pink inside.

**3.** Meanwhile, combine sesame oil, vinegar and hot pepper sauce; toss with lettuces, and salt and pepper to taste. Arrange on large serving platter.

**4.** Arrange grilled chicken on lettuces. Garnish with cherry tomatoes and olives. **Makes 6 servings.**

**MAKE AHEAD:** Through step 1 for up to one day.

*PER SERVING:*

225 calories

29 g protein

7 g total fat
    1 g saturated fat
    73 mg cholesterol

12 g carbohydrate
    1 g dietary fibre

419 mg sodium

509 mg potassium

GOOD: Vitamin C
EXCELLENT: Folate

Asian Chicken (page 98)

# Chicken and Snow Peas in Black Bean Sauce

*You can find the fermented (or salted) black beans (often in a plastic bag) in Chinese food stores. If not available, don't substitute black turtle beans but rather add ¼ cup (50 mL) bottled black bean sauce and reduce chicken stock to ¼ cup (50 mL). Serve with rice or noodles.*

| | | |
|---|---|---|
| 1 lb | boneless skinless chicken breasts | 500 g |
| 1 tbsp | vegetable oil | 15 mL |
| 3 tbsp | Chinese fermented black beans | 50 mL |
| 2 | cloves garlic, minced | 2 |
| 1 tbsp | minced gingerroot | 15 mL |
| ¼ tsp | crushed red pepper flakes | 1 mL |
| 2 cups | snow peas, trimmed | 500 mL |

**Sauce**

| | | |
|---|---|---|
| ½ cup | chicken stock or water | 125 mL |
| 2 tbsp | sodium-reduced soy sauce | 25 mL |
| 1 tbsp | sherry | 15 mL |
| 2 tsp | granulated sugar | 10 mL |
| 1½ tsp | cornstarch | 7 mL |
| 1 tsp | sesame oil | 5 mL |

**1.** Sauce: Combine stock, soy sauce, sherry, sugar, cornstarch and sesame oil; set aside.

**2.** Slice chicken thinly; set aside.

**3.** In large nonstick skillet, heat oil over high heat; stir-fry black beans, garlic, ginger and red pepper flakes for 15 seconds.

**4.** Add chicken; stir-fry for 2 minutes. Add snow peas; stir-fry for 2 minutes.

**5.** Stir sauce; add to skillet and stir-fry over medium heat for 1 minute or until chicken is no longer pink inside. **Makes 4 servings**.

 **MAKE AHEAD:** Through step 2, covered and refrigerated for up to four hours.

Fish Mediterranean, made with Red Snapper (page 110)
Lemon Parsley Rice Pilaf (page 181)

***Nutritional Note***
Use as little as possible of pure fats—butter, margarine, lard, shortening and oil. Use nonstick pans, and when browning, add the absolute minimum of fat. Instead of frying, choose other methods, such as grilling, broiling, baking, poaching or microwaving.

When stir-frying, add water instead of extra oil to prevent scorching. To maximize flavor, add a bit of sesame oil just before serving.

*PER SERVING:*
  221 calories
  29 g protein
  6 g total fat
    1 g saturated fat
    66 mg cholesterol
  10 g carbohydrate
    2 g dietary fibre
  436 mg sodium
  473 mg potassium

GOOD: Vitamin C

# Asian Chicken

*This is a great dish for casual entertaining or when you want something a little different. Set the table with a platter of chicken, one of lettuce and one with remaining ingredients. Give each person some sauce. Diners make up their own lettuce rolls filled with chicken, noodles and herbs. (Pictured opposite page 96.)*

(Pictured opposite page 96.)

Asian Sauce (recipe page 99)

| | | |
|---|---|---|
| 6 | boneless skinless chicken breasts, cut in strips | 6 |
| ½ lb | rice vermicelli noodles | 250 g |
| 2 | heads Boston or soft leaf lettuce | 2 |
| 1 | cucumber, halved lengthwise and thinly sliced | 1 |
| 3 cups | bean sprouts | 750 mL |
| ½ cup | fresh mint leaves | 125 mL |
| ½ cup | fresh coriander leaves | 125 mL |

**1.** Spread ⅓ cup (75 mL) of the Asian Sauce over chicken; cover and refrigerate for 4 hours.

**2.** In large saucepan of boiling water, cook noodles for 1 minute or according to package directions; drain and rinse under cold water. Drain again and toss with 2 tbsp (25 mL) of Asian Sauce.

**3.** On platter, arrange lettuce leaves. On another platter, arrange cucumber, bean sprouts, mint, coriander and noodles. Divide remaining sauce among 6 small dishes.

**4.** In nonstick skillet, stir-fry chicken over high heat for 3 to 5 minutes or until no longer pink inside; transfer to serving platter.

**5.** Let each person spread some Asian Sauce on a lettuce leaf, then top with some chicken, noodles, bean sprouts, cucumber, mint and coriander leaves. Using fingers, roll up and eat. **Makes 6 servings**.

**MAKE AHEAD:** Through step 2 for up to one day. Step 3, covered and refrigerated for up to four hours.

---

## Summer Barbecue Asian Chicken

Follow Asian Chicken recipe except: Marinate whole skinless boneless chicken breasts. Grill chicken over high heat for about 4 minutes on each side or until meat is no longer pink inside. Cut into strips; place on serving plate.

## *Mostly Make-Ahead Oriental Dinner*

- Hot and Sour Soup (page 62)
- Asian Chicken
- Nectarine and Orange Compote (page 234)
  OR
  Fresh Fruit Plate
- Gingerbread Cake (page 212)

PER SERVING:
377 calories
32 g protein
3 g total fat
  1 g saturated fat
  68 mg cholesterol
56 g carbohydrate
  2 g dietary fibre
704 mg sodium
667 mg potassium

GOOD: Iron
EXCELLENT: Folate

# Asian Sauce

*This is delicious as a marinade or as a sauce with chicken, pork, Chinese noodle dishes, shrimp or scallops.*

| | | |
|---|---|---|
| ½ cup | hoisin sauce | 125 mL |
| 2 tbsp | sodium-reduced soy sauce | 25 mL |
| 2 tbsp | rice vinegar | 25 mL |
| 2 tbsp | liquid honey | 25 mL |
| 1 tbsp | minced gingerroot | 15 mL |
| 1 tbsp | minced fresh garlic | 15 mL |
| | Crushed red pepper flakes (optional) | |

**1.** Combine hoisin sauce, soy sauce, vinegar, honey, gingerroot, garlic, and red pepper flakes to taste, if using. **Makes about 1 cup (250 mL).**

**MAKE AHEAD:** Sauce can be covered and refrigerated for up to two weeks.

*Tip*
This sauce is thick and quite sweet. With pasta you might want to add more vinegar to taste.

---

### LIGHT AND LEAN BARBECUES

Barbecuing is a great way to cook light and lean. To keep barbecues lean, follow these easy tips:

• Choose lean cuts of meat:
  Beef: flank, rump, sirloin tip, round
  Pork: centre loin, leg, tenderloin
  Lamb: loin, leg, tenderloin

• Thaw completely before cooking to reduce cooking time, and avoid charring food on the outside before it's cooked inside.

• Remove all visible fat from meat.

• Choose marinades with little or no oil or reduce oil to a minimum in your own recipes. In some cases, you can substitute water, stock or fruit juice for most of the oil.

• Keep your accompaniments light. Serve lots of fresh vegetables and salads and leave off the butter and mayonnaise. Try Creamy Tomato Pickle Sauce (page 127) on burgers and Light Tartar Sauce (page 114) on fish.

•Serve meat portions no larger than 3½ ounces (100 grams) per person—about the size of a deck of cards.

• Remove skin from chicken, turkey and fish before eating.

*PER SERVING*
*(1 TBSP/15 ML):*
  29 calories
  1 g protein
  1 g total fat
    0 g saturated fat
    0 mg cholesterol
  6 g carbohydrate
    0 g dietary fibre
  231 mg sodium
  12 mg potassium

# Barbecued Curried Chicken Breasts

*Yogurt and curry powder are the basis for this flavorful marinade. Serve with Barbecued Potato Packets (page 150) or Potato Salad with Yogurt Herb Dressing (page 87) and asparagus, green beans or sliced tomatoes.*

## Baked Spicy Chicken

Marinate chicken as in Barbecued Curried Chicken Breasts. Then cover chicken with fresh brown bread crumbs (see sidebar, page 193); bake in 350°F (180°C) oven for 45 minutes or until no longer pink inside.

## Chicken Salad

Curried Chicken Breasts are delicious cold, so in the summer, I like to grill extra then slice the meat and serve it as part of a salad plate or over greens tossed with Asian Sauce (page 99).

| | | |
|---|---|---|
| ¼ cup | low-fat yogurt | 50 mL |
| 2 tbsp | vegetable oil | 25 mL |
| 2 tbsp | lime or lemon juice | 25 mL |
| 2 tbsp | liquid honey | 25 mL |
| 2 tbsp | curry powder | 25 mL |
| 1 tbsp | minced fresh garlic | 15 mL |
| ½ tsp | salt | 2 mL |
| 6 | skinless chicken breasts | 6 |

**1.** Combine yogurt, oil, lime juice, honey, curry powder, garlic and salt; brush over chicken. Cover and refrigerate for 4 hours.

**2.** Grill chicken over medium heat for 15 to 20 minutes on each side or until no longer pink inside. **Makes 6 servings**.

**MAKE AHEAD:** Through step 1 for up to one day.

# Chicken and Vegetable Stew with Parsley Dumplings

*This one-pot chicken dinner (pictured opposite page 65) is a light version of an old-fashioned favorite. Add ½ cup (125 mL) white wine to the stew when adding peas, if desired.*

| | | |
|---|---|---|
| 4 | skinless chicken breasts (2 lb/1 kg) or 2 lb (1 kg) skinless chicken parts | 4 |
| 4 | small potatoes, quartered | 4 |
| 2 | each carrots and onions, quartered | 2 |
| 2 | stalks celery, sliced | 2 |
| 1½ cups | cubed peeled rutabaga | 375 mL |
| 1½ cups | cubed peeled sweet potato | 375 mL |
| 4 cups | water or chicken stock | 1 L |
| ½ tsp | each dried thyme, sage and salt | 2 mL |
| ¼ tsp | pepper | 1 mL |
| 1 cup | frozen peas | 250 mL |

## Dumplings

| | | |
|---|---|---|
| 1 cup | all-purpose flour | 250 mL |
| 2 tbsp | chopped fresh parsley | 25 mL |
| 2 tbsp | soft margarine or butter | 25 mL |
| 1½ tsp | baking powder | 7 mL |
| ¼ tsp | salt | 1 mL |
| ½ cup | low-fat milk | 125 mL |

**1.** In large saucepan, combine chicken, potatoes, carrots, onions, celery, rutabaga, sweet potato, water, thyme, sage, salt and pepper; bring to boil over high heat. Reduce heat to medium-low; simmer, covered, for 20 minutes. Stir in peas.

**2.** Dumplings: In food processor or by hand, combine flour, parsley, margarine, baking powder and salt until mixture is in coarse crumbs. Stir in milk; drop by tablespoonfuls (15 mL) onto hot stew to make 4 to 6 mounds.

**3.** Cover and simmer (don't boil hard and don't lift lid) for 15 minutes or until dumplings have risen. **Makes 4 servings**.

**MAKE AHEAD:** Through step 1 (except peas), covered and refrigerated for up to 24 hours.

### Where's the Salt?

There are many ways to control the sodium in your diet. Look at these three ways to make Chicken and Vegetable Stew with Parsley Dumplings:

| | Sodium/ serving (mg) |
|---|---|
| Made with chicken stock | 1562 |
| Made with water | 794 |
| Made with water, omit salt in stew and in dumplings | 364 |

### Where's the Fat?

Compare:

| Recipe made with 2 lb/1 kg | Fat/ serving (g) |
|---|---|
| Chicken breasts, skinless | 9 |
| Whole chicken, skin removed | 13 |
| Whole chicken, including skin | 38 |

*PER SERVING (MADE WITH WATER AND CHICKEN BREASTS):*

537 calories
38 g protein
9 g total fat
   2 g saturated fat
   71 mg cholesterol
77 g carbohydrate
   9 g dietary fibre
794 mg sodium
1299 mg potassium

GOOD: Calcium
EXCELLENT: Vitamin A; Vitamin C; Folate; Iron

# Turkey Vegetable Casserole

*This is a delicious way to use up cooked turkey or chicken and makes a great dish for a buffet.*

***Make-Ahead Buffet Menu***
- Turkey Vegetable Casserole
- Tossed Salad Greens with Mustard Garlic Vinaigrette (page 88)
- Green Bean Salad with Buttermik Dressing (page 79)
  OR
  Asparagus and Mushroom Salad (page 78)
- Fresh Breads
- Chocolate Mocha Ice Cream Pie (page 218)
  OR
  Lemon Mousse with Raspberry Sauce (page 221)

| | | |
|---|---|---|
| 1 cup | long grain rice | 250 mL |
| 1½ tsp | soft margarine or butter | 7 mL |
| ½ cup | coarsely chopped fresh parsley | 125 mL |
| 1 | onion, chopped | 1 |
| 3 | cloves garlic, minced | 3 |
| 1½ cups | finely chopped carrots | 375 mL |
| 1½ cups | chopped celery | 375 mL |
| ½ lb | mushrooms, thinly sliced (3 cups/750 mL) | 250 g |
| 4 cups | cooked turkey chunks (1 lb/500 g) | 1 L |

### Herb Cream Sauce

| | | |
|---|---|---|
| 2 tbsp | soft margarine or butter | 25 mL |
| ¼ cup | all-purpose flour | 50 mL |
| 2½ cups | low-fat milk | 625 mL |
| ½ tsp | each dried tarragon, salt and pepper | 2 mL |
| ¼ tsp | dried thyme | 1 mL |

### Topping

| | | |
|---|---|---|
| ½ cup | fresh whole wheat bread crumbs | 125 mL |
| ¼ cup | chopped fresh parsley | 50 mL |

**1.** In saucepan, bring 2 cups (500 mL) water to boil; add rice and ½ tsp (2 mL) of the margarine. Reduce heat, cover and simmer for 20 minutes. Toss with 2 tbsp (25 mL) of the parsley.

**2.** Meanwhile, in large nonstick saucepan, melt remaining margarine over low heat; cook onion, garlic and carrots for 5 minutes. Add celery, mushrooms and remaining parsley; cook, stirring, for 5 to 10 minutes or until softened. Stir in turkey.

**3.** Herb Cream Sauce: In saucepan, melt margarine over medium-low heat; whisk in flour and cook, stirring, for 1 minute. Gradually add milk, whisking constantly; cook for 1 to 2 minutes or until bubbling and thickened. Add tarragon, salt, pepper and thyme. Stir sauce into turkey mixture; spoon into greased 13- x 9-inch (3.5 L) baking dish.

**4.** Topping: Combine bread crumbs and parsley; sprinkle over casserole. Bake in 325°F (160°C) oven for 40 to 50 minutes or until heated through. **Makes 8 servings.**

 **MAKE AHEAD:** Through step 3, covered and refrigerated for up to two days, or cooled in refrigerator then frozen for up to two weeks. Thaw in refrigerator for two days; let stand at room temperature for 25 minutes before sprinkling with topping and baking.

*PER SERVING:*

298 calories
23 g protein
8 g total fat
    3 g saturated fat
    49 mg cholesterol
32 g carbohydrate
    2 g dietary fibre
320 mg sodium
558 mg potassium

GOOD: Folate; Iron
EXCELLENT: Vitamin A

# Roast Turkey with Sausage, Apple and Herb Stuffing

*Traditional roast turkey is still my family's favorite for Christmas and Thanksgiving dinners. Serve it with flavorful Giblet Gravy (page 106).*

| | | |
|---|---|---|
| 14 lb | turkey | 6.5 kg |
| | Sausage, Apple and Herb Stuffing (page 105) | |
| 4 | sprigs fresh rosemary or thyme | 4 |

**1.** Remove neck and giblets from body cavities of turkey. Discard gizzard and heart. Cover and refrigerate neck and liver for gravy. Rinse turkey under cold running water; dry skin and cavities.

**2.** Loosely stuff neck and body cavities with stuffing. Fold neck skin over cavity and skewer to back. Secure legs by tying with string. Lift wings and fold behind back or tie to sides of turkey with string. Place rosemary sprigs between body of turkey and each leg and wing.

**3.** Place turkey on rack in roasting pan with breast side up. Cover with loose tent of lightly greased foil, dull side out, leaving sides open. Roast in 325°F (160°C) oven for 5½ to 6 hours or until juices run clear when turkey is pierced and thermometer inserted into thigh reads 185°F (85°C). Remove foil for last 30 minutes of cooking, so turkey can brown.

**4.** Remove from oven and let stand, covered with foil, for 30 minutes before carving. **Makes 14 servings.**

## Buying Turkey

Avoid pre-basted turkeys or ones injected with fat. You are paying a high price for added fat, which is usually hydrogenated or saturated.

## Thawing Turkey

Leave in original wrapper. Cover with cold water and allow 1 hour per pound (500 g); change water occasionally.

Or, in refrigerator, allow 1 day for every 5 lb (2.2 kg).

*PER SERVING (3½ OZ/100 G LIGHT MEAT AND STUFFING):*

229 calories
33 g protein
5 g total fat
  2 g saturated fat
  73 mg cholesterol
12 g carbohydrate
  2 g dietary fibre
245 mg sodium
389 mg potassium

GOOD: Iron

---

### TURKEY COOKING TIMES

Roast in 325° F (160° C) oven 20 minutes per pound, 40 minutes per kilogram (small turkeys require a little more, large ones a little less) or until meat thermometer inserted into thigh reads 185° F (85° C) or, if stuffed, thermometer inserted into stuffing reads 165° F (75° C).

Many factors affect the cooking time. Fresh turkeys take longer than thawed. A 10 lb (4.5 kg) stuffed turkey takes about 3½ hours, a 20 lb (9 kg) turkey, 6 to 6½ hours. Don't overcook as it will be dry.

# Sausage, Apple and Herb Stuffing

*In the fall, I often use McIntosh apples; in the winter, Golden Delicious or Spy. Stuff the bird just before cooking.*

| | | |
|---|---|---|
| ¼ lb | bulk turkey sausage | 125 g |
| 6 cups | day-old whole wheat bread cubes (about 9 slices) | 1.5 L |
| ½ cup | chopped celery | 125 mL |
| ½ cup | chopped onion | 125 mL |
| 2 | small apples, peeled and chopped | 2 |
| 2 tbsp | each chopped fresh sage and basil (or ½ tsp/2 mL each dried) | 25 mL |
| 1½ tsp | dried savory | 7 mL |
| 2 tsp | chopped fresh thyme or oregano (or ½ tsp/2 mL dried) | 10 mL |
| ½ tsp | each salt and pepper | 2 mL |

**1.** In small nonstick skillet, cook turkey sausage over medium heat for 5 to 7 minutes or until no longer pink, breaking up meat with fork.

**2.** In large bowl, combine sausage, bread, celery, onion, apples, sage, basil, savory, thyme, salt and pepper. **Makes about 8 cups (2 L), enough for one 14 lb (6.5 kg) turkey or 14 servings.**

**MAKE AHEAD:** Stuffing can be refrigerated in airtight container for up to two days or frozen for up to four weeks. Thaw slightly in refrigerator to stuff the turkey.

## Take Care

To avoid illness from bacteria, do not stuff a turkey or chicken until just before cooking. Don't leave the turkey carcass on the kitchen counter while the dishes are being done. Remove leftover stuffing from bird and refrigerate stuffing and turkey as soon as possible.

*Per Serving:*

71 calories
3 g protein
2 g total fat
   1 g saturated fat
   3 mg cholesterol
12 g carbohydrate
   2 g dietary fibre
181 mg sodium
84 mg potassium

# Giblet Gravy

*Liver adds a delicious flavor to this gravy. Liver is high in cholesterol, but the actual amount per serving in this recipe is very small and not worth worrying about.*

|          | Turkey neck and liver             |          |
|----------|-----------------------------------|----------|
| ¼ cup    | pan drippings from turkey         | 50 mL    |
| 6 tbsp   | all-purpose flour                 | 90 mL    |
|          | Water, cooking liquids and pan juices |      |
|          | Salt and pepper                   |          |

**1.** In small saucepan, cover neck with water; simmer, covered, for 2 hours. Add liver; simmer for 20 minutes. Drain, reserving cooking liquid in large measure. Remove meat from neck and chop along with liver; refrigerate.

**2.** Pour pan juices from cooked turkey into bowl, leaving all particles in pan. Let fat rise to top of liquids; skim off fat and pour ¼ cup (50 mL) of the fat into roasting pan. Add pan juices to reserved cooking liquid, adding water if necessary to make 4 cups (1 L). Sprinkle flour into pan; cook over low heat, stirring to scrape up any brown bits, for 1 minute.

**3.** Gradually add reserved liquid, whisking continuously until boiling and thickened. Stir in chopped liver and neck meat. Season with salt and pepper to taste. **Makes 4½ cups (1.125 L).**

| HOW MUCH TURKEY TO BUY | | |
|------------------------|------|----------------------------------------|
| **Purchased weight** | | **Number of 3 oz (90 g)** |
| **lb** | **kg** | **servings of cooked turkey** |
| 9 | 4 | 17 |
| 12 | 5.5 | 24 |
| 14 | 6.5 | 29 |
| 22 | 10 | 42 |

# Lemon Pepper Turkey Loaf

*This tasty turkey loaf is absolutely delicious served either hot with mashed potatoes, baked squash and green beans, or cold in a sandwich.*

| | | |
|---|---|---|
| 1 | pkg (300 g) frozen spinach, thawed | 1 |
| 1 lb | lean ground turkey | 500 g |
| 1 | small onion, chopped | 1 |
| 1 | egg, lightly beaten | 1 |
| 1 | slice whole wheat bread, crumbled | 1 |
| 1 | clove garlic, minced | 1 |
| 3 tbsp | freshly grated Parmesan cheese | 50 mL |
| 2 tsp | grated lemon rind | 10 mL |
| ½ tsp | each salt and pepper | 2 mL |
| Pinch | nutmeg | Pinch |

**1.** Squeeze spinach dry; chop finely.

**2.** In bowl, combine spinach, turkey, onion, egg, bread crumbs, garlic, cheese, lemon rind, salt, pepper and nutmeg; mix gently.

**3.** Transfer to 6-cup (1.5 L) baking dish, smoothing top.

**4.** Bake in 350°F (180°C) oven for 40 minutes or until no longer pink in centre and meat thermometer registers 185°F (85°C). Let stand for 10 minutes. Pour off any liquid. **Makes 4 servings.**

**MAKE AHEAD:** Through step 3, covered and refrigerated for up to three hours.

***To Garnish***

To garnish loaf, before baking, arrange slices from 1 peeled and thinly sliced lemon over top.

***Nutritional Note***

Commercial ground chicken or turkey often contains skin, which adds extra fat. For the leanest product, ask your butcher for some made without skin, or buy boneless skinless breast meat and grind your own.

*PER SERVING:*

268 calories
26 g protein
14 g total fat
    4 g saturated fat
    114 mg cholesterol
9 g carbohydrate
    2 g dietary fibre
538 mg sodium
440 mg potassium

GOOD: Calcium; Iron
EXCELLENT: Vitamin A; Folate

# Thai Barbecued Turkey Scaloppine

## Scaloppine

Scaloppine are thin slices of meat, usually veal. Turkey is an excellent, less expensive alternative and if you can't find turkey scaloppine, buy turkey or chicken breast and cut it into thin slices.

## Easy Barbecue Dinner

• Thai Barbecued Turkey Scaloppine
• Jiffy Chinese Noodles (page 164)
• Green Beans
• Sliced Tomatoes with Fresh Basil

THAI FISH SAUCE

*PER SERVING:*

150 calories

27 g protein

3 g total fat
    1 g saturated fat
    61 mg cholesterol

2 g carbohydrate
    0.1 g dietary fibre

301 mg sodium

304 mg potassium

*Serve these tasty slices with rice or noodles and a salad such as Purple Vegetable Slaw (page 83) or Ginger Stir-Fried Zucchini (page 147).*

| | | |
|---|---|---|
| 2 tbsp | chopped fresh coriander or parsley | 25 mL |
| 2 tbsp | fish sauce or sodium-reduced soy sauce | 25 mL |
| 4 tsp | lemon juice | 20 mL |
| 1 tbsp | water | 15 mL |
| 1 tsp | granulated sugar | 5 mL |
| 1 tsp | vegetable oil | 5 mL |
| ¼ tsp | pepper | 1 mL |
| ¼ tsp | crushed red pepper flakes* | 1 mL |
| 1 lb | turkey scaloppine | 500 g |

**1.** Combine coriander, fish sauce, lemon juice, water, sugar, oil, pepper and red pepper flakes; mix well.

**2.** Place turkey in shallow dish; pour marinade over top. Cover and refrigerate for 1 hour, turning occasionally.

**3.** Place on greased grill over high heat; grill for about 2 minutes on each side or until no longer pink inside. **Makes 4 servings**.

* Or chili paste to taste

**MAKE AHEAD:** Through step 2 for up to 24 hours.

# FISH AND SEAFOOD

Steamed Ginger Fish Fillets

Fish Mediterranean

Lemon Tarragon Sole Fillets

Baked Breaded Fish Fillets with Almonds

Lemon Sesame Tuna Fillets

Barbecued Trout with Light Tartar Sauce

Barbecued Salmon Fillets

Baked Whole Salmon Stuffed with
Mushrooms and Artichokes

Creamy Dill Sauce

Shrimp and Chicken Jambalaya

Spicy Scallops

Salmon Salad Fajitas

Good
TRY MARINATE IN
A PLASTIC BAG FIRST

# Steamed Ginger Fish Fillets

*If you don't have a steamer, place a rack in a wok, add water and bring to a boil. Place fish on a heatproof plate on rack; cover and steam.*

| | | |
|---|---|---|
| ¾ lb | cod or halibut fillets | 375 g |
| 1 tbsp | chopped gingerroot | 15 mL |
| 3 | green onions, diagonally sliced | 3 |
| 1 tsp | vegetable oil | 5 mL |
| 1 tsp | minced fresh garlic | 5 mL |
| 1 tbsp | sodium-reduced soy sauce | 15 mL |

**1.** Place fillets in steamer; sprinkle with ginger and onions. Cover tightly and steam for 5 minutes or until fish is opaque. Transfer to plates.

**2.** In small skillet, heat oil over medium heat; cook garlic for 30 seconds. Stir in soy sauce; drizzle over fish. **Makes 4 servings.**

*PER SERVING:*
89 calories
16 g protein
2 g total fat
    0.2 g saturated fat
    36 mg cholesterol
2 g carbohydrate
    0.4 g dietary fibre
175 mg sodium
218 mg potassium

**Buying Fish**
Fresh fish:
• should not have a strong smell
• should have firm flesh that springs back when touched
• should have clear bright convex eyes (not sunken)

Frozen fish:
If fish is frozen as soon as caught, it is often better than fresh. I like the fillets that have been individually frozen.
   Keep higher-fat fish (salmon, mackerel, lake trout) for a maximum of two months in the freezer; lean fish up to 6 months.

# Fish Mediterranean

*Any kind of fish fillet is delicious topped with this zesty sauce. Cooking time will vary depending on the thickness of the fish. (Pictured opposite page 97.)*

| | | |
|---|---|---|
| 1 lb | red snapper, sole or other fillets | 500 g |

**Sauce**

| | | |
|---|---|---|
| ½ tsp | olive oil | 2 mL |
| 1 tbsp | chopped green onion or shallots | 15 mL |
| ½ tsp | minced fresh garlic | 2 mL |
| ¾ cup | drained canned tomatoes, chopped | 175 mL |
| ¼ tsp | dried basil (or 1 tsp/5 mL chopped fresh) | 1 mL |
| 2 tbsp | chopped black olives | 25 mL |
| 1½ tsp | capers | 7 mL |
| | Pepper | |

**1.** In skillet of gently simmering water, cover and poach fish over medium heat for 5 minutes or until fish is opaque. Drain well; transfer to platter and keep warm.

**2.** Sauce: Meanwhile, in small saucepan, heat oil over medium heat; cook onion and garlic for 2 minutes. Add tomatoes and basil; simmer for 3 minutes, stirring occasionally. Stir in olives, capers, and pepper to taste.

**3.** Spoon sauce over fish. **Makes 4 servings**.

**MAKE AHEAD:** Sauce, step 2, can be made up to one hour before serving and gently reheated.

*PER SERVING:*

132 calories
24 g protein
3 g total fat
  1 g saturated fat
  42 mg cholesterol
3 g carbohydrate
  1 g dietary fibre
175 mg sodium
572 mg potassium

# Lemon Tarragon Sole Fillets

*I love this easy way to cook any kind of fish fillets or steaks. It's a lighter version of my mother's West Coast method.*

| | | |
|---|---|---|
| 2 tbsp | light mayonnaise | 25 mL |
| 2 tbsp | low-fat yogurt | 25 mL |
| 1 tsp | all-purpose flour | 5 mL |
| ½ tsp | dried tarragon | 2 mL |
| 1 tsp | finely chopped lemon rind | 5 mL |
| 1 lb | sole fillets | 500 g |

**1.** In small bowl, mix together mayonnaise, yogurt, flour, tarragon, and lemon rind.

**2.** Arrange fillets in single layer on baking sheet; spread with mayonnaise mixture.

**3.** Broil 6 to 8 inches (15 to 20 cm) from heat for 5 to 10 minutes or until fish is opaque. (Time will vary depending on thickness of fish; ¼ inch / 1 cm thick fillets will take only 5 minutes.) **Makes 4 servings**.

**MAKE AHEAD:** Through step 2, covered and refrigerated for up to two hours.

**Olives**

Olives can be high in fat and sodium so should be used in moderation. Black olives are usually lower in fat and sodium than green olives. Choose ones packed in brine rather than oil.

*PER SERVING:*

134 calories
22 g protein
4 g total fat
  1 g saturated fat
  61 mg cholesterol
2 g carbohydrate
  0.1 g dietary fibre
148 mg sodium
327 mg potassium

# Baked Breaded Fish Fillets with Almonds

*You can use any kind of fresh or frozen and thawed fillets in this easy-to-make fish dish. Whole wheat bread crumbs instead of white bread crumbs not only add fibre but are much more attractive in color. (Pictured opposite page 160.)*

| | | |
|---|---|---|
| 1 | egg, lightly beaten | 1 |
| ¼ cup | low-fat milk | 50 mL |
| 1⅓ cups | fresh whole wheat bread crumbs | 325 mL |
| 1 tsp | dried oregano or basil | 5 mL |
| ¼ tsp | each salt and pepper | 1 mL |
| 1 lb | sole or haddock fillets | 500 g |
| 2 tbsp | lemon juice | 25 mL |
| 2 tbsp | water | 25 mL |
| 1 tbsp | soft margarine or butter, melted | 15 mL |
| 3 tbsp | sliced almonds | 50 mL |
| 3 tbsp | chopped green onions | 50 mL |

**1.** In shallow dish, combine egg and milk.

**2.** On plate, mix crumbs, oregano, salt and pepper.

**3.** Dip fish in egg mixture, then in crumbs. Arrange in single layer on greased baking sheet.

**4.** Combine lemon juice, water and margarine; drizzle over fish. Sprinkle with almonds. Bake, uncovered, in 425°F (220°C) oven for 10 minutes or until fish is opaque.

**5.** Sprinkle with onions. **Makes 4 servings**.

*Per Serving:*

224 calories
26 g protein
9 g total fat
   2 g saturated fat
   110 mg cholesterol
10 g carbohydrate
   1 g dietary fibre
379 mg sodium
549 mg potassium

**Make Ahead:** Through step 3 for up to 30 minutes , covered and refrigerated.

# Lemon Sesame Tuna Fillets

*Tuna is tender and moist as long as it isn't overcooked, when it becomes dry. Cook until light pink in the centre.*

| | | |
|---|---|---|
| 4 | tuna fillets or steaks, 1-inch (2.5 cm) thick (1½ lb/750 g) | 4 |
| 1 | green onion, chopped | 1 |
| Pinch | pepper | Pinch |

**Lemon-Soy Marinade**

| | | |
|---|---|---|
| 2 tbsp | lemon juice | 25 mL |
| 1 tbsp | sodium-reduced soy sauce | 15 mL |
| 1 tbsp | sesame or vegetable oil | 25 mL |

**1.** Lemon-Soy Marinade: Combine lemon juice, soy sauce and oil; pour over tuna fillets in baking dish. Cover and refrigerate for at least 30 minutes.

**2.** Bake in 400°F (200°C) oven for 10 to 12 minutes or until fish is opaque and is slightly pink in centre.

**3.** Sprinkle with green onion and pepper. **Makes 4 servings.**

**MAKE AHEAD:** Through step 1 for up to four hours; remove from refrigerator 10 minutes before cooking.

---

### COOKING FISH

Fish is tender and doesn't require a long cooking time. It is cooked as soon as the flesh becomes opaque throughout.

• Measure fish at the thickest part.

• Allow 10 minutes cooking time per inch (2.5 cm) thickness for fresh fish, 20 minutes per inch if frozen. If wrapped in foil, add 5 minutes for fresh, 10 minutes for frozen. This applies to all fish and all cooking methods (if in oven, cook at 450° F/230° C).

• To Microwave Fish: Place fish on microwaveable dish. Cover and microwave on High for 3 to 5 minutes per pound (500 g). Let stand for 2 to 3 minutes.

---

### Grilled Tuna Fillet Burgers

Prepare Lemon Sesame Tuna Fillets using 4 oz (125 g) fillets ½ inch (1 cm) thick. Grill for 5 to 7 minutes and serve in toasted whole wheat bun with lettuce and sliced tomato.

*PER SERVING:*

262 calories
40 g protein
10 g total fat
   2 g saturated fat
   65 mg cholesterol
1 g carbohydrate
   0.1 g dietary fibre
128 mg sodium
445 mg potassium

---

EXCELLENT: Vitamin A

# Barbecued Trout with Light Tartar Sauce

## Oven-Baked Trout

Prepare trout as in Barbecued Trout recipe. Bake on baking sheet in 450°F (230°C) oven for 10 minutes for every inch (2.5 cm) of thickness of fish.

## Foil-Steamed Trout

Prepare trout as in Barbecued Trout recipe. Wrap in foil and bake as in Oven-Baked Trout, adding 5 minutes to baking time.

### *Light Tartar Sauce*

Light Tartar Sauce also is delicious with any fish or with a chicken or turkey burger.

*This fish can also be cooked in foil; just peel off the foil after cooking to remove the skin. A few capers or a little Dijon mustard, chopped green onions or chives can be added to the Tartar Sauce. Garnish trout with lemon slices and fresh dill.*

| | | |
|---|---|---|
| 4 | sprigs fresh dill | 4 |
| 4 | rainbow trout (about 9 oz/255 g each) | 4 |
| | Salt and pepper | |

**Light Tartar Sauce**

| | | |
|---|---|---|
| ¼ cup | low-fat yogurt | 50 mL |
| ¼ cup | light mayonnaise | 50 mL |
| ¼ cup | finely chopped dill pickle | 50 mL |
| 2 tbsp | chopped fresh dill | 25 mL |
| | Salt and pepper | |

**1.** Light Tartar Sauce: Stir together yogurt, mayonnaise, pickle, dill, and salt and pepper to taste.

**2.** Place dill sprig in each trout cavity; sprinkle cavity with salt and pepper.

**3.** Place trout on greased grill over high heat; cover and grill, turning once, for 10 to 15 minutes or until fish is opaque. Serve with Tartar Sauce. **Makes 4 servings**.

**MAKE AHEAD:** Through step 1, covered and refrigerated for up to three days. Through step 2, covered and refrigerated for up to six hours.

PER SERVING:

284 calories

41 g protein

11 g total fat
  2 g saturated fat
  111 mg cholesterol

3 g carbohydrate
  0.1 g dietary fibre

273 mg sodium

1009 mg potassium

GOOD: Calcium
EXCELLENT: Iron

# Barbecued Salmon Fillets

*Barbecued salmon fillet or steak is one of my favorite summer meals: it's fast, easy and tastes terrific. Sometimes I don't do anything to the salmon; its delicate flavor and smoky taste from the barbecue is all it needs. Sometimes I marinate it in a teriyaki-type sauce; other times I add a little lemon juice, or use this recipe.*

| | | |
|---|---|---|
| 2 tbsp | lemon juice or white wine vinegar | 25 mL |
| 1 tbsp | vegetable oil | 15 mL |
| 1 tsp | crumbled dried rosemary (or 2 tsp 10 mL fresh) | 5 mL |
| 4 | salmon fillets (about 1½ lb/750 g total) | 4 |
| | Salt and pepper | |

**1.** Combine lemon juice, oil and rosemary. Pour over salmon; marinate for 15 minutes at room temperature.

**2.** Spray grill or broiler pan with nonstick coating; cook salmon about 4 inches (10 cm) from medium-high heat, turning halfway through cooking time, for 10 minutes per inch (2.5 cm) of thickness or until fish is opaque. (If fillet is thin and you put the top down on the barbecue, turning may not be necessary.) Season with salt and pepper to taste. **Makes 4 servings.**

**MAKE AHEAD:** Through step 1, covered and refrigerated for up to four hours; remove from refrigerator 10 minutes before cooking.

*Grilling Salmon*

I usually start to cook the salmon skin side down on the grill, however, others do the reverse. Each way has advantages, so choose for yourself.

*PER SERVING:*

250 calories
34 g protein
12 g total fat
  2 g saturated fat
  94 mg cholesterol
0.2 g carbohydrate
  0 g dietary fibre
75 mg sodium
836 mg potassium

# Baked Whole Salmon Stuffed with Mushrooms and Artichokes

*This easy-to-prepare fish looks and tastes wonderful. Garnish the platter with fresh dill sprigs or parsley and lemon slices. Use any combination of mushrooms—regular, oyster, portobello, cremini. If you're lucky enough to have leftovers, this dish is also delicious cold.*

| | | |
|---|---|---|
| 5½ lb | whole salmon, cleaned, scaled, head and tail on | 2.5 kg |

**Stuffing**

| | | |
|---|---|---|
| 1 tsp | olive oil | 5 mL |
| ¼ lb | each regular, brown, shiitake and oyster mushrooms, chopped | 125 g |
| 1 | can (14 oz/398 g) artichokes, drained and coarsely chopped | 1 |
| ½ cup | lightly packed chopped fresh dill | 125 mL |
| | Creamy Dill Sauce (page 117) | |

**1.** Stuffing: In nonstick skillet, heat oil over medium-high heat; cook mushrooms, stirring often, for about 5 minutes or until softened. Stir in artichokes; cook for 1 minute. Remove from heat; stir in dill.

**2.** Lightly stuff cavity of salmon with mushroom mixture. Using heavy needle and thread, stitch opening of fish together.

**3.** Place fish on ungreased baking sheet. Bake, uncovered, in 450°F (230°C) oven for 50 minutes or until small cut in centre of fish shows meat is opaque. Pass Creamy Dill Sauce separately. **Makes 12 servings**.

**MAKE AHEAD:** Through step 2, covered and refrigerated for up to 6 hours. Remove from refrigerator 30 minutes before baking, or increase baking time 5 to 10 minutes.

### Nutritional Content of Fish

Fish is a good nutritional buy. It's high in protein and low or relatively low in fat, unless it is breaded and fried. It is also a source of many vitamins and minerals.

*Fish with 5 g of fat or less per 3 oz (90 g) serving:* sole, bluefish, cod, halibut, haddock, grouper, red snapper, rockfish, Pacific Ocean perch, walleye, pollock, monkfish.

*PER SERVING:*

199 calories

26 g protein

8 g total fat
   1 g saturated fat
   67 mg cholesterol

5 g carbohydrate
   1 g dietary fibre

75 mg sodium

765 mg potassium

# Creamy Dill Sauce

*Serve with Salmon Stuffed with Mushrooms and Artichokes
(page 116) or any grilled or poached fish.*

| | | |
|---|---|---|
| ½ cup | low-fat yogurt | 125 mL |
| ½ cup | low-fat quark (7%)* | 125 mL |
| ½ cup | chopped fresh dill | 125 mL |
| 2 tbsp | capers | 25 mL |
| | Salt and pepper | |

**1.** In small bowl, combine yogurt, quark, dill and capers. Season
with salt and pepper to taste. **Makes 1¼ cups (300 mL).**

\* See page 38, About Quark. If it's unavailable, purée low-fat cottage cheese
for a substitute.

**MAKE
AHEAD:** Sauce can be covered and
refrigerated for up to two days.

CAPERS

---

### OMEGA-3 FATTY ACIDS

As long as we stick to 3½ oz (100 g) portions, I don't think the fat
content of fish should be of too much concern because of the
merits of Omega-3 fatty acids found in fish oils.

Omega-3 fatty acids do not reduce blood cholesterol levels,
as some have claimed, but may have a very positive effect in
reducing the risk of blood clots, the level of blood triglycerides
and help in reducing blood pressure. Health professionals do
not recommend taking supplements. Instead, they suggest we
get our Omega-3 fatty acids from eating fish.

*PER SERVING
(1 TBSP/15 ML):*

12 calories

1 g protein

1 g total fat
  0.3 g saturated fat
  2 mg cholesterol

1 g carbohydrate
  0 g dietary fibre

19 mg sodium

22 mg potassium

# Shrimp and Chicken Jambalaya

*This make-ahead version of a Creole classic is medium-hot. Add more pepper or hot pepper sauce if you want your mouth on fire. Instead of shrimp, you could add ½ lb (250 g) lean smoked cubed ham. This recipe was part of a Christmas buffet menu I developed for* Canadian Living *magazine.*

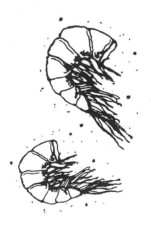

| 1 tbsp | soft margarine or butter | 15 mL |
|---|---|---|
| 2 cups | chopped onion | 500 mL |
| 2 cups | chopped celery | 500 mL |
| 1 | sweet green pepper, chopped | 1 |
| 3 oz | diced smoked ham or sausage (andouille or kielbasa) | 75 g |
| 1½ lb | boneless skinless chicken breasts, cubed | 750 g |
| 1½ tsp | minced fresh garlic | 7 mL |
| 2 | bay leaves | 2 |
| 2 tsp | dried oregano | 10 mL |
| 1 tsp | dried thyme | 5 mL |
| ½ tsp | each salt, cayenne and black pepper | 2 mL |
| 1 | can (28 oz/796 mL) tomatoes | 1 |
| 1 | can (7½ oz/213 mL) tomato sauce | 1 |
| 4 cups | chicken stock | 1 L |
| 2½ cups | long grain white rice | 625 mL |
| 1 lb | medium raw shrimp, peeled | 500 g |
| 1 | sweet red pepper, chopped | 1 |
| ½ cup | chopped green onions | 125 mL |
| ½ cup | chopped fresh parsley | 125 mL |

**1.** In large Dutch oven, melt margarine over medium-high heat; cook onion and celery for 3 minutes. Add green pepper, ham, chicken, garlic, bay leaves, oregano, thyme, salt, cayenne and pepper; cook, stirring, for 3 minutes.

**2.** Add tomatoes, tomato sauce and stock; bring to boil. Stir in rice and shrimp; boil for 1 minute. Bake, covered, in 350°F (180°C) oven for 25 minutes or until rice is tender. Discard bay leaves.

**3.** Stir in red pepper and green onions; sprinkle with parsley. **Makes 8 servings.**

**MAKE AHEAD:** Through step 2, cooled, covered and refrigerated for up to one day. To reheat, stir in 1 cup (250 mL) hot water; bake, covered, in 350°F (180°C) oven for 1 hour and 15 minutes or until hot.

*PER SERVING:*

468 calories

41 g protein

6 g total fat
  1 g saturated fat
  125 mg cholesterol

61 g carbohydrate
  4 g dietary fibre

1186 mg sodium

1040 mg potassium

EXCELLENT: Vitamin A; Vitamin C; Folate; Iron

# Spicy Scallops

*Hot Chinese chili paste adds a little fiery flavor to scallops. Serve with rice and stir-fried bok choy or broccoli. I like to use the regular-size scallops, not the tiny bay scallops.*

| | | |
|---|---|---|
| 2 tsp | vegetable oil | 10 mL |
| 1 tbsp | minced gingerroot | 15 mL |
| 3 tbsp | chopped green onion | 50 mL |
| 1 lb | scallops | 500 g |

**Sauce**

| | | |
|---|---|---|
| 2 tbsp | sherry | 25 mL |
| 1 tbsp | sodium-reduced soy sauce | 15 mL |
| 1 tbsp | sesame oil | 15 mL |
| 1 tsp | granulated sugar | 5 mL |
| ½ tsp | chili paste or hot pepper sauce | 2 mL |

**1.** Sauce: Stir together sherry, soy sauce, oil, sugar and chili paste. Set aside.

**2.** In nonstick skillet, heat oil over high heat; stir-fry ginger and onion for 10 seconds. Add scallops; stir-fry for 1 minute.

**3.** Stir in sauce; stir-fry for 3 to 5 minutes or just until scallops are opaque throughout. **Makes 4 servings**.

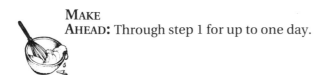

**MAKE AHEAD:** Through step 1 for up to one day.

**Nutritional Note**

Scallops are a treat for anyone, but they're especially so for someone on a low-calorie, low-fat or low-cholesterol diet. Three ounces (90 g) of steamed scallops (about 7 scallops) has only 1 gram of fat, 100 calories and 48 mg of cholesterol.

Be careful not to overcook scallops. They cook very quickly and soon become overcooked and dry.

*PER SERVING:*

166 calories

19 g protein

7 g total fat
  1 g saturated fat
  37 mg cholesterol

5 g carbohydrate
  0.2 g dietary fibre

308 mg sodium

404 mg potassium

# Salmon Salad Fajitas

*There is a fabulous combination of flavors and textures in this easy-to-make meal (pictured opposite page 33). Avocados are high in fat and even though it is unsaturated fat, they should be eaten in small amounts.*

**Other Fish Recipes**
- Fish 'n' Vegetable Chowder (page 69)
- Seafood Vegetable Chowder (page 69)
- Fettuccine Alfredo with Salmon (page 158)
- Summer Shrimp and Tomato Pasta (page 160)
- Linguine with Scallops and Leeks (page 161)
- Seafood Pasta Salad (page 172)
- Bulgur Pilaf with Shrimp and Snow Peas (page 183)

| | | |
|---|---|---|
| 1 | can (7.5 oz/213 g) salmon, drained | 1 |
| ¼ cup | low-fat yogurt | 50 mL |
| 2 tbsp | light mayonnaise | 25 mL |
| ¼ tsp | chili powder | 1 mL |
| 1 | medium carrot, grated | 1 |
| 1 | green onion, chopped | 1 |
| 1 | tomato, diced | 1 |
| 1 | small avocado, peeled and cut in chunks | 1 |
| ¼ cup | chopped fresh coriander | 50 mL |
| | Salt and pepper | |
| 4 | soft 8-inch (20 cm) flour tortillas | 4 |
| 4 | large leaves leaf lettuce | 4 |

**1.** In bowl, combine salmon, yogurt, mayonnaise and chili powder. Add carrot, onion, tomato, avocado and coriander. Season with salt and pepper to taste; stir gently.

**2.** Stack tortillas; wrap in foil and warm in 350°F (180°C) oven for 5 minutes.

**3.** Lay each tortilla flat; top with lettuce leaf. Spoon salmon mixture down one side of tortilla; roll up. **Makes 4 servings**.

*Per Serving:*

328 calories

15 g protein

16 g total fat
   3 g saturated fat
   13 mg cholesterol

34 g carbohydrate
   3 g dietary fibre

414 mg sodium

695 mg potassium

GOOD: Folate; Calcium; Iron

EXCELLENT: Vitamin A

**MAKE AHEAD:** Through step 1, covered and refrigerated for up to two hours.

# MEAT

Garlic-Soy Marinated Beef Strips

Beef and Asparagus Stir-Fry

Beef Fajitas

Hoisin-Garlic Flank Steak

Burgers with Creamy Tomato
Pickle Sauce

Meat Loaf with Herbs

Beef Filet Roasted with
Mustard Peppercorn Crust

Pork Tenderloin Teriyaki

Lettuce Wrap Pork

Chalupas

Chick-Pea and Pork Curry

Skillet Sausage and Rice Paella

Honey Garlic Roast Pork

Chutney-Glazed Ham

Lemon Grass Marinated Leg of Lamb

Onions Stuffed with Lamb and Spinach

Lamb and Feta Pita Pockets

Moroccan Rabbit Tagine

## WHERE'S THE BEEF?

People often tell me that they have improved their eating habits and cut out red meat. Others confess reluctantly that, although they'd like to eat more healthfully, they're not about to give up steak. These people are buying into a popular misconception that red meat isn't part of a healthy diet.

I'm not recommending plate-size steaks fried in butter, but 4 oz (125 g) of grilled sirloin is a different matter. Meat is a concentrated source of many nutrients including Vitamin $B_{12}$, which we can't get from conventional vegetables, and heme iron, which is more easily absorbed than the iron we get from vegetables.

### Cook the Low-Fat Way
- Trim all visible fat.
- Use a nonstick pan to brown meats, or cook in a heavy pan to prevent burning.
- Grill, broil or roast on a rack, or microwave instead of frying.
- Pour or spoon off any visible fat from stews or baked dishes. Or prepare a day ahead, refrigerate and remove hardened fat.

### Choose Leaner Cuts
*Beef:* round steak (inside is leanest), sirloin and sirloin tip, rump, eye of round, strip loin, tenderloin, flank
*Pork:* ham, tenderloin, back bacon, leg (roast, chop and cutlets) and loin
*Lamb:* leg, loin

### Eat Higher-Fat Meats Less Often
Breaded and fried meats, sausages, bologna, side bacon, spareribs, regular ground meats (unless drained) and short ribs are all high in fat.

### What's the Right Amount?
The new Canada's Food Guide to Healthy Eating recommends two to three servings daily of meat or alternatives: one serving is $1\frac{1}{2}$ oz to 3 oz (50 g to 100 g) of meat, fish or poultry (3 oz is about the size of a deck of cards); 1 to 2 eggs; $\frac{1}{2}$ cup to 1 cup (125 mL to 250 mL) cooked beans; $\frac{1}{3}$ cup (75 mL) tofu; or 2 tbsp (25 mL) peanut butter.

# Garlic-Soy Marinated Beef Strips

*This is a good choice for buffets or barbecues when you don't want to use a fork. Soak wooden skewers in water for 15 minutes before threading with beef. Top round steak is a lean cut that works well here. You could also use lean boneless pork. Serve with Thai Peanut Sauce (see sidebar) or use the sauce with Lettuce Wrap Pork on page 131.*

| ¼ cup | sodium-reduced soy sauce | 50 mL |
|-------|--------------------------|-------|
| 2 tbsp | dry sherry | 25 mL |
| 2 tbsp | packed brown sugar | 25 mL |
| 1 tbsp | minced fresh garlic | 15 mL |
| 1 lb | lean beef, 1-inch (2.5 cm) thick | 500 g |

**1.** In 13- x 9-inch (3 L) baking dish, stir together soy sauce, sherry, sugar and garlic until sugar dissolves.

**2.** Slice beef into ¼-inch (5 mm) thick strips about 7 inches (18 cm) long and 1 inch (2.5 cm) wide. Thread strips onto skewers; place in soy sauce mixture, turning to coat. Cover and refrigerate 4 for hours, turning occasionally.

**3.** Broil or grill for about 2 minutes on each side or until desired doneness, brushing with remaining marinade. **Makes 6 servings**.

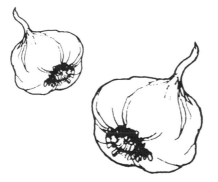

**MAKE AHEAD:** Through step 2, covered and refrigerated for up to 24 hours.

## Thai Peanut Sauce

In blender or food processor, combine 1 cup (250 mL) dry-roasted unsalted peanuts, 1⅓ cups (325 mL) water, 3 cloves garlic, 2 tbsp (25 mL) packed brown sugar, 2 tbsp (25 mL) lime juice, 1 tbsp (15 mL) low-sodium soy sauce, ¼ tsp (1 mL) red pepper flakes and 1 piece (1 inch/2.5 cm) gingerroot, peeled and thinly sliced; process for 2 minutes.

Pour into top of double boiler over boiling water; cook for 30 minutes, stirring occasionally. (Sauce can be covered and refrigerated up to 2 weeks.) Serve warm. **Makes 2 cups (500 mL).** *PER SERVING (1 TBSP/15 ML):* about 30 calories, 1 g protein, 2 g total fat, 2 g carbohydrate, 16 mg sodium, 37 mg potassium

*PER SERVING:*

132 calories

17 g protein

4 g total fat
    1 g saturated fat
    37 mg cholesterol

6 g carbohydrate
    0.1 g dietary fibre

363 mg sodium

270 mg potassium

GOOD: Iron

# Beef and Asparagus Stir-Fry

*Make the most of asparagus season with this fast, easy dinner. To save time, buy beef ready-cut for stir-frying. Pork, chicken or turkey can also be used. Serve over rice or noodles.*

### Buying Beef for Stir-Frying

Choose any lean cut of beef: round, flank, sirloin, sirloin tip, rump, eye of round, strip loin, tenderloin.

### Slicing Beef for Stir-Frying

For easier slicing, partially freeze beef before cutting.

| | | |
|---|---|---|
| 1 lb | asparagus | 500 g |
| ¾ lb | lean boneless beef | 375 g |
| 1 tbsp | vegetable oil | 15 mL |
| 1 tbsp | minced gingerroot | 15 mL |
| 2 | cloves garlic, minced | 2 |
| ¼ cup | water | 50 mL |
| 3 | green onions, diagonally sliced | 3 |

**Sauce**

| | | |
|---|---|---|
| ⅓ cup | water | 75 mL |
| 2 tbsp | sherry | 25 mL |
| 2 tbsp | sodium-reduced soy sauce | 25 mL |
| 2 tbsp | cider vinegar | 25 mL |
| 1 tbsp | cornstarch | 15 mL |
| 1 tsp | granulated sugar | 5 mL |
| Pinch | crushed red pepper flakes | Pinch |

**1.** Sauce: Combine water, sherry, soy sauce, vinegar, cornstarch, sugar and red pepper flakes.

**2.** Cut asparagus diagonally into 1½-inch (4 cm) lengths; cut beef into thin slices.

**3.** In large nonstick skillet, heat oil over high heat; stir-fry ginger and garlic for 30 seconds. Add meat and stir-fry until no longer pink; transfer to plate.

**4.** Add asparagus; stir-fry for 30 seconds. Add water; cover and cook for 3 minutes or until tender-crisp.

**5.** Return meat mixture to pan along with green onions and sauce; cook, stirring, for 1 minute or until thickened. **Makes 4 servings**.

*Per Serving:*

195 calories
22 g protein
7 g total fat
   2 g saturated fat
   40 mg cholesterol
11 g carbohydrate
   2 g dietary fibre
311 mg sodium
611 mg potassium

GOOD: Iron
EXCELLENT: Folate

**MAKE AHEAD:** Through step 2, covered and refrigerated for up to eight hours.

# Beef Fajitas

*This family pleaser is a cinch to make. If you have pickled jalapeño peppers on hand, add them to taste instead of red pepper flakes.*

| | | |
|---|---|---|
| 6 | soft 8-inch (20 cm) flour tortillas | 6 |
| 1 tsp | vegetable oil | 5 mL |
| ½ lb | lean ground beef | 250 g |
| 1 | onion, chopped | 1 |
| 1 | sweet red or green pepper, cut in thin strips | 1 |
| 2 | cloves garlic, minced | 2 |
| 1 tsp | ground coriander | 5 mL |
| ¼ tsp | ground cumin | 1 mL |
| Pinch | crushed red pepper flakes | Pinch |
| ½ cup | each shredded lettuce, tomato salsa, low-fat yogurt, low-fat shredded cheese | 125 mL |
| ¼ cup | chopped fresh coriander | 50 mL |

**1.** Stack tortillas and wrap in foil; heat in 325°F (160°C) oven for 5 to 10 minutes or until warmed through.

**2.** Meanwhile, in large nonstick skillet, heat oil over high heat; cook beef and onion, breaking up meat with spoon, for 1 minute.

**3.** Add red pepper, garlic, ground coriander, cumin and red pepper flakes; cook for 5 minutes or until beef is no longer pink.

**4.** Spoon mixture evenly onto centre of each tortilla; top with lettuce, salsa, yogurt, cheese and coriander. Roll up. **Makes 3 servings**.

**MAKE AHEAD:** Step 2 and 3, covered and refrigerated for up to three hours; reheat in microwave or over low heat.

## Chicken or Turkey Fajitas

Substitute lean ground chicken or turkey for beef.

*PER SERVING:*

570 calories
31 g protein
23 g total fat
    9 g saturated fat
    57 mg cholesterol
62 g carbohydrate
    3 g dietary fibre
784 mg sodium
684 mg potassium

GOOD: Vitamin A
EXCELLENT: Vitamin C; Calcium; Iron

# Hoisin-Garlic Flank Steak

*This oriental marinade tenderizes a lean cut of beef while adding extra flavor. The longer it marinates, the more tender the steak.*

| | | |
|---|---|---|
| 1 lb | flank steak | 500 g |

## Oriental Marinade

| | | |
|---|---|---|
| 2 tbsp | hoisin sauce | 25 mL |
| l tbsp | each rice vinegar,* sherry and liquid honey | 15 mL |
| 1 tsp | sesame oil | 5 mL |
| 1 tsp | grated orange rind | 5 mL |
| 3 | cloves garlic, minced | 3 |
| Pinch | crushed red pepper flakes | Pinch |

**1.** Place meat in shallow dish or plastic bag.

**2.** Oriental Marinade: Combine hoisin sauce, vinegar, sherry, honey, sesame oil, orange rind, garlic and red pepper flakes; pour over meat. Cover and refrigerate for at least 1 hour or up to 24 hours.

**3.** Discarding marinade, grill or broil steak for 5 to 8 minutes on each side or until medium-rare.

**4.** Let stand for 3 minutes before slicing thinly on an angle across the grain. **Makes 4 servings**.

\* If rice vinegar isn't available, use cider vinegar or wine vinegar.

### Cooking Tip
Instead of using salt to add zip or counting on fat-marbled cuts for tenderness, let marinades tenderize and add flavor to lean meats.

*PER SERVING:*

222 calories
27 g protein
10 g total fat
  4 g saturated fat
  46 mg cholesterol
5 g carbohydrate
  0.1 g dietary fibre
160 mg sodium
367 mg potassium

**MAKE AHEAD:** Through step 2. Or to serve cold, through step 3, covered and refrigerated for up to one day; slice just before serving.

# Burgers with Creamy Tomato Pickle Sauce

*Growing up in Vancouver, I enjoyed White Spot's hamburgers with their Triple O sauce, which nobody could beat. Here's my lower-calorie, lower-fat version. Add lettuce, sliced onion and tomato, and a dollop of this sauce.*

| 1 lb | medium ground beef | 500 g |
|---|---|---|
| 4 | hamburger buns | 4 |
| 4 | slices each tomato and onion | 4 |

**Creamy Tomato Pickle Sauce**

| ¼ cup | low-fat yogurt | 50 mL |
|---|---|---|
| 2 tbsp | light mayonnaise | 25 mL |
| 2 tbsp | ketchup | 25 mL |
| 1 tbsp | sweet pickle relish | 15 mL |
| 1 tbsp | chopped green onion or chives | 15 mL |

**1.** Creamy Tomato Pickle Sauce: Combine yogurt, mayonnaise, ketchup, relish and green onion.

**2.** Shape beef into 4 patties.

**3.** Place patties on grill; grill over high heat for about 5 minutes on each side or until no longer pink inside.

**4.** Toast buns if desired; spread with sauce. Top with hamburger, tomato and onion. **Makes 4 servings**.

**MAKE AHEAD:** Through step 2, covered and refrigerated for up to one day.

---

### HAMBURGER DISEASE OR BARBECUE SYNDROME

This is the common name for a type of food poisoning caused by bacteria often found in ground meats. It can be very serious and result in kidney damage. For this reason, it is important to cook all ground meats until they are well done.

You can eat roasts and steaks a little rare, as long as they are well cooked on the outside. However rolled roasts should be cooked like ground meat, so that no pink remains.

Be sure to have a clean plate to put the cooked meat on, and clean utensils, and not the ones already used for the raw meat.

---

***Nutritional Note***
Someone on a low-fat diet should use extra-lean beef and omit the mayonnaise in the sauce. Fat content would then be 12 g per serving.

*PER SERVING:*

434 calories

26 g protein

19 g total fat
   6 g saturated fat
   59 mg cholesterol

40 g carbohydrate
   2 g dietary fibre

546 mg sodium

483 mg potassium

---

GOOD: Folate
EXCELLENT: Iron

# Meat Loaf with Herbs

*Here's an updated version of everyone's favorite meat loaf. Serve with Salsa (page 34), or Mango Salsa (page 51).*

| | | |
|---|---|---|
| 1 | slice bread, crumbled | 1 |
| ¼ cup | low-fat milk | 50 mL |
| 1 | onion, minced | 1 |
| 1 | stalk celery (with leaves), minced | 1 |
| ½ cup | chopped fresh parsley | 125 mL |
| ¼ cup | minced sweet green or red pepper | 50 mL |
| ½ tsp | dried thyme leaves | 2 mL |
| 1 | clove garlic, minced | 1 |
| 1 | egg, lightly beaten | 1 |
| ¼ cup | ketchup | 50 mL |
| 1½ tsp | Worcestershire sauce | 7 mL |
| ¼ tsp | each salt and pepper | 1 mL |
| 1 lb | lean ground beef | 500 g |

**1.** In large bowl, combine bread crumbs and milk. Stir in onion, celery, parsley, green pepper, thyme, garlic, egg, ketchup, Worcestershire sauce, salt and pepper; mix well. Add beef; mix lightly. Transfer to 9- x 5-inch (2 L) loaf pan.

**2.** Bake in 350°F (180°C) oven for 1 hour or until meat thermometer registers 170°F (75°C); drain off fat. Let stand for 10 minutes; cut into thick slices. **Makes 4 servings**.

**MAKE AHEAD:** Through step 1, covered and refrigerated for up to three hours. Or, through step 2 and serve cold.

### Tomato Paste

Most of us have ketchup on our cupboard shelves, however, tomato paste is lower in salt. For those on a low-sodium diet, substitute 2 tbsp (25 mL) tomato paste for the ketchup in this meatloaf. This will reduce the sodium to 282 mg per serving. To reduce sodium by half again, omit salt.

### Nutritional Note

Choose lean or extra lean ground meats in dishes where you can't pour off the fat. Anyone on a low-fat diet should use extra lean ground meats whenever possible.

*PER SERVING:*

253 calories
24 g protein
11 g total fat
    4 g saturated fat
    114 mg cholesterol
13 g carbohydrate
    1 g dietary fibre
482 mg sodium
451 mg potassium

GOOD: Folate; Iron

| FAT CONTENT OF GROUND BEEF | | |
|---|---|---|
| **Ground Beef:** | **Maximum % fat (by raw weight)** | |
| Regular | 30 | |
| Medium | 23 | |
| Lean | 17 | |
| Extra Lean | 10 | |
| **Compare 120 g beef patty, broiled:** | **Fat (g)** | **% calories from fat** |
| Regular | 18 | 65 |
| Medium | 16 | 61 |
| Lean | 13 | 54 |
| Extra Lean | 10 | 46 |

Beef Filet Roasted with Mustard Peppercorn Crust (page 129)
Portobello Mushrooms with Sweet Peppers (page 148)
tiny new potatoes; steamed asparagus

# Beef Filet Roasted with Mustard Peppercorn Crust

*This most tender cut of beef is the perfect choice for a special dinner. Serve with asparagus or green beans, sautéed mushrooms and sweet peppers and baked or tiny new potatoes or couscous. (Pictured opposite page 128.)*

| | | |
|---|---|---|
| 2½ lb | beef tenderloin | 1.2 kg |
| ¼ cup | Dijon mustard | 50 mL |
| 2 tsp | minced fresh garlic | 10 mL |
| 2 tbsp | black peppercorns | 25 mL |

**1.** Trim any fat or muscle covering from meat; place in roasting pan.

**2.** Combine mustard and garlic; spread over beef.

**3.** In food processor or with mallet, crush peppercorns; pat onto mustard coating. Let stand for 1 hour.

**4.** Roast in 425°F (220°C) oven for 10 minutes. Reduce heat to 350°F (180°C); roast for 25 minutes or until medium-rare. Remove and let stand for 10 minutes before carving. **Makes 8 servings**.

**Make Ahead:** Through step 3, covered and refrigerated for up to 24 hours. Remove from refrigerator one hour before roasting, or if roasting directly from refrigerator, add at least five minutes to roasting time.

| BEEF DONENESS | |
|---|---|
| **For:** | **Meat Thermometre Registers:** |
| Rare | 140° F (60° C) |
| Medium Rare | 150° F (65° C) |
| Medium | 160° F (70° C) |
| Well done | 170° F (75° C) |

### On Buying Filet

The terms used in the meat stores are often confusing. The thicker end of the tenderloin is often called the Châteaubriand and the thinner end is called the filet. I ask for the tenderloin from the wide end, and sometimes buy "tenderloin butt" which is from the sirloin end.

### To Serve Cold

Roast as directed for Beef Filet; let cool completely before slicing and serving cold.

*Per Serving:*

206 calories
28 g protein
9 g total fat
   3 g saturated fat
   67 mg cholesterol
1 g carbohydrate
   0.1 g dietary fibre
163 mg sodium
435 mg potassium

Excellent: Iron

Overleaf: Grilled Salmon Ribbons with Sesame and Coriander (page 48)
Thai Pork Skewers (page 49); Thai Peanut Sauce (page 123)
Easy Couscous Vegetable Salad (page 77)
Asparagus and Mushroom Salad (page 78)
Make-Ahead Party Thai Noodles (page 165)
Lemon Grass Marinated Leg of Lamb (page 137)

# Pork Tenderloin Teriyaki

*Pork tenderloin, one of the leanest cuts of pork, is delicious marinated, then grilled just until moist and juicy. Serve with Grilled Fall Vegetables (page 149).*

| | | |
|---|---|---|
| 2 tbsp | sodium-reduced soy sauce | 25 mL |
| 2 tbsp | sherry | 25 mL |
| 1 tbsp | vegetable oil | 15 mL |
| l tbsp | finely chopped gingerrroot | 15 mL |
| 1 tsp | granulated sugar | 5 mL |
| l | clove garlic, minced | 1 |
| 2 | pork tenderloins (about 9 oz/255 g each) | 2 |

**1.** Combine soy sauce, sherry, oil, ginger, sugar and garlic.

**2.** Place pork in plastic bag; pour in marinade. Refrigerate for 2 hours.

**3.** Reserving marinade, place pork on greased grill over medium-high heat. Grill for 18 to 25 minutes or until meat thermometer registers 160°F (70°C) for medium or 170°F (75°C) for well done, turning occasionally and brushing with marinade during last 10 minutes.

**4.** Remove from grill; tent with foil and let stand for 5 minutes. Slice diagonally into thin slices. **Makes 6 servings**.

### Oven-Roasted Pork Tenderloin Teriyaki

In roasting pan or on baking sheet, roast marinated pork in 350°F (180°C) oven for 40 to 50 minutes or until meat thermometer registers 160°-170°F (70°-75°C). Time is based on meat coming straight from refrigerator. If meat is at room temperature, cooking time will be less.

PER SERVING:

133 calories

18 g protein

5 g total fat
   1 g saturated fat
   43 mg cholesterol

2 g carbohydrate
   0.1 g dietary fibre

204 mg sodium

358 mg potassium

**MAKE AHEAD:** Through step 1, covered and refrigerated for up to two days. Through step 2 for up to 24 hours.

# Lettuce Wrap Pork

*Whenever we go out for Chinese food in Vancouver, my niece and nephew, Ashley and Jayson Elliott, always pick a dish similar to this. Serve as an appetizer or as part of a main course and let diners wrap their own.*

| | | |
|---|---|---|
| 6 | dried Chinese mushrooms | 6 |
| 2 tsp | sesame oil | 10 mL |
| ¾ lb | lean ground pork | 375 g |
| 10 | water chestnuts, chopped | 10 |
| 1 | stalk celery, chopped | 1 |
| 3 | green onions, chopped | 3 |
| ½ tsp | minced gingerroot | 2 mL |
| 2 tbsp | rice vinegar or sherry | 25 mL |
| 2 tbsp | hoisin sauce | 25 mL |
| 1 tbsp | sodium-reduced soy sauce | 15 mL |
| 12 | leaves iceberg lettuce | 12 |

**Sauce***

| | | |
|---|---|---|
| 2 tbsp | each hoisin sauce, rice vinegar or sherry and sodium-reduced soy sauce | 25 mL |
| 1 tsp | minced gingerroot | 5 mL |

**1.** Sauce: In small serving dish, combine hoisin sauce, vinegar, soy sauce and ginger.

**2.** Remove tough stems from mushrooms. Cover mushrooms with hot water and let soak for 15 minutes; drain and chop.

**3.** In nonstick skillet, heat oil over high heat; stir-fry pork for 3 minutes; pour off any liquid. Add water chestnuts, celery, onions, ginger and mushrooms; stir-fry until pork is no longer pink. Stir in vinegar, and hoisin and soy sauces.

**4.** Spoon onto platter; surround with lettuce. Let each person spoon a little pork mixture onto a lettuce leaf, drizzle with sauce and roll up to enclose filling. **Makes 4 main-course servings**.

\* Use this sauce as a dipping sauce with Garlic-Soy Marinated Beef Strips (page 123).

**MAKE AHEAD:** Through step 3, covered and refrigerated for up to one day; reheat in microwave or over medium heat.

### Oriental Dinner Menu
• Hot and Sour Soup (page 62)
• Lettuce Wrap Pork
• Thai Noodles with Chicken and Broccoli (page 167)
• Garlic-Soy Marinated Beef Strips (page 123)
  OR
  Spicy Scallops (page 87)
• Chinese Vegetable Fried Rice (page 178)
• Snow Peas with Mushrooms (page 143)
• Nectarine and Orange Compote (page 234)

### Nutritional Note
Anyone on a sodium-restricted diet can omit the sauce in this recipe and reduce the sodium to less than 350 mg.

*PER SERVING:*

278 calories
19 g protein
13 g total fat
    4 g saturated fat
    41 mg cholesterol
21 g carbohydrate
    2 g dietary fibre
757 mg sodium
580 mg potassium

EXCELLENT: Folate

# Chalupas

*This recipe from my friend Janie Sims is great for a cottage meal or for after skiing or skating. Let each person pile this spicy bean and pork combo over tortilla chips and top with the traditional Mexican toppings. If pinto beans are unavailable, use one or a combination of: dried cranberry or romano beans or kidney beans. Sometimes I also include black beans and white pea beans. One pound of dried beans is about 2⅓ cups (575 mL).*

| | | |
|---|---|---|
| 1 lb | lean boneless pork loin | 500 g |
| 6 cups | boiling water | 1.5 L |
| 1 lb | pinto beans | 500 g |
| 2 | large cloves garlic, minced | 2 |
| 2 tbsp | chili powder | 25 mL |
| 1 tbsp | ground cumin or cumin seeds | 15 mL |
| 1 tbsp | hot pepper sauce | 15 mL |
| 1 tsp | dried oregano | 5 mL |
| 16 | large flour tortillas | 16 |
| | Toppings | |

**1.** In large baking dish, combine pork, water, beans, garlic, chili powder, cumin, hot pepper sauce and oregano. Cover and bake in 250°F (125°C) oven for 6 hours or until beans are tender and most of the liquid is absorbed and meat falls apart when stirred.

**2.** Toast tortillas in 350°F (180°C) oven for 10 minutes or until crisp; break into chip-size pieces and place in serving bowl.

**3.** Let each person spoon some bean mixture over tortilla pieces, then top with toppings. **Makes 8 servings.**

### Toppings

Toppings could include individual bowls of chopped lettuce, green onions, diced tomatoes, chopped green pepper, low-fat yogurt or light sour cream, salsa and shredded Cheddar cheese.

### Low Sodium

Cooking your own beans instead of using canned, and using lean pork instead of the traditional salt pork or smoked pork hock with beans, means lower sodium.

### Chalupas

Actually, in Mexico, Chalupas are round corn tortillas fried with the edges curled up in a little boat shape.

PER SERVING
*WITHOUT TOPPINGS*
*(WITH TOPPINGS\*)*

645 (698) calories
34 (38) g protein
11 (13) g total fat
  3 (4) g saturated fat
  33 (39) mg cholesterol
103 (108) g carbohydrate
  15 (16) g dietary fibre
502 (668) mg sodium
1070 (1257) mg potassium

GOOD: Vitamin C
EXCELLENT: Folate;
Calcium; Iron

\* Includes 2 tbsp (25 mL) each chopped green pepper, tomatoes and yogurt and 1 tbsp (15 mL) each salsa and shredded Cheddar cheese.

**MAKE AHEAD:** Through step 2 for up to two days. Refrigerate bean mixture.

# Chick-Pea and Pork Curry

*Ground beef also works well in this tasty curry. Serve over rice.*

| | | |
|---|---|---:|
| ½ lb | ground pork | 250 g |
| 2 tsp | minced fresh garlic | 10 mL |
| 1 | white of leek (or 1 onion), chopped | 1 |
| 2 tsp | minced gingerroot | 10 mL |
| 1 tbsp | all-purpose flour | 15 mL |
| 1 tsp | curry powder | 5 mL |
| ¼ tsp | each ground coriander, cumin and salt | 1 mL |
| Pinch | cayenne pepper | Pinch |
| 1½ cups | cubed peeled butternut squash | 375 mL |
| 1 cup | coarsely shredded carrot | 250 mL |
| 1 cup | cubed peeled potato | 250 mL |
| 1 cup | water | 250 mL |
| 1 | can (19 oz/540 mL) chick-peas, drained | 1 |
| 1 | apple, cored and chopped | 1 |

**1.** In nonstick saucepan, brown pork over medium heat; pour off fat.

**2.** Add garlic, leek and ginger; cook for 2 minutes.

**3.** Add flour, curry powder, coriander, cumin, salt and cayenne; cook, stirring, for 1 minute.

**4.** Add squash, carrot, potato and water; bring to boil. Reduce heat, cover and simmer for 10 minutes. Add ½ cup (125 mL) water if too dry.

**5.** Add chick-peas and apple; cover and cook until vegetables are tender. **Makes 4 servings.**

**MAKE AHEAD:** Curry can be covered and refrigerated for up to 24 hours.

### Variations

Ground pork adds flavor and is inexpensive. Ground beef, chicken or turkey can also be used, or for a vegetarian meal, omit ground meats and instead sauté garlic, leek and ginger in 1 tbsp (15 mL) vegetable oil.

*PER SERVING:*

327 calories
19 g protein
9 g total fat
   3 g saturated fat
   27 mg cholesterol
45 g carbohydrate
   6 g dietary fibre
394 mg sodium
634 mg potassium

GOOD: Iron
EXCELLENT: Vitamin A; Folate

# Skillet Sausage and Rice Paella

## Chicken and Rice Paella

Substitute pieces of skinless chicken (1 lb/500 g) for sausage. Fat per serving would then be cut in about half.

### Nutritional Note

Whole grain rice is a good choice for this dish as it cooks in 20 to 25 minutes and has more nutrients than white rice. If you have time, use brown rice. Cook for 20 minutes, add green pepper and tomatoes, cook another 20 minutes or until rice is tender.

*Hot and spicy Italian sausage is perfect in this easy rice dish. You can also use sweet (mild) Italian sausages, but then add more hot pepper sauce or a pinch of red pepper flakes.*

| | | |
|---|---|---|
| ¾ lb | hot Italian sausages (2), thickly sliced | 375 g |
| 1 | onion, chopped | 1 |
| 2 | cloves garlic, minced | 2 |
| 2 cups | boiling water or chicken stock | 500 mL |
| 1 cup | long grain rice | 250 mL |
| 1 | sweet green pepper, cut in chunks | 1 |
| 2 | tomatoes, coarsely chopped | 2 |
| 1 | bay leaf | 1 |
| ¼ tsp | turmeric | 1 mL |
| Dash | hot pepper sauce | Dash |
| 1 cup | frozen peas, thawed | 250 mL |
| | Salt and pepper | |

**1.** In large nonstick skillet, cook sausages over medium heat for 10 minutes or until browned. Pour off fat.

**2.** Add onion and garlic; cook until softened. Add water, stirring up brown bits from bottom of pan.

**3.** Stir in rice, green pepper, tomatoes, bay leaf, turmeric and hot pepper sauce; cover and simmer for 20 minutes or until rice is tender.

**4.** Stir in peas, and salt and pepper to taste. Discard bay leaf. **Makes 4 servings**.

*Per Serving:*

394 calories
19 g protein
13 g total fat
    4 g saturated fat
    36 mg cholesterol
51 g carbohydrate
    4 g dietary fibre
333 mg sodium
424 mg potassium

Good: Folate
Excellent: Vitamin C

**Make Ahead:** Through step 3, covered and refrigerated for up to 24 hours. Reheat in microwave or over medium heat.

# Honey Garlic Roast Pork

*For easy entertaining, this is one of my all-time favorites. While it's roasting, rich aromas fill your kitchen. Serve with Mango Salsa (page 51) or chutney.*

| | | |
|---|---|---|
| 4 lb | boneless pork loin roast | 2 kg |

**Marinade**

| | | |
|---|---|---|
| 2 tbsp | sodium-reduced soy sauce | 25 mL |
| 2 tbsp | sherry | 25 mL |
| 2 tbsp | liquid honey | 25 mL |
| 2 tbsp | minced gingerroot | 25 mL |
| 2 | cloves garlic, minced | 2 |

**1.** Marinade: Combine soy sauce, sherry, honey, ginger and garlic.

**2.** Trim any fat from meat. Place roast in large plastic bag and pour marinade over. Tie bag shut and refrigerate for at least 4 hours, rotating bag occasionally.

**3.** Remove roast from bag, reserving marinade and leaving as much ginger and garlic bits as possible clinging to roast. Set roast on rack in roasting pan. Roast, uncovered and basting occasionally with marinade, in 325°F (160°C) oven for 2 hours or until meat thermometer registers 160°F (70°C). Let stand for 15 minutes before carving. **Makes 12 servings**.

 **MAKE AHEAD:** Through step 2 for up to two days.

### About Pork

Pork used to be cooked until well done to ensure it was safe. Today, trichinosis from pork is virtually nonexistent in Canada. According to Agriculture Canada, this organism, if present, is destroyed when pork is cooked to an internal temperature of 137° F (58° C), well below the recommended 160° F (70° C). Also, because pork is leaner, it should be cooked at a lower oven temperature to medium (internal 160°F/70° C) with just a hint of pink remaining. Cooking to a higher temperature will dry it out and make it tough. Of course, ground pork and sausage should be cooked thoroughly (see page 127).

*PER SERVING:*

209 calories
23 g protein
11 g total fat
    4 g saturated fat
    53 mg cholesterol
4 g carbohydrate
    0.1 g dietary fibre
139 mg sodium
370 mg potassium

# *Chutney-Glazed Ham*

*Serve with Mango Salsa (page 51) or chutney.*

*I often cook a ham when I want an easy meal to feed a crowd as well as have some leftovers. Ham is a good choice because it is easy to serve and to eat, and you don't have to worry about over- or under-cooking it (as I sometimes do with other meats). Serve with Mango Salsa (page 51) or chutney.*

| | | |
|---|---|---|
| 7 lb | part-skinned, semi-boneless ham (shank or butt) | 3.5 kg |

**Glaze**

| | | |
|---|---|---|
| ½ cup | packed brown sugar | 125 mL |
| ¼ cup | chutney | 50 mL |
| ¼ cup | plum or peach jam | 50 mL |
| 1 tbsp | Dijon mustard | 15 mL |
| 1 tbsp | wine vinegar | 15 mL |
| 1 | clove garlic, minced | 1 |
| Dash | hot pepper sauce | Dash |

**1.** Glaze: Combine sugar, chutney, jam, mustard, vinegar, garlic and hot pepper sauce; set aside.

**2.** Remove skin and all but ¼ inch (5 mm) thick layer of fat on ham. Place, fat side up, in roasting pan. Bake in 325°F (160°C) oven for 1 hour and 45 minutes for fully cooked ham, or 2 hours and 15 minutes for cook-before-eating ham.

**3.** Brush with half of the glaze; bake for another 30 minutes. Brush with remaining glaze; bake for 15 minutes or until meat thermometer reaches 130°F (55°C) for ready-to-eat ham or 160°F (70°C) for cook-before-eating ham. Remove from oven and let stand for 10 minutes before slicing. Serve hot or cold. **Makes 12 servings**.

---

**Buffet Dinner for 50 Guests**

- Thai Shrimp Salad in Pita Pockets (triple recipe, page 43)
- Clam Dip with Herbs and crudités (page 35) or any other dip
- Chutney-Glazed Ham (buy a whole semi-boneless ham, about 20 lb / 10 kg; double glaze recipe)
- Mango Salsa (page 51)
- Party Thai Noodles, (5 times the recipe, page 165)
- Green Beans (about 5 lb / 2.2 kg)
- Tossed Salad Greens with Mustard Garlic Vinaigrette (page 88)
- Elizabeth Baird's Chocolate Angel Food Cake (make 2, page 214)
- Fresh Fruit Salad
- Vanilla Cream (page 239)
- Light Lemon Squares (make 2, page 208)

*PER SERVING (3½ OZ / 100 G):*

174 calories
25 g protein
6 g total fat
    2 g saturated fat
    55 mg cholesterol
4 g carbohydrate
    0.1 g dietary fibre
1338 mg sodium
333 mg potassium

**MAKE AHEAD:** For cold ham, cover and refrigerate cooked ham for up to two days.

# Lemon Grass Marinated Leg of Lamb

*This is one of my favorite meats for entertaining. As well as having fabulous flavor, it's marinated in advance, it cooks fairly quickly and it's boneless for easy serving. In the summer, we barbecue it; in the winter, we broil. (Pictured opposite page 129.)*

| 1 | boneless butterflied leg of lamb (about 3 lb / 1.5 kg boned) | 1 |

**Marinade**

| 3 | stalks lemon grass* | 3 |
| 1 tbsp | finely chopped onion | 15 mL |
| 3 tbsp | lemon juice | 50 mL |
| 2 tbsp | fish sauce or sodium-reduced soy sauce | 25 mL |
| 1½ tsp | minced fresh garlic | 7 mL |
| 1 tsp | packed brown sugar | 5 mL |
| ½ tsp | hot pepper sauce | 2 mL |

**1.** Marinade: Cut off top two-thirds of each lemon grass stalk; trim off outside leaves and roots. Finely chop remaining stalk; combine with onion, lemon juice, fish sauce, garlic, sugar and hot pepper sauce.

**2.** Trim any fat from lamb; place lamb in bowl or plastic bag; pour marinade over. Cover and refrigerate for at least 12 hours, turning occasionally.

**3.** Remove lamb from refrigerator about 1 hour before cooking. Broil about 6 inches (15 cm) from heat for 12 minutes on each side for medium-rare, 15 to 20 minutes on each side for well-done. Meat thermometer should register 150°F (65° C) for medium-rare, 160°F (70°C) for medium or 170°F (75°C) for well-done. Remove from heat; let stand for 10 minutes. Slice thinly across the grain. **Makes 8 servings**.

* See Information on Ingredients (page 32). If fresh lemon grass is unavailable, use 2 tbsp (25 mL) dried, or grated rind from 1 lemon.

 **Make Ahead:** Through step 2 for up to two days.

## Barbecued Leg of Lamb

Grill over high heat for 15 to 20 minutes on each side for medium-rare, 25 to 30 minutes on each side for well-done.

## Lamb Tenderloins or Loins

Marinate up to 2 lb (1 kg) of tenderloins in this marinade for 1 hour or up to 2 days. Grill or broil over high heat for 3 to 4 minutes for tenderloins, 6 minutes for loins, or until still pink inside, turning once or twice.

### Lamb

If buying a leg of frozen lamb, it is best to let it thaw in the refrigerator for 2 days. Lamb is juicy and tender when cooked just until it is pink or medium-rare. If it is overcooked, it will be dried out and not as tender.

PER SERVING:

  193 calories
  29 g protein
  7 g total fat
    3 g saturated fat
    105 mg cholesterol
  0.4 g carbohydrate
    0 g dietary fibre
  78 mg sodium
  198 mg potassium

GOOD: Iron

# Onions Stuffed with Lamb and Spinach

*Tender, juicy onions are filled with a tasty Middle Eastern stuffing. Use any kind of large onion—Spanish, red or regular cooking onions—3½ to 4 inches (9 to 10 cm) in diameter (or use 8 medium onions). Serve with couscous, cooked rice or bulgur.*

| | | |
|---|---|---|
| 5 | large onions | 5 |
| ½ lb | lean ground lamb | 250 g |
| ¼ tsp | each cinnamon, allspice and ground cumin | 1 mL |
| 2 cups | packed chopped fresh spinach | 500 mL |
| 1 | egg | 1 |
| 1 cup | coarse fresh bread crumbs | 250 mL |
| | Salt and pepper | |
| 1 cup | hot broth (lamb* or beef) | 250 mL |

**1.** Peel onions; cut slice off top, then off root end so they will stand. Cut cone shape into top of onion; remove cone. Using melon baller or teaspoon, hollow out onion to make ½-inch (1 cm) thick shell; chop removed onion to make 1½ cups (375 mL).

**2.** Blanch shells in boiling water for 5 minutes. Remove and drain upside down on rack.

**3.** In nonstick pan, cook lamb over medium heat, stirring to break up, for 3 minutes or until browned; pour off fat. Add chopped onion, cinnamon, allspice and cumin; cook until onion is tender.

**4.** Add spinach and cook until wilted. Remove from heat. Stir in egg, bread crumbs, and salt and pepper to taste. Spoon into onion shells.

**5.** Pour hot broth into pan. Bake in 375°F (190°C) oven for 30 minutes. Cover with foil and bake for 10 minutes longer or until onion is tender. **Makes 5 servings.**

\* See lamb broth recipe (page 70).

 **MAKE AHEAD:** Through step 4, covered and refrigerated for up to four hours.

*PER SERVING:*

190 calories

13 g protein

8 g total fat
  3 g saturated fat
  73 mg cholesterol

19 g carbohydrate
  3 g dietary fibre

258 mg sodium

463 mg potassium

GOOD: Vitamin A; Iron
EXCELLENT: Folate

# Lamb and Feta Pita Pockets

*Pork or beef can also be used in this tasty filling for pitas.*

| | | |
|---|---|---|
| 4 | 6-inch (16 cm) pita breads | 4 |
| ¾ lb | lean ground lamb | 375 g |
| 1 | onion, minced | 1 |
| 2 tsp | minced fresh garlic | 10 mL |
| 1 | stalk celery, chopped | 1 |
| 1 | pkg (300 g) chopped frozen spinach, thawed and squeezed dry | 1 |
| 2 tsp | dried oregano | 10 mL |
| | Salt and pepper | |
| ½ cup | crumbled feta cheese | 125 mL |
| | Lettuce leaves (optional) | |
| 1 | tomato, diced | 1 |
| ½ cup | low-fat yogurt | 125 mL |

**1.** Cut pitas in half; slide knife into each half to form pocket. Warm in 325°F (160°C) oven for 5 minutes.

**2.** Meanwhile, in large nonstick skillet, cook lamb, onion, garlic and celery over medium-high heat for 5 minutes or until vegetables are tender. Pour off any liquid.

**3.** Add spinach, oregano, and salt and pepper to taste; cook for 2 minutes or until heated through.

**4.** Remove from heat. Crumble in cheese.

**5.** Line each pita with lettuce (if using); spoon in lamb mixture. Top with tomato and yogurt. **Makes 4 servings.**

**MAKE AHEAD:** Through step 3, covered and refrigerated for up to four hours. Reheat in microwave or over medium heat.

## Lamb and Spinach with Rice

Instead of a filling for pitas, this is also a quick and easy supper dish served over hot rice. Top the lamb mixture with the diced tomato, then drizzle with yogurt.

*PER SERVING:*

427 calories

27 g protein

16 g total fat
   7 g saturated fat
   71 mg cholesterol

44 g carbohydrate
   4 g dietary fibre

521 mg sodium

711 mg potassium

GOOD: Vitamin C
EXCELLENT: Vitamin A; Folate; Calcium; Iron

# Moroccan Rabbit Tagine

*A letter from the Ontario Commercial Rabbit Growers Association telling me of the nutritional benefits of rabbit meat made me want to include a rabbit recipe. This one, unlike most traditional rabbit dishes, is low in added fat and spiked with North African seasonings. Serve with plain couscous (see page 188), rice or bulgur.*

## Moroccan Chicken Tagine

Substitute 3 lb (1.5 kg) bone-in skinless chicken pieces for rabbit.

## Tagine

A tagine is a North African stew usually served over couscous. I don't know if they make a rabbit tagine, but this one tastes wonderful.

| | | |
|---|---|---|
| 2 tsp | vegetable oil | 10 mL |
| 2 tsp | chopped fresh garlic | 10 mL |
| 2 | onions, sliced | 2 |
| 2 tbsp | chopped gingerroot | 25 mL |
| 1 tsp | each ground coriander, cumin and turmeric | 5 mL |
| ½ tsp | cinnamon | 2 mL |
| ¼ tsp | each salt and pepper | 1 mL |
| 1 | skinned rabbit (3 lb/1.5 kg), cut in pieces | 1 |
| 3 cups | chopped peeled sweet potato | 750 mL |
| 2 cups | chopped peeled carrots | 500 mL |
| 2 cups | chopped peeled parsnips | 500 mL |
| 1 | can (28 oz/796 mL) tomatoes | 1 |
| 1 cup | pitted prunes | 250 mL |
| ¼ cup | chopped fresh parsley and/or coriander | 50 mL |

**1.** In large flameproof casserole, heat oil over medium-high heat; cook garlic, onions, ginger, ground coriander, cumin, turmeric, cinnamon, salt and pepper, stirring often, for 3 minutes.

**2.** Add rabbit; cook for 5 minutes or until lightly browned. Add potato, carrots, parsnips and tomatoes; bring to boil.

**3.** Bake, covered, in 325°F (160°C) oven for 35 minutes.

**4.** Add prunes; bake for 5 minutes or until rabbit is tender, meat easily falls away from bone and vegetables are fork-tender. Stir in parsley and/or coriander. **Makes 6 servings**.

**MAKE AHEAD:** Through step 3, covered and refrigerated for up to one day or frozen for up to two weeks. Thaw completely. Reheat in 350°F (180°C) oven, uncovered, for 30 to 40 minutes or until bubbly.

*PER SERVING:*

444 calories

39 g protein

12 g total fat
　3 g saturated fat
　98 mg cholesterol

46 g carbohydrate
　8 g dietary fibre

398 mg sodium

1193 mg potassium

EXCELLENT: Vitamin A; Vitamin C; Folate; Iron

# VEGETABLES

Sesame Carrots

Snow Peas with Mushrooms

Sherried Green Beans with
Sweet Red Peppers

Green Beans with Herbs and Pine Nuts

Spinach with Lemon and Nutmeg

Cauliflower with Fresh Dill

Ginger Stir-Fried Zucchini

Portobello Mushrooms with
Sweet Peppers

Grilled Fall Vegetables

Barbecued Potato Packets

Rosemary Garlic Roasted Potatoes

Buttermilk Mashed Potatoes

Sweet Potato and Apple Purée

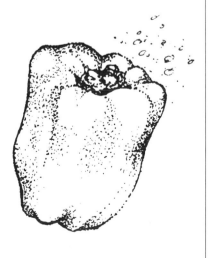

# Sesame Carrots

*The crunch of sesame seeds really adds a delicious dimension to familiar carrots. (Pictured on cover.)*

| 6 | carrots (1 lb/500 g) | 6 |
|---|---|---|
| 1 tbsp | sesame seeds | 15 mL |
| 2 tbsp | orange juice | 25 mL |
| 1 tsp | grated gingerroot | 5 mL |
| 1 tsp | sesame oil | 5 mL |
| 1 tsp | sodium-reduced soy sauce | 5 mL |
| | Salt and pepper | |

**1.** Peel carrots; cut into sticks. (You should have about 4 cups/1 L.)

**2.** In small skillet, cook sesame seeds over medium heat for 2 minutes or until golden, shaking pan occasionally.

**3.** Combine orange juice, ginger, sesame oil and soy sauce.

**4.** Steam carrots for about 8 minutes or until tender-crisp. (Or toss carrots with 2 tbsp/25 mL water; cover and microwave at High for 5 minutes.)

**5.** Toss with sesame seeds and ginger mixture. Season with salt and pepper to taste. **Makes 4 servings**.

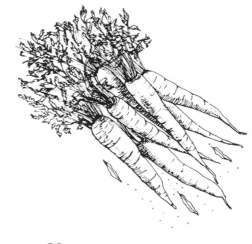

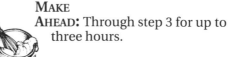

**MAKE AHEAD:** Through step 3 for up to three hours.

## Sesame Broccoli and Carrots

Prepare Sesame Carrots recipe, add one bunch broccoli and use 2 tbsp (25 mL) sesame seeds. Trim tough ends from broccoli. Peel stalks and slice diagonally. Separate head into florets. Steam broccoli then toss with carrots and ginger mixture. Makes 8 servings.

### Beta Carotene

Carrots, raw or cooked, are an excellent source of beta carotene, an antioxidant vitamin. Health professionals recommend we eat more dark green and orange vegetables as they are rich in vitamins.

*PER SERVING:*

67 calories
2 g protein
3 g total fat
   0.4 g saturated fat
   0 mg cholesterol
10 g carbohydrate
   2 g dietary fibre
99 mg sodium
225 mg potassium

EXCELLENT: Vitamin A

# Snow Peas with Mushrooms

*Use any kind or combination of mushrooms in this colorful, easy vegetable dish (pictured opposite page 64). If using dried wild mushrooms, soak in warm water to soften before cooking. A few ounces of dried wild mushrooms mixed with some fresh brown mushrooms is a nice combination.*

| | | |
|---|---|---|
| 1 lb | snow peas | 500 g |
| 1 tbsp | olive oil | 15 mL |
| ½ lb | mushrooms, thickly sliced | 250 g |
| | Salt and pepper | |

**1.** Remove stem and string from snow peas.

**2.** In large nonstick skillet, heat oil over medium-high heat; cook mushrooms, stirring or shaking pan, for 8 to 10 minutes or until browned, tender and any liquid has evaporated.

**3.** Blanch snow peas in boiling water for 2 to 4 minutes or until tender; drain well.

**4.** Toss peas with mushrooms. Season with salt and pepper to taste. **Makes 8 servings**.

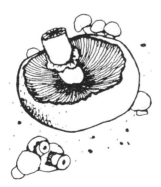

**MAKE AHEAD:** Through step 3 for up to four hours. After blanching snow peas, cool in ice water and drain thoroughly. Reheat in boiling water for 30 seconds. Reheat mushrooms in skillet over medium heat before step 4.

### Vitamins

There is a lot of attention now being paid to the role of vitamins in protecting us against heart disease and certain cancers. It is important to get our vitamins from food and not to rely on supplements, as food contains fibre, energy and other important nutrients not found in supplements. Dark green and orange vegetables and orange fruits are rich sources of vitamins.

*PER SERVING:*

43 calories
2 g protein
2 g total fat
   0.3 g saturated fat
   0 mg cholesterol
5 g carbohydrate
   2 g dietary fibre
3 mg sodium
200 mg potassium

GOOD: Vitamin C

# Sherried Green Beans with Sweet Red Peppers

*This colorful vegetable dish goes well with any meats, fish or poultry. If fresh red peppers aren't available, substitute ½ cup (125 mL) diced bottled red peppers.*

| | | |
|---|---|---|
| ½ cup | water | 125 mL |
| ¼ cup | dry sherry | 50 mL |
| 2 tbsp | sodium-reduced soy sauce | 25 mL |
| 1 tbsp | minced gingerroot | 15 mL |
| 2 tsp | cornstarch | 10 mL |
| 1 tbsp | sesame oil | 15 mL |
| 1½ lb | green beans, ends and strings removed | 750 kg |
| 1 cup | diced sweet red pepper | 250 mL |

**1.** In saucepan, combine water, sherry, soy sauce, ginger and cornstarch; cook over medium-high heat, stirring constantly, until boiling and thickened. Remove from heat. Stir in sesame oil.

**2.** In separate saucepan of boiling water, cook beans for 6 to 8 minutes or until tender-crisp; drain. Pour hot sauce over beans; mix gently. Transfer to serving dish; sprinkle red pepper on top. **Makes 10 servings**.

## Microwave Method for Sauce

In microwaveable dish, combine water, sherry, soy sauce, ginger and cornstarch; microwave at High for 3 to 4 minutes, stirring after each minute, until boiling and thickened. Let cool slightly. Add sesame oil.

*Per Serving:*

- 44 calories
- 1 g protein
- 2 g total fat
  - 0.2 g saturated fat
  - 0 mg cholesterol
- 6 g carbohydrate
  - 2 g dietary fibre
- 100 mg sodium
- 208 mg potassium

Good: Vitamin C

**Make Ahead:** Through step 1 for up to three hours; reheat over medium-high heat, stirring continuously, or microwave at High for one minute, until hot.

# Green Beans with Herbs and Pine Nuts

*Green beans are a tasty and colorful addition to most dinners.*

| | | |
|---|---|---|
| 2 tbsp | pine nuts or sunflower seeds | 25 mL |
| 1½ lb | green beans, trimmed | 750 g |
| ¼ cup | chopped fresh dill or parsley | 50 mL |
| 1 tbsp | soft margarine or butter, melted | 15 mL |
| 2 tsp | lemon juice | 10 mL |
| | Salt and pepper | |

**1.** Toast nuts in 350°F (180°C) oven for 5 minutes or until golden.

**2.** In large saucepan of boiling water, cook beans for 5 minutes or until tender-crisp. Drain thoroughly.

**3.** Add dill and margarine; toss gently. Add lemon juice, and salt and pepper to taste; toss again. Sprinkle with pine nuts. **Makes 10 servings**.

**MAKE AHEAD:** Through step 2; immediately plunge into cold water, then drain. Wrap in clean tea towel and refrigerate for up to six hours. Reheat in boiling water for one minute or until heated through; drain and continue with step 3.

***Fresh Herbs***
Be generous with fresh herbs: they liven up everything from pasta to salad dressings. In the winter, when it's costly to have a variety of fresh herbs on hand, splurge on one kind and use it over a few days, then buy another the next shopping trip. If parsley is the only fresh herb available, use it and add other dried herbs to taste.

*Per Serving:*
45 calories
2 g protein
2 g total fat
   1 g saturated fat
   3 mg cholesterol
6 g carbohydrate
   2 g dietary fibre
14 mg sodium
221 mg potassium

# Spinach with Lemon and Nutmeg

*Spinach adds a pretty color to a plate and goes well with almost any fish, meat or poultry. This quick-cooking method maximizes the spinach's nutrients.*

| | | |
|---|---|---|
| 1 | bunch or pkg (10 oz/284 g) spinach | 1 |
| 2 tsp | lemon juice | 10 mL |
| 1 tsp | soft margarine or butter, melted | 5 mL |
| Pinch | nutmeg | Pinch |
| | Salt and pepper | |

**1.** Rinse spinach and shake off excess water.

**2.** In large saucepan, cover and cook spinach with just the water clinging to leaves over medium heat for 2 minutes or just until wilted; drain well.

**3.** Sprinkle with lemon juice, margarine, nutmeg, and salt and pepper to taste. **Makes 3 servings.**

# Cauliflower with Fresh Dill

*Fresh dill goes well with most vegetables and is very good with cauliflower. This dish is also good served cold and makes a wonderful addition to a summer salad plate.*

| | | |
|---|---|---|
| 1 | medium head cauliflower | 1 |
| 2 tbsp | lemon juice | 25 mL |
| 1 tbsp | olive oil | 15 mL |
| 1/3 cup | chopped fresh dill | 75 mL |
| | Salt and pepper | |
| | Chopped sweet red pepper or tomato (optional) | |

**1.** Remove leaves and stem from cauliflower; cut cauliflower into florets. Cook in large pot of boiling water, covered, for 10 minutes or until tender; drain. Transfer to serving dish.

**2.** Mix lemon juice with oil; pour over cauliflower and stir to mix. Sprinkle with dill, and salt and pepper to taste. Garnish with red pepper (if using). **Makes 6 servings.**

# Ginger Stir-Fried Zucchini

*Add carrots, cauliflower, red onion, bean sprouts or any seasonal vegetables to this easy stir-fry.*

| | | |
|---|---|---|
| 1 tsp | vegetable oil | 5 mL |
| 2 cups | sliced zucchini | 500 mL |
| Half | red onion, sliced | Half |
| 2 tsp | chopped gingerroot | 10 mL |
| 1 tbsp | sodium-reduced soy sauce | 15 mL |
| 1 tsp | dark sesame oil | 5 mL |
| | Salt and pepper | |

**1.** In nonstick skillet, heat oil over medium-high heat; stir-fry zucchini, onion and ginger for 1 minute.

**2.** Add 1 tbsp (15 mL) water; cover and steam for 1 to 2 minutes or until tender-crisp, adding more water if necessary to prevent scorching.

**3.** Stir in soy sauce and oil. Season with salt and pepper to taste. **Makes 4 servings**.

***Nutritional Note***

Choose cooking methods that preserve nutrients. Steam or microwave vegetables, and use their nutrient-rich cooking liquid in soups or recipes calling for stock or broth.

*Per Serving:*

51 calories
1 g protein
2 g total fat
    0.3 g saturated fat
    0 mg cholesterol
7 g carbohydrate
    2 g dietary fibre
124 mg sodium
227 mg potassium

# Portobello Mushrooms with Sweet Peppers

### Grilled Portobello Mushrooms

These are delicious on the grill and because of their size, easy to barbecue. Cut into ¼-inch (5 mm) thick slices; brush lightly with olive oil and grill over medium heat for 4 to 6 minutes or until tender, turning once.

### Portobello Mushrooms

These mushrooms are dark brown with 5- to 10-inch (12 to 25 cm) wide caps with prominent gills underneath. Because mushrooms are open and dirt is often in the gills, they need to be washed by quickly swishing through a bowl of water. When cooked, they turn mostly black.

*Huge portobello mushrooms have much more flavor than regular mushrooms and are easy to cook. Thanks to mushroom lover Dave Nichol and Ontario mushroom farmer Lou Argo, they are easy to find in Ontario and, I hope, across Canada. If unavailable, use large, old-fashioned brown mushrooms. (Pictured opposite page 128.)*

| 1 lb | portobello mushrooms | 500 g |
| 2 tbsp | soft margarine, butter or olive oil | 25 mL |
| 1 | clove garlic, minced (optional) | 1 |
| 1 | each sweet red and yellow pepper, cut in strips | 1 |
| | Salt and pepper | |

**1.** Wash mushrooms quickly in a little water; pat dry. Cut into ¼-inch (5 mm) thick slices.

**2.** In large nonstick skillet, heat margarine over high heat; cook garlic, red and yellow peppers and mushrooms, shaking pan or stirring often, for 7 to 10 minutes or until vegetables are tender and any liquid from mushrooms has nearly disappeared.

**3.** Sprinkle with salt and pepper to taste. **Makes 6 servings**.

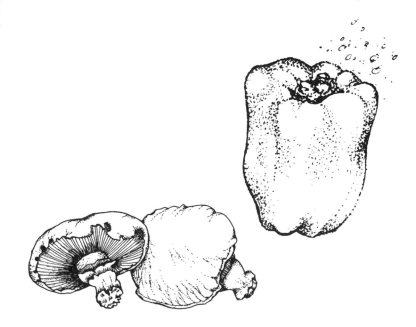

PER SERVING:

58 calories
2 g protein
4 g total fat
   1 g saturated fat
   0 mg cholesterol
5 g carbohydrate
   2 g dietary fibre
52 mg sodium
251 mg potassium

EXCELLENT: Vitamin C

# Grilled Fall Vegetables

*Steaming the eggplant first shortens the grilling time and keeps it moist, which means you don't need to brush it with oil. Serve this side dish hot or at room temperature.*

| | | |
|---|---|---|
| 1 | eggplant (about 12 oz/375 g) | 1 |
| 2 | zucchini (about 7 inches/18 cm each) | 2 |
| 2 tbsp | olive oil | 25 mL |
| 3 | sweet peppers (red, green and yellow) | 3 |
| 2 tbsp | balsamic vinegar | 25 mL |
| 2 tbsp | chopped fresh thyme (or ¼ tsp/1 mL dried) | 25 mL |
| 1 tbsp | water | 15 mL |
| | Salt and pepper | |

**1.** Cut eggplant into ½-inch (1 cm) thick slices. Place in steamer in single layer; steam for 4 minutes.

**2.** Cut zucchini diagonally into ¼-inch (5 mm) thick slices; brush with 1 tsp (5 mL) of the oil.

**3.** Seed and cut peppers lengthwise into 8 pieces.

**4.** Grill vegetables, in batches if necessary, over high heat for 4 to 6 minutes on each side or until tender but firm. Transfer to serving bowl.

**5.** Whisk together remaining oil, vinegar, thyme, water, and salt and pepper to taste. Pour over hot vegetables and toss to coat. **Makes 6 servings**.

**MAKE AHEAD:** Vegetables can be covered and refrigerated for up to one day. Serve at room temperature.

## Grilled Peppers

One of my favorite vegetables is grilled sweet red peppers. The problem is cooking them enough to be tender without burning—the minute you forget to watch they burn.

My husband, Bob, does the barbecuing and has tried a number of ways to grill peppers, from cooking over high heat and turning often, to his latest, which is to grill peppers cut in quarters about 10 minutes over medium-low heat, turning once. Then he moves them to the other side of the barbecue, not over the heat, where they continue to cook while he barbecues the meat on the other side.

Total cooking time varies with the outdoor temperature but is about 20 to 30 minutes.

*PER SERVING:*

80 calories
1 g protein
5 g total fat
   1 g saturated fat
   0 mg cholesterol
10 g carbohydrate
   3 g dietary fibre
4 mg sodium
366 mg potassium

GOOD: Vitamin A
EXCELLENT: Vitamin C

# Barbecued Potato Packets

*Just scrub tender new potatoes, leaving the skin on for texture and nutrients. Instead of dried herbs, you can use 1 tbsp (15 mL) of any fresh herbs such as rosemary, basil, thyme, dill and/or oregano.*

| 4 | new potatoes, thinly sliced | 4 |
|---|---|---|
| 1 | onion, thinly sliced | 1 |
| 1 | clove garlic, minced | 1 |
| 1 tbsp | olive oil | 15 mL |
| ¼ tsp | each dried thyme, rosemary, salt and pepper | 1 mL |

**1.** Toss potatoes with onion, garlic, oil, thyme, rosemary, salt and pepper.

**2.** Divide among 4 pieces of greased heavy-duty foil; wrap well to seal.

**3.** Grill over medium heat for 20 minutes or until tender. **Makes 4 servings**.

**MAKE AHEAD:** Through step 2, refrigerated for up to four hours.

PER SERVING:

165 calories

3 g protein

4 g total fat
  0.5 g saturated fat
  0 mg cholesterol

31 g carbohydrate
  3 g dietary fibre

153 mg sodium

515 mg potassium

# Rosemary Garlic Roasted Potatoes

*Cook these the same time you are roasting any meat or poultry. With these potatoes, the oven temperature can vary depending on what else is in the oven.*

| 6 cups | peeled potato wedges (about 2 lb/1 kg) | 1.5 L |
|---|---|---|
| 1 tbsp | olive oil | 15 mL |
| 2 tsp | chopped fresh garlic | 10 mL |
| 2 tsp | chopped fresh or dried rosemary | 10 mL |
| | Salt and pepper | |

**1.** In large shallow baking dish, toss potatoes with oil, garlic, rosemary, and salt and pepper to taste.

**2.** Bake, uncovered, in 325°F (160°C) oven for 1 hour or until fork-tender. **Makes 6 servings**.

PER SERVING:

118 calories

2 g protein

2 g total fat
  0.3 g saturated fat
  0 mg cholesterol

23 g carbohydrate
  2 g dietary fibre

6 mg sodium

370 mg potassium

# Buttermilk Mashed Potatoes

*These creamy potatoes are fabulous. I'm often asked what to do with leftover buttermilk: this is one of the best ways I know. Instead of mashing, a potato ricer or food mill also works well.*

| 10 | medium potatoes (about 3 lb/1.5 kg), peeled and quartered | 10 |
|---|---|---|
| 2 cups | buttermilk | 500 mL |
| 1 tbsp | soft margarine or butter | 15 mL |
| ¼ cup | chopped green onion | 50 mL |
| Pinch | nutmeg | Pinch |
| | Salt and pepper | |

**1.** In large saucepan, cover potatoes with cold water; bring to boil and cook for 20 minutes or until fork-tender. Drain; return to low heat for 3 minutes to dry.

**2.** Mash potatoes to remove all lumps. Gradually beat in buttermilk and margarine. Stir in green onion and nutmeg. Season with salt and pepper to taste. **Makes 12 servings**.

**MAKE AHEAD:** Through step 2; spoon into lightly greased 8-cup (2 L) baking dish. Let cool, cover and refrigerate for up to three days. Do not freeze. To serve: Let stand at room temperature for 30 minutes before reheating, covered, in 350°F (180°C) oven for 50 minutes.

---

### OVEN-ROASTED VEGETABLES

Sunday night, I like to cook a chicken or roast. To go along with it, I usually roast onions (halved), and parsnips, carrots, potatoes, sweet potatoes and leeks cut in ½-inch (1 cm) thick pieces. I place them in a shallow pan and toss with enough meat-pan juices to keep them from sticking. Roast in 325°F (160°C) oven, or whatever temperature meat requires, for 60 to 90 minutes.

While the meat rests at room temperature for 15 minutes before carving, raise the oven temperature to 450° F (230° C) if the vegetables are not yet cooked, and cook until tender.

---

## Oven-Baked Fries

Cut 4 (unpeeled) potatoes into wedges or ½ inch (1 cm) thick strips; toss with 1 tbsp (15 mL) vegetable oil, ½ tsp (2 mL) each paprika and chili powder. Bake on baking sheet in 475°F (240°C) oven for 25 to 30 minutes or until golden, turning occasionally. Toss with salt. Makes 4 servings. You can do this with peeled turnip, parsnips and sweet potatoes too.

## New Potatoes with Herbs

Scrub 4 new potatoes; halve or quarter if large. Boil for 12 to 14 minutes or until tender. Drain and toss with 2 tbsp (25 mL) chopped fresh parsley or dill, 2 tsp (10 mL) olive oil, and salt and pepper to taste. **Makes 4 servings**. *PER SERVING:* about 160 calories, 3 g protein, 2 g fat, 32 g carbohydrate

*PER SERVING:*
97 calories
3 g protein
1 g total fat
  0.4 g saturated fat
  1 mg cholesterol
19 g carbohydrate
  1 g dietary fibre
60 mg sodium
339 mg potassium

# Sweet Potato and Apple Purée

*This make-ahead dish goes well with roast chicken, turkey, ham or pork. Instead of apples, you can use 2 cups (500 mL) unsweetened applesauce.*

| | | |
|---|---|---|
| 3 lb | sweet potatoes, peeled and cubed (about 6 medium) | 1.5 kg |
| 3 | large tart apples, peeled and chopped | 3 |
| ¼ cup | water | 50 mL |
| 2 tbsp | soft margarine or butter | 25 mL |
| | Nutmeg, salt and pepper | |
| 2 tbsp | toasted sunflower seeds (optional) | 25 mL |

**1.** In saucepan of boiling water, cook potatoes for 15 minutes or until tender when pierced with fork. Drain and return to saucepan.

**2.** In small saucepan, combine apples with water; cover and simmer for 5 to 6 minutes or until tender.

**3.** Using potato masher or in food processor, purée potatoes and apples until smooth. Stir in margarine, and nutmeg, salt and pepper to taste.

**4.** Transfer to serving dish; sprinkle sunflower seeds on top (if using). **Makes 12 servings**.

### To Toast Sunflower Seeds

Bake on baking sheet in 350°F (180°C) oven for 5 minutes or until golden.

### Nutritional Note

Sweet potatoes are packed with beta carotene, which the body converts to Vitamin A. They are also high in fibre and Vitamin C. Try baking them in the oven or microwave as you would regular potatoes.

PER SERVING:

150 calories

2 g protein

2 g total fat
 0.4 g saturated fat
 0 mg cholesterol

32 g carbohydrate
 4 g dietary fibre

38 mg sodium

235 mg potassium

GOOD: Vitamin C
EXCELLENT: Vitamin A

**MAKE AHEAD:** Through step 3; transfer to 8-cup (2 L) baking dish; cover and refrigerate for up to three days, or freeze for up to two weeks. Let stand at room temperature for one hour, or thaw in refrigerator for 24 hours. Reheat, uncovered, in 350°F (180°C) oven for 30 minutes or until heated through.

# PASTA

Pasta with Chick-Peas, Tomatoes
and Herbs

Pasta with Tomatoes, Cheese
and Jalapeños

Spaghettini with Ham and Cheese

Macaroni and Cheese

Light Fettuccine Alfredo with Fresh Herbs

Linguine with Mushrooms
and Green Peppers

Summer Shrimp and Tomato Pasta

Linguine with Scallops and Leeks

Pasta Provençal with Tofu

Singapore Noodles with Pork

Jiffy Chinese Noodles

Make-Ahead Party Thai Noodles

Szechuan Beef with Noodles

Thai Noodles with Chicken
and Broccoli

Singapore Noodle and Chicken Salad

Spicy Noodle Salad

Pasta Salad with Sun-Dried Tomatoes

Pasta and Ham Salad with
Tomato Basil Dressing

Seafood Pasta Salad

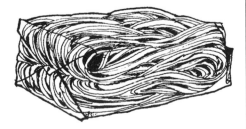

# Pasta with Chick-Peas, Tomatoes and Herbs

*Keep the makings for this easy, inexpensive yet tasty dinner on your shelf for when the refrigerator is bare and you need to have dinner ready in minutes.*

| | | |
|---|---|---|
| 2 cups | penne pasta (or 8 oz/250 g corkscrew or other pasta) | 500 mL |
| 1 tbsp | olive oil | 15 mL |
| 1 | large clove garlic, minced | 1 |
| 1 | can (19 oz/540 mL) tomatoes (undrained), chopped | 1 |
| 1 tsp | each dried basil and oregano | 5 mL |
| 1 | can (19 oz/540 mL) chick-peas, drained and rinsed | 1 |
| ¼ cup | chopped fresh basil or parsley | 50 mL |
| ¼ cup | freshly grated Parmesan cheese | 50 mL |

**1.** In large pot of boiling water, cook pasta until tender but firm, 7 to 10 minutes; drain and transfer to large bowl.

**2.** Meanwhile, in saucepan, heat oil over medium heat; cook garlic for 30 seconds. Add tomatoes, dried basil, oregano and chick-peas; simmer for 5 minutes.

**3.** Add fresh basil; simmer for 5 minutes. Pour over hot pasta and toss to mix. Sprinkle cheese over each serving. **Makes 4 servings**.

***Chick-peas***

Chick-peas are high in fibre and iron. They also contribute calcium and protein.

*PER SERVING:*

444 calories

19 g protein

8 g total fat
   2 g saturated fat
   5 mg cholesterol

75 g carbohydrate
   7 g dietary fibre

543 mg sodium

508 mg potassium

GOOD: Vitamin C; Calcium; Iron
EXCELLENT: Folate

**MAKE AHEAD:** Sauce, step 2, can be covered and refrigerated for up to two days.

# Pasta with Tomatoes, Cheese and Jalapeños

*Keep a jar of pickled jalapeños in your refrigerator to add zing to this easy pasta. Vary the amount or kind of hot pepper, depending upon your tastes. Serve with toasted whole wheat buns and a green salad.*

| | | |
|---|---|---|
| 1 lb | linguine or other pasta | 500 g |
| 2 tbsp | minced fresh garlic | 25 mL |
| 1 cup | coarsely chopped parsley | 250 mL |
| 2 tbsp | chopped pickled jalapeño peppers | 25 mL |
| 2 tbsp | olive oil | 25 mL |
| 3 | large tomatoes, chopped | 3 |
| 1 cup | freshly grated Parmesan or Romano cheese | 250 mL |

**1.** In large pot of boiling water, cook linguine until tender yet firm; drain.

**2.** Meanwhile, in food processor, chop garlic, parsley and peppers until fine.

**3.** In nonstick skillet, heat oil over high heat; cook garlic mixture and tomatoes for 1 minute or until hot. Toss with linguine. Add cheese and toss to mix. **Makes 6 servings**.

### Leftovers
Any leftovers of this pasta dish can be covered and refrigerated; to reheat, add a spoonful or two of water, cover and microwave until hot.

### Canned Tomatoes
Use 1 can (28 oz/ 796 mL) tomatoes, undrained (chopped), instead of fresh. Cook garlic mixture in oil for 1 minute; add tomatoes and simmer, uncovered, for 5 minutes. Toss with pasta and cheese.

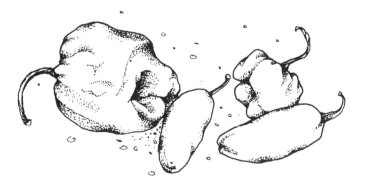

*Per Serving:*

424 calories
18 g protein
11 g total fat
   4 g saturated fat
   13 mg cholesterol
63 g carbohydrate
   5 g dietary fibre
326 mg sodium
355 mg potassium

Good: Vitamin A; Folate; Calcium; Iron
Excellent: Vitamin C

# Spaghettini with Ham and Cheese

*Any shape or kind of pasta is fine in this recipe. Danbo cheese, low-fat mozzarella or light Cheddar-type cheese work well here. Instead of zucchini, you can use a grated carrot, chopped green onions or frozen peas.*

| | | |
|---|---|---|
| ½ lb | spaghettini | 250 g |
| 1 cup | low-fat cottage cheese | 250 mL |
| 1 cup | shredded low-fat cheese | 250 mL |
| ¼ cup | low-fat milk | 50 mL |
| ¼ tsp | each salt and pepper | 1 mL |
| Pinch | nutmeg | Pinch |
| 2 | small zucchini, halved lengthwise and thinly sliced | 2 |
| ¾ cup | julienned ham (4 oz/125 g) | 175 mL |
| 2 tbsp | chopped fresh parsley | 25 mL |

**1.** In large pot of boiling water, cook pasta until tender yet firm; drain and return to saucepan.

**2.** Meanwhile, in food processor or pressing through sieve, purée cottage cheese. Combine with shredded cheese, milk, salt, pepper and nutmeg; add to hot pasta.

**3.** Add zucchini and ham; cook over medium-low heat, stirring, for 1 minute or until heated through.

**4.** Sprinkle with parsley. **Makes 4 servings**.

## Nutritional Note

For a fat-restricted diet, use ½ cup (125 mL) shredded Danbo cheese. The fat content will be 5 g per serving.

*Per Serving:*

405 calories
30 g protein
9 g total fat
    5 g saturated fat
    37 mg cholesterol
49 g carbohydrate
    4 g dietary fibre
925 mg sodium
420 mg potassium

Good: Folate
Excellent: Calcium

# Macaroni and Cheese

*Good*

*This creamy dish is made lower in fat by thickening the sauce
with cornstarch instead of the traditional butter-flour mixture
and using lower-fat cheeses.*

| | | |
|---|---|---|
| 2 cups | macaroni | 500 mL |
| 1 | onion, coarsely chopped | 1 |
| 2 cups | low-fat milk | 500 mL |
| 2 tbsp | cornstarch | 25 mL |
| 1 tsp | dry mustard | 5 mL |
| 1 cup | shredded fat-reduced old Cheddar-style cheese | 250 mL |
| 1 cup | shredded Danbo or skim milk cheese | 250 mL |
| | Salt and pepper | |
| 1 | tomato, thinly sliced | 1 |

**Topping**

| | | |
|---|---|---|
| ½ cup | fresh bread crumbs | 125 mL |
| 2 tbsp | freshly grated Parmesan cheese | 25 mL |
| 1 tbsp | soft margarine or butter, melted | 15 mL |

**1.** In large pot of boiling water, cook macaroni for 5 minutes; add onion and cook for 5 minutes or until macaroni is tender but firm; drain.

**2.** In separate large saucepan, combine milk, cornstarch and mustard; cook, stirring, over medium heat until thickened.

**3.** Stir in Cheddar-style and Danbo cheeses until melted. Stir in macaroni; season with salt and pepper to taste. Transfer to 13- x 9-inch (3 L) baking dish. Top evenly with tomato slices.

**4.** Topping: Combine bread crumbs, cheese and margarine; sprinkle over macaroni.

**5.** Bake, uncovered, in 350°F (180°C) oven for 20 minutes or until bubbly. **Makes 5 servings.**

**MAKE AHEAD:** Through step 4, covered and refrigerated for up to four hours.

### Cooking Pasta

Cook pasta in a large pot of boiling water, uncovered. If there isn't enough water, the pasta could stick together. There is no need to add oil to the water to prevent the pasta from sticking.

I don't add salt to the cooking water. Rather, I taste the pasta after the sauce has been added to see if it needs salt. Usually the salt from cheese or canned tomatoes is enough.

*PER SERVING:*

406 calories
24 g protein
14 g total fat
   8 g saturated fat
   36 mg cholesterol
46 g carbohydrate
   3 g dietary fibre
442 mg sodium
310 mg potassium

GOOD: Vitamin A
EXCELLENT: Calcium

# Light Fettuccine Alfredo with Fresh Herbs

*This is the easiest and fastest way to make a creamy pasta dish—it's also delicious. Evaporated milk is creamier than 2% milk and works well in this dish.*

| | | |
|---|---|---|
| ½ lb | fettuccine | 250 g |
| 1 tbsp | olive oil | 15 mL |
| 1 | clove garlic, minced | 1 |
| 1 cup | 2% evaporated milk | 250 mL |
| ½ cup | freshly grated Parmesan cheese | 125 mL |
| ¼ cup | chopped fresh parsley | 50 mL |
| ¼ cup | packed chopped fresh basil (or 1 tsp/5 mL dried) | 50 mL |
| | Nutmeg, salt and pepper | |

**1.** In large pot of boiling water, cook fettuccine until tender but firm; drain and return to saucepan.

**2.** Meanwhile, in small nonstick skillet, heat oil over medium-high heat; cook garlic for 1 minute. (Alternatively, in microwave-able dish, microwave garlic and oil on Medium for 30 seconds.)

**3.** Add garlic mixture, evaporated milk, cheese, parsley and basil to drained pasta. Cook, stirring, over medium heat until sauce is heated through and thickened slightly, about 3 minutes. Season with nutmeg, salt and pepper to taste. **Makes 3 servings**.

## Fettuccine Alfredo with Salmon

Stir in 1 can (7.5 oz/ 213 g) salmon, drained, before seasoning with salt and pepper only.

### Nutritional Note

Traditional Fettuccine Alfredo recipes usually call for butter and whipping cream. This one has one-third of the fat yet is creamy and flavorful.

*Per Serving:*

478 calories
23 g protein
13 g total fat
    5 g saturated fat
    20 mg cholesterol
67 g carbohydrate
    4 g dietary fibre
408 mg sodium
390 mg potassium

Good: Vitamin C; Folate
Excellent: Calcium

# Linguine with Mushrooms and Green Peppers

*I like to use a combination of different mushrooms—brown, portobello or wild—in this pasta. If you use dried mushrooms, soak them first in hot water and add the soaking liquid to the pasta cooking water. I use evaporated milk because it is thick like cream, however you can also use regular whole milk.*

| | | |
|---|---|---|
| 1 lb | linguine | 500 g |
| 1 tbsp | olive oil | 15 mL |
| 1 | large onion, chopped | 1 |
| 2 tsp | chopped fresh garlic | 10 mL |
| 1 lb | mushrooms, sliced | 500 g |
| 1 | sweet red, green or yellow pepper, thinly sliced | 1 |
| 1 cup | 2% evaporated milk | 250 mL |
| 1 cup | chopped fresh parsley | 250 mL |
| ½ cup | freshly grated Parmesan cheese | 125 mL |
| | Salt and pepper | |

**1.** In large pot of boiling water, cook linguine until tender yet firm; drain.

**2.** Meanwhile, in large nonstick skillet, heat oil over medium heat; cook onion and garlic until softened. Add mushrooms; cook, stirring often, for 5 minutes or until tender. Add sweet pepper; cook for 2 minutes.

**3.** Stir in milk; bring to boil. Stir in parsley and cheese; toss with hot pasta. Season with salt and pepper to taste. **Makes 6 servings**.

*Leftovers*
Any leftovers of this dish can be covered and refrigerated for up to two days. Reheat, covered, in microwave.

*Per Serving:*

411 calories
18 g protein
7 g total fat
   3 g saturated fat
   10 mg cholesterol
69 g carbohydrate
   6 g dietary fibre
210 mg sodium
516 mg potassium

Good: Vitamin A; Folate; Iron
Excellent: Vitamin C; Calcium

# Summer Shrimp and Tomato Pasta

*This is one of my favorite meals during tomato season. It works fine with any kind or shape of pasta. (Pictured opposite page 192.)*

**Nutritional Note**

Someone on a cholesterol-restricted diet should substitute raw scallops or cooked mussels for the shrimp, and cook for 2 to 4 minutes or until scallops are opaque.

If using scallops instead of shrimp, cholesterol will be 42 mg per serving.

| | | |
|---|---|---|
| 1 lb | spaghetti or other pasta | 500 g |
| 1 tbsp | olive oil | 15 mL |
| 4 tsp | minced fresh garlic | 20 mL |
| 3 | large tomatoes, coarsely chopped | 3 |
| 1 lb | cooked peeled large shrimp | 500 g |
| ⅓ cup | each coarsely chopped fresh basil and parsley | 75 mL |
| ¼ cup | freshly grated Parmesan cheese | 50 mL |
| | Salt and pepper | |

**1.** In large pot of boiling water, cook pasta until tender but firm; drain and return to pot.

**2.** Meanwhile, in nonstick skillet, heat oil over medium-high heat; cook garlic, stirring, for 1 minute.

**3.** Add tomatoes; cook, stirring, for 2 minutes. Add shrimp; cook until heated through, about 2 minutes.

**4.** Add to hot pasta along with basil, parsley, Parmesan, and salt and pepper to taste; toss to mix. **Makes 4 servings**.

PER SERVING:

677 calories

50 g protein

10 g total fat
   3 g saturated fat
   241 mg cholesterol

94 g carbohydrate
   7 g dietary fibre

363 mg sodium

624 mg potassium

GOOD: Vitamin C; Folate; Calcium
EXCELLENT: Vitamin A; Iron

Baked Breaded Fish Fillets with Almonds, made with Cod (page 112)
Purple Vegetable Slaw (page 83)

# Linguine with Scallops and Leeks

*For a really delicious dish, grate your own Parmesan cheese: it has much more flavor than if you buy it grated and is easy to grate in a food processor or with a regular grater. Serve with baby carrots, a tossed salad and garlic bread.*

| | | |
|---|---|---|
| 1 tbsp | soft margarine or butter | 15 mL |
| 2 cups | chopped leeks (white and light green parts only) | 500 mL |
| 1 tbsp | all-purpose flour | 15 mL |
| 1½ cups | low-fat milk | 375 mL |
| ½ cup | dry white wine | 125 mL |
| 1 lb | scallops | 500 g |
| ¼ cup | chopped Italian (flat leaf) parsley | 50 mL |
| 2 tbsp | chopped fresh chives or green onions | 25 mL |
| 1 lb | linguine | 500 g |
| ½ cup | freshly grated Parmesan cheese | 125 mL |

**1.** In large nonstick skillet, melt margarine over low heat; cook leeks, covered, for 10 minutes or until tender. (If mixture sticks to pan, add 1 tbsp/15 mL water, or more.)

**2.** Sprinkle flour over leeks; cook, stirring, for 1 minute. Gradually add milk, stirring constantly; bring to simmer. Cook, stirring, for 2 to 3 minutes or until thickened. Gradually whisk in wine until smooth.

**3.** Add scallops to hot leek mixture; cook over low heat for 2 to 3 minutes or until scallops are opaque. Stir in parsley and chives.

**4.** Meanwhile, in large pot of boiling water, cook linguine until tender but firm; drain and return to saucepan.

**5.** Pour leek mixture into hot pasta; add Parmesan cheese and toss gently. **Makes 4 servings.**

 **MAKE AHEAD:** Through step 2 for up to three hours.

*PER SERVING:*

680 calories
42 g protein
11 g total fat
    4 g saturated fat
    54 mg cholesterol
96 g carbohydrate
    5 g dietary fibre
507 mg sodium
689 mg potassium

GOOD: Vitamin A; Folate; Iron
EXCELLENT: Calcium

Potato, Bean and Tomato Stew with Basil (page 187)
Muesli Soda Bread (page 205)

# Pasta Provençal with Tofu

*Use medium-size pasta shells or penne. Zucchini, grilled eggplant or black olives can also be added.*

| | | |
|---|---|---|
| ½ lb | penne | 250 g |
| 1 tbsp | olive oil | 15 mL |
| 1 | large onion, chopped | 1 |
| 1 | sweet green pepper, chopped | 1 |
| 4 tsp | minced fresh garlic | 20 mL |
| ½ lb | mushrooms, sliced | 250 g |
| 1 | can (28 oz/796 mL) tomatoes, chopped | 1 |
| Pinch | red pepper flakes | Pinch |
| 1¼ cups | diced extra-firm tofu | 300 mL |
| ⅓ cup | chopped fresh parsley | 75 mL |
| ⅓ cup | chopped fresh basil (or 1½ tsp/7 mL dried) | 75 mL |
| ¼ cup | freshly grated Parmesan cheese | 50 mL |

**1.** In pot of boiling water, cook pasta for 7 to 10 minutes or until tender but firm; drain.

**2.** Meanwhile, in large nonstick saucepan, heat oil over medium heat; cook onion, green pepper, garlic and mushrooms for 5 to 8 minutes or until tender. Add tomatoes and red pepper flakes; boil for 6 minutes or until thickened slightly.

**3.** Add tofu, parsley and basil. Toss with pasta; sprinkle with Parmesan. **Makes 4 servings**.

### Herbs and Spices

I go easy on the amounts of spices, herbs and seasonings in these recipes, assuming that anyone who likes spicier tastes will add more. It's much easier to add spice than to take it away!

*Per Serving:*

420 calories

21 g protein

11 g total fat
   3 g saturated fat
   5 mg cholesterol

62 g carbohydrate
   8 g dietary fibre

457 mg sodium

901 mg potassium

GOOD: Vitamin A
EXCELLENT: Vitamin C; Folate; Calcium; Iron

**MAKE AHEAD:** Sauce, step 2, covered and refrigerated for up to one day.

# Singapore Noodles with Pork

*Prepare these spicy noodles in a variety of ways: use chicken or beef instead of pork; for a side dish, omit pork; for vegetarians, substitute diced firm tofu for the pork; for special occasions, add large shrimp. Instead of red pepper, use two large carrots, cut in thin strips.*

| | | |
|---|---|---|
| ¼ cup | rice wine vinegar or lemon juice | 50 mL |
| ¼ cup | sodium-reduced soy sauce | 50 mL |
| 2 tbsp | packed brown sugar | 25 mL |
| ½ tsp | chili paste or hot pepper sauce* | 2 mL |
| ½ lb | medium rice vermicelli noodles or very thin regular noodles | 250 g |
| 1 tbsp | vegetable oil | 15 mL |
| 1 tbsp | curry powder | 15 mL |
| 1 tbsp | minced fresh garlic | 15 mL |
| 1 tbsp | minced gingerroot | 15 mL |
| 1 | sweet red pepper, thinly sliced | 1 |
| ½ lb | lean pork, cut in thin strips | 250 g |
| 4 cups | bean sprouts | 1 L |
| 1½ cups | frozen peas, thawed | 375 mL |
| ½ cup | diagonally sliced green onions | 125 mL |
| ¼ cup | chopped fresh coriander | 50 mL |

**1.** Combine vinegar, soy sauce, sugar and chili paste; set aside.

**2.** Cook noodles according to package directions; drain.

**3.** Meanwhile, in large nonstick skillet, heat oil over medium-high heat; stir in curry powder, garlic and gingerroot for 10 seconds. Add red pepper; stir-fry for 1 minute.

**4.** Add pork; stir-fry for 3 minutes or until no longer pink.

**5.** Add noodles, bean sprouts, peas and soy sauce mixture; cook, stirring, for 2 minutes or until heated through. Transfer to platter; sprinkle with onions and coriander. **Makes 4 servings.**

\* See Information on Ingredients, page 32.

### Mild or Hot?
These Singaporc Noodles are quite mild. Add more chili paste or hot pepper sauce to taste to spice them up, if you like.

*PER SERVING:*

432 calories
20 g protein
7 g total fat
  1 g saturated fat
  32 mg cholesterol
76 g carbohydrate
  5 g dietary fibre
585 mg sodium
693 mg potassium

GOOD: Vitamin A
EXCELLENT: Vitamin C; Folate; Iron

# Jiffy Chinese Noodles

*My kids love these noodles. In fact, they heat any leftovers in the microwave to eat after school. I try to keep a package of steamed Chinese or chow mein noodles (not canned) in my refrigerator so I can make this in 10 minutes. I often add whatever vegetables I have on hand. Sometimes I add strips of cooked chicken, pork, beef or shrimp.*

| | | |
|---|---|---|
| 1 | pkg (350 g) steamed Chinese noodles or thin fresh pasta | 1 |
| ½ cup | Asian Sauce (page 99) | 125 mL |
| 2 cups | bean sprouts | 500 mL |
| 2 | carrots, grated | 2 |
| ½ cup | diagonally sliced green onions | 125 mL |
| ¼ cup | chopped fresh coriander or parsley | 50 mL |

**1.** In saucepan of boiling water, cook noodles for 2 to 3 minutes or until tender but firm; drain and return to pan or serving bowl.

**2.** Add sauce, bean sprouts, carrots, green onions and coriander; toss to mix well. **Makes 8 servings.**

## Sweet or Tart?

Depending on your taste and on the kind of pasta you use, you might want to add more rice vinegar to the Asian Sauce or to the pasta-vegetable mixture.

*Per Serving:*

173 calories

7 g protein

2 g total fat
   0.2 g saturated fat
   32 mg cholesterol

34 g carbohydrate
   3 g dietary fibre

246 mg sodium

156 mg potassium

Excellent: Vitamin A

**Make Ahead:** Through step 2, covered and refrigerated for up to two days; microwave to reheat.

# Make-Ahead Party Thai Noodles

*These are particularly suitable for a buffet or when entertaining as they can be made in advance and reheated. (Pictured opposite page 129.)*

| | | |
|---|---|---|
| ½ lb | spaghetti | 250 g |
| Half | each sweet red and yellow pepper, cut in thin strips | Half |
| ½ cup | chopped fresh coriander | 125 mL |
| ⅓ cup | chopped green onion | 75 mL |
| 4 cups | bean sprouts | 1 L |

**Sauce**

| | | |
|---|---|---|
| ¼ cup | rice vinegar or cider vinegar | 50 mL |
| ¼ cup | hoisin sauce | 50 mL |
| 2 tbsp | hot water | 25 mL |
| 1 tbsp | sesame oil | 15 mL |
| 1 tbsp | sodium-reduced soy sauce | 15 mL |
| 1 tbsp | minced gingerroot | 15 mL |
| 1½ tsp | packed brown sugar | 7 mL |
| 1½ tsp | minced fresh garlic | 7 mL |
| ½ tsp | dry mustard | 2 mL |
| ½ tsp | chili paste or hot pepper sauce | 2 mL |

**1.** In large pot of boiling water, cook pasta until tender but firm; drain. Transfer to 12-cup (3 L) baking dish.

**2.** Sauce: Combine vinegar, hoisin sauce, water, sesame oil, soy sauce, gingerroot, sugar, garlic, mustard and chili paste. Set one-third of the sauce aside; stir remaining sauce into noodles.

**3.** Stir in red and yellow peppers, coriander, onion and bean sprouts.

**4.** Add remaining sauce; bake, covered, in 350°F (180°C) oven for 20 to 30 minutes or until hot. **Makes 8 servings**.

**MAKE AHEAD:** Through step 3, covered and refrigerated for up to 24 hours. To reheat, let stand at room temperature for one hour; bake as in Step 4 for 30 to 40 minutes.

***Entertaining Note***

This is the recipe I've served most often this past year when entertaining. I've also taken it to a pot luck. I've served it with the Honey Garlic Roast Pork (page 135) at a dinner for eight, another time with the Lemon Grass Marinated Leg of Lamb (page 137).

For a buffet dinner, I have served it with the Chutney Glazed Ham (page 136) and the Sesame Carrots (page 142).

*PER SERVING:*

168 calories
6 g protein
3 g total fat
  0.3 g saturated fat
  0 mg cholesterol
30 g carbohydrate
  2 g dietary fibre
238 mg sodium
179 mg potassium

GOOD: Vitamin C; Folate

# Szechuan Beef with Noodles

*Vacuum-packed chow mein or Cantonese-style steamed noodles are fast and easy to prepare. They are the ones I like to use in this recipe. If unavailable, use vermicelli or other thin noodles. Don't use the canned chow mein noodles because they are fried and high in fat.*

| | | |
|---|---|---|
| 1 tbsp | vegetable oil | 15 mL |
| 2 | onions, sliced | 2 |
| 4 | cloves garlic, minced | 4 |
| 4 tsp | minced gingerroot | 20 mL |
| ¾ lb | lean beef, thinly sliced | 375 g |
| 3 | tomatoes, cut in chunks | 3 |
| 2 | sweet green peppers, cut in strips | 2 |
| ¼ cup | oyster sauce* | 50 mL |
| 2 tbsp | sodium-reduced soy sauce | 25 mL |
| 1½ tsp | chili paste | 7 mL |
| 4 cups | bean sprouts | 1 L |
| ¾ lb | fresh chow mein noodles** or vermicelli | 375 g |
| 2 tbsp | chopped peanuts | 25 mL |
| 6 | green onions, diagonally sliced | 6 |

**1.** In wok or large deep nonstick skillet, heat oil over high heat; stir-fry onions for 2 minutes. Add garlic, ginger and beef; stir-fry for 2 minutes or until beef is browned.

**2.** Add tomatoes, green peppers, oyster sauce, soy sauce and chili paste; stir-fry for 2 minutes. Stir in bean sprouts.

**3.** Meanwhile, in large pot of boiling water, cook chow mein noodles for 2 minutes or until heated through; drain. (If using vermicelli, cook for 6 to 8 minutes or until tender but firm; drain.)

**4.** Toss with beef mixture. Sprinkle with peanuts and green onions. **Makes 4 servings**.

\* See Information on Ingredients, page 32.
\*\* Often available in the fresh vegetable section of the supermarket.

*PER SERVING:*

535 calories

37 g protein

13 g total fat
    3 g saturated fat
    103 mg cholesterol

72 g carbohydrate
    10 g dietary fibre

809 mg sodium

1133 mg potassium

GOOD: Vitamin A
EXCELLENT: Vitamin C;
Folate; Iron

# Thai Noodles with Chicken and Broccoli

*Serve this dish as a main course, or omit the chicken and serve with fish, poultry or any grilled meats.*

| | | |
|---|---|---|
| ½ lb | spaghettini or thin noodles | 250 g |
| 4 cups | broccoli florets (1 bunch) | 1 L |
| 2 | carrots, cut in julienne strips | 2 |
| 1 tbsp | vegetable oil | 15 mL |
| 1 tbsp | minced gingerroot | 15 mL |
| 3 | cloves garlic, minced | 3 |
| ¾ lb | boneless skinless chicken breasts, cut in thin strips | 375 g |
| ¼ cup | chopped fresh coriander | 50 mL |

**Sauce**

| | | |
|---|---|---|
| ½ cup | chicken stock | 125 mL |
| 3 tbsp | cider vinegar or rice wine vinegar | 50 mL |
| 3 tbsp | sodium-reduced soy sauce | 50 mL |
| 3 tbsp | peanut butter | 50 mL |
| 1 tbsp | granulated sugar | 15 mL |
| 1 tbsp | sesame oil | 15 mL |
| 1½ tsp | chili paste or hot pepper sauce | 7 mL |

**1.** Sauce: Whisk together stock, vinegar, soy sauce, peanut butter, sugar, sesame oil and chili paste. Set aside.

**2.** In large pot of boiling water, cook noodles for 5 minutes. Add broccoli and carrots; cook for 2 to 3 minutes or until noodles are tender yet firm. Drain and set aside.

**3.** In large nonstick skillet, heat oil over high heat; stir-fry ginger and garlic for 30 seconds. Add chicken; stir-fry for 3 to 5 minutes or until no longer pink inside.

**4.** Stir sauce; add to skillet and bring to boil. Remove from heat; toss with noodles and vegetables. Sprinkle with coriander. Serve in large bowls. **Makes 4 servings**.

**MAKE AHEAD:** Through step 1 for up to four hours.

*PER SERVING:*

506 calories
34 g protein
15 g total fat
   2 g saturated fat
   49 mg cholesterol
59 g carbohydrate
   6 g dietary fibre
631 mg sodium
790 mg potassium

GOOD: Iron
EXCELLENT: Vitamin A; Vitamin C; Folate

# Singapore Noodle and Chicken Salad

*Here's a delicious way to use up leftover barbecued chicken, roast chicken or turkey. Blanched asparagus and/or green beans are nice additions to the salad.*

| | | |
|---|---|---|
| ¼ lb | thin noodles (capellini, spaghettini or rice vermicelli) | 125 g |
| ¼ cup | unsalted peanuts | 50 mL |
| 2 | cloves garlic | 2 |
| 2 tsp | chopped gingerroot | 10 mL |
| 1 tsp | granulated sugar | 5 mL |
| ¼ cup | water | 50 mL |
| 1 tbsp | sesame oil | 15 mL |
| 1 tbsp | sodium-reduced soy sauce | 15 mL |
| 1 tbsp | lime juice | 15 mL |
| ½ tsp | hot chili paste or red pepper flakes | 2 mL |
| 2 | green onions, chopped | 2 |
| 1 cup | thin strips cooked chicken | 250 mL |
| 1 cup | blanched julienned carrots | 250 mL |
| ¼ cup | chopped fresh coriander | 50 mL |

**1.** In large pot of boiling water, cook noodles until tender but firm. Drain and rinse under cold water; drain well.

**2.** In food processor, coarsely chop peanuts; set 2 tbsp (25 mL) aside. To food processor, add garlic, ginger and sugar; process for 30 seconds. Add water, sesame oil, soy sauce, lime juice and chili paste; process to mix.

**3.** Toss sauce with noodles. Add green onions, chicken and carrots; toss to mix.

**4.** Arrange on serving platter; sprinkle with coriander and reserved peanuts. **Makes 6 servings**.

**MAKE AHEAD:** Through step 3, covered and refrigerated for up to one day.

*PER SERVING:*

189 calories
11 g protein
8 g total fat
   1 g saturated fat
   21 mg cholesterol
20 g carbohydrate
   2 g dietary fibre
111 mg sodium
225 mg potassium

EXCELLENT: Vitamin A

# Spicy Noodle Salad

*This is a wonderful salad for a luncheon, buffet or summer supper. Use any thin noodle or medium rice noodles. For a main course, add shrimp, sliced grilled chicken or a can of salmon. Thinly sliced cabbage is a good addition.*

| | | |
|---|---|---|
| ½ lb | thin noodles (capellini, spaghettini or rice vermicelli) | 250 g |
| 1 cup | grated carrot | 250 mL |
| 1 cup | frozen peas, thawed | 250 mL |
| 1 | sweet red pepper, cut in thin strips | 1 |
| 2 cups | bean sprouts | 500 mL |
| ¼ cup | chopped fresh coriander or parsley | 50 mL |

## Dressing

| | | |
|---|---|---|
| ¼ cup | rice vinegar or lemon juice | 50 mL |
| ¼ cup | water | 50 mL |
| 2 tbsp | sodium-reduced soy sauce | 25 mL |
| 4 tsp | minced gingerroot | 20 mL |
| 1 tbsp | sesame oil | 15 mL |
| 1 | clove garlic, minced | 1 |
| ½ tsp | granulated sugar | 2 mL |
| ½ tsp | hot pepper sauce | 2 mL |

**1.** In large pot of boiling water, cook noodles until tender but firm; drain. Rinse thoroughly under cold water; drain.

**2.** Dressing: In salad bowl, combine vinegar, water, soy sauce, ginger, oil, garlic, sugar and hot pepper sauce.

**3.** Add noodles and toss. Add carrot, peas, red pepper, bean sprouts and coriander; toss. **Makes 8 servings.**

**MAKE AHEAD:** Salad can be covered and refrigerated for up to two hours; remove from refrigerator 20 minutes before serving.

***Sodium-Reduced Soy Sauce***

To make your own sodium-reduced soy sauce, mix 1 tbsp (15 mL) regular soy sauce with 1 tbsp (15 mL) water.

***Easy Barbecue Supper***

- Herb and Buttermilk Barbecued Chicken (page 93)
- Spicy Noodle Salad
- Sliced Tomato Platter
- Focaccia or French baguette
- Blueberries with Vanilla Cream (page 239)

*PER SERVING:*

158 calories
6 g protein
2 g total fat
   0.3 g saturated fat
   0 mg cholesterol
29 g carbohydrate
   3 g dietary fibre
151 mg sodium
194 mg potassium

GOOD: Folate
EXCELLENT: Vitamin A; Vitamin C

# Pasta Salad with Sun-Dried Tomatoes

*Sun-dried tomatoes add flavor, color and a chewy texture to this salad. Use the dry-packed tomatoes because they are lower in fat than the ones packed in oil. For variety, add artichoke hearts, celery, carrots, cauliflower, cooked chicken or ham.*

| | | |
|---|---|---|
| ½ lb | penne, fusilli or macaroni (about 2 cups/500 mL) | 250 g |
| 1 cup | dry-packed sun-dried tomatoes | 250 mL |
| 1 cup | chopped green onions | 250 mL |
| ½ cup | chopped fresh parsley | 125 mL |
| 2 tbsp | freshly grated Parmesan cheese (optional) | 25 mL |

### Vinaigrette

| | | |
|---|---|---|
| ¼ cup | balsamic or cider vinegar | 50 mL |
| ¼ cup | orange juice | 50 mL |
| ¼ cup | olive oil | 50 mL |
| 1 | clove garlic, minced | 1 |
| 2 tsp | Dijon mustard | 10 mL |
| 1 tsp | each dried basil and oregano | 5 mL |
| | Salt and pepper | |

**1.** In large pot of boiling water, cook pasta until tender but firm; drain and rinse under cold water. Drain thoroughly.

**2.** Pour hot water over tomatoes and let stand for 1 minute; drain, then coarsely chop. In large bowl, combine pasta, tomatoes, onions, parsley, and cheese (if using).

**3.** Vinaigrette: Combine vinegar, orange juice, oil, garlic, mustard, basil and oregano; mix well. Pour over salad and toss to mix. Season with salt and pepper to taste. **Makes 8 servings**.

**MAKE AHEAD:** Salad can be covered and refrigerated for up to two days.

---

***Easy Summer Lunch***
- Pasta Salad with Sun-Dried Tomatoes
- Whole Wheat Rolls
- Sliced Cucumbers
- Sliced Turkey Platter
- Melon with Berries

SUN-DRIED TOMATOES

*Per Serving:*

197 calories

5 g protein

8 g total fat
   1 g saturated fat
   0 mg cholesterol

28 g carbohydrate
   3 g dietary fibre

189 mg sodium

382 mg potassium

# Pasta and Ham Salad with Tomato Basil Dressing

*Instead of ham, you can add any leftover barbecued meats or chicken, or for a vegetarian meal, omit ham and add feta cheese.*

| | | |
|---|---|---|
| 2½ cups | penne or other short pasta (½ lb/250 g) | 625 mL |
| ¼ lb | ham, cubed | 125 g |
| 10 | black olives, pitted and sliced | 10 |
| ⅓ cup | chopped fresh basil or parsley | 75 mL |
| 1 cup | Tomato Basil Dressing (page 86) | 250 mL |

**1.** In large pot of boiling water, cook penne until tender but firm, 7 to 9 minutes; drain and cool under cold water. Drain.

**2.** In salad bowl, toss pasta, ham, olives and basil with dressing. **Makes 4 servings.**

**MAKE AHEAD:** Salad can be covered and refrigerated for up to 24 hours.

***Summer Sunday Lunch***
- Pasta and Ham Salad
- Garlic Bread
- Roasted Sweet Peppers (page 182) drizzled with balsamic vinegar
- Berries with Orange Cream (page 236)
- Apricot Streusel Cake (page 211)

***Nutritional Note***

For a sodium-reduced diet, omit ham and olives.

*PER SERVING:*

348 calories
14 g protein
11 g total fat
   2 g saturated fat
   16 mg cholesterol
47 g carbohydrate
   4 g dietary fibre
641 mg sodium
301 mg potassium

GOOD: Iron

# Seafood Pasta Salad

*Serve this at a special luncheon, at a buffet or for a summer supper. Use any short corkscrew or tubular pasta. If fresh crab is available, I would use it instead of frozen.*

| | | |
|---|---|---|
| 2 cups | penne or short pasta | 500 mL |
| ½ lb | sea scallops (not bay scallops) | 250 g |
| ¼ lb | snow peas, trimmed and strings removed | 125 g |
| ½ lb | cooked medium or small shrimp | 250 g |
| ¼ lb | frozen cooked crabmeat, thawed, drained and broken into chunks | 125 g |
| Half | sweet red pepper, diced | Half |
| ⅓ cup | chopped purple or green onion | 75 mL |
| 1 cup | Yogurt Herb Dressing (page 87) | 250 mL |
| | Salt and pepper | |

**1.** In large pot of boiling water, cook penne until tender but firm, 7 to 10 minutes. Drain and rinse under cold water; drain.

**2.** In pot of boiling water, cook scallops for about 3 minutes or until opaque in centre; drain.

**3.** In pot of boiling water, cook snow peas for 1 minute; drain. Rinse under cold water; drain. Slice in half diagonally.

**4.** In salad bowl, combine penne, scallops, snow peas, shrimp, crabmeat, red pepper, onion and dressing; toss gently. Add salt and pepper to taste. **Makes 8 servings.**

### To Cook Shrimp

Shrimp are more flavorful when cooked in their shell, rather than peeled and deveined first. Cook in large pot of boiling water for 1 to 2 minutes or until shrimp turn pink; drain and cool under cold water. Remove shell and small dark vein running down back of shrimp.

*Per Serving:*

261 calories
24 g protein
5 g total fat
   1 g saturated fat
   85 mg cholesterol
29 g carbohydrate
   1 g dietary fibre
575 mg sodium
375 mg potassium

Good: Vitamin C; Folate

**Make Ahead:** Through step 4 except for adding snow peas; cover and refrigerate for up to one day. Wrap cooked snow peas in paper towels and refrigerate; add to salad up to one hour before serving (otherwise they will turn yellow).

# GRAINS, LEGUMES AND MEATLESS MAIN DISHES

Spinach Rice Casserole

Green Vegetable Risotto

Indian Rice with Lentils
and Mushrooms

Spanish Rice with Coriander

Chinese Vegetable Fried Rice

Wild Rice Pilaf

Rice with Black Beans and Ginger

Lemon Parsley Rice Pilaf

Bulgur with Red Onion and Pimiento

Bulgur Pilaf with Shrimp and Snow Peas

Quinoa-Stuffed Peppers

Barley and Corn Casserole

Bean and Sausage Casserole

Potato, Bean and Tomato Stew with Basil

Winter Vegetable Curry with Couscous

Quick and Easy Spiced Couscous

Crustless Vegetable Quiche

Marinated Baked Tofu

Vegetable Tofu Stir-Fry

Tomato, Eggplant and Zucchini Gratin

Apricot-Raisin Muesli

# Spinach Rice Casserole

*Avoid the pitfall of high-fat vegetarian dishes by using a flavorful lower-fat cheese. Serve with Tomato, Eggplant and Zucchini Gratin (page 193) and toasted whole wheat bread.*

| | | |
|---|---|---|
| 1 cup | long grain brown or white rice | 250 mL |
| 1 tbsp | olive oil | 15 mL |
| 1 | medium onion, chopped | 1 |
| 1 | clove garlic, minced | 1 |
| 1 lb | spinach leaves | 500 g |
| 3 | eggs, beaten | 3 |
| 1½ cups | shredded Danbo or light-style Swiss cheese | 375 mL |
| ½ cup | low-fat milk | 125 mL |
| ⅓ cup | chopped fresh parsley | 75 mL |
| ¾ tsp | salt | 4 mL |
| ½ tsp | each dried basil and thyme | 2 mL |
| Pinch | each cayenne and pepper | Pinch |
| ¼ cup | toasted slivered almonds | 50 mL |
| 2 tbsp | freshly grated Parmesan cheese | 25 mL |

**1.** In pot of boiling water, cook rice 20 minutes for white, 40 minutes for brown; drain and rinse under cold water. Transfer to large bowl.

**2.** Meanwhile, in skillet, heat oil over medium heat; cook onion and garlic until tender. In saucepan, cook spinach in small amount of water just until wilted; drain, squeeze dry and chop.

**3.** To rice, stir in onion mixture, spinach, eggs, Danbo, milk, parsley, salt, basil, thyme, cayenne and pepper. Transfer to greased 11- x 7-inch (2 L) glass baking dish. Sprinkle with almonds and Parmesan cheese.

**4.** Bake, covered, in 350°F (180°C) oven for 25 minutes. Uncover and bake for another 10 minutes or until golden. **Makes 6 servings**.

**MAKE AHEAD:** Through step 3, covered and set aside for up to two hours.

## Nutritional Note

Danbo Light is a Danish cheese with good flavor and texture that has an 8% butterfat content, making it one of the lower-fat cheeses. Use it in sandwiches and cooking.

When you substitute 1 cup (250 mL) of shredded 8% b.f. cheese for 1 cup (250 mL) of 17% b.f. cheese in a recipe serving four, each person's fat intake is reduced by 3 g.

## Fresh Herbs

Instead of dried basil and thyme in this recipe, you can use 2 tbsp (25 mL) chopped fresh basil and 1 tbsp (15 mL) chopped fresh thyme.

PER SERVING:
  327 calories
  19 g protein
  15 g total fat
    5 g saturated fat
    126 mg cholesterol
  32 g carbohydrate
    5 g dietary fibre
  576 mg sodium
  561 mg potassium

EXCELLENT: Vitamin A; Folate; Calcium; Iron

# Green Vegetable Risotto

*Shannon Graham, who has worked with me on all my books, came up with this delicious rice dish, which has less fat than a traditional risotto. Serve as a vegetarian main dish or as a side dish with chicken, a green salad and whole grain bread.*

| | | |
|---|---|---|
| 2 tbsp | soft margarine or butter | 25 mL |
| ½ cup | sliced green onions | 125 mL |
| 1 cup | Arborio rice or long grain white rice | 250 mL |
| 4 cups | simmering chicken stock | 1 L |
| 1 cup | sliced green beans | 250 mL |
| 12 | snow peas | 12 |
| 1 cup | coarsely chopped zucchini | 250 mL |
| ¼ cup | chopped fresh parsley | 50 mL |
| ¼ cup | freshly grated Parmesan cheese | 50 mL |
| | Pepper | |

**1.** In large nonstick skillet, melt half of the margarine over medium heat; cook green onions until softened, about 3 minutes.

**2.** Add rice and stir to coat.

**3.** Add about half of the chicken stock, ¼ cup (50 mL) at a time, cooking and stirring until each addition is absorbed before adding next, about 8 minutes in total.

**4.** Stir in green beans; cook for 2 minutes. Stir in snow peas and zucchini.

**5.** Stir in remaining stock, ¼ cup (50 mL) at a time, cooking and stirring until each addition is absorbed before adding next, 10 to 15 minutes in total or until rice is creamy and firm.

**6.** Stir in parsley, Parmesan, remaining margarine, and pepper to taste. Serve immediately. **Makes 4 main-course servings, 8 side-dish servings**.

**MAKE AHEAD:** Risotto should always be eaten as soon as it's cooked, but leftovers are delicious reheated the next day.

## Arborio

Arborio is an Italian rice mainly used in risotto.

## About Risotto

Risotto is an Italian rice dish made by adding hot liquid to rice in small amounts, then stirring until all liquid has been absorbed before adding more liquid. The rice is creamy on the outside and al dente or firm on the inside. It takes about 25 minutes to make.

Some cooks recommend using a parboiled long grain rice if arborio isn't available.

*PER SERVING (SIDE DISH):*

162 calories
6 g protein
5 g total fat
    1 g saturated fat
    2 mg cholesterol
23 g carbohydrate
    1 g dietary fibre
487 mg sodium
251 mg potassium

# Indian Rice with Lentils and Mushrooms

*Easy to make, this rice dish is delicious.*

*V. Good*

| | | |
|---|---|---|
| 1 tbsp | soft margarine or butter | 15 mL |
| 2½ cups | sliced onions | 625 mL |
| 3 cups | vegetable or chicken stock | 750 mL |
| 2 cups | mushrooms, quartered | 500 mL |
| 1 cup | whole grain or basmati rice | 250 mL |
| ½ cup | green lentils | 125 mL |
| 1 tbsp | minced gingerroot | 15 mL |
| 1 tsp | curry powder *used more at least 1 tsp. more* | 5 mL |
| ¼ tsp | cinnamon | 1 mL |
| 2 | cloves garlic, minced | 2 |
| ½ cup | chopped fresh parsley | 125 mL |
| | Salt and pepper | |

**1.** In heavy nonstick skillet, melt margarine over low heat; cook onions, stirring occasionally, for 25 minutes or until very tender and lightly browned.

**2.** Meanwhile, in saucepan, combine stock, mushrooms, rice, lentils, gingerroot, curry powder, cinnamon and garlic; bring to boil. Reduce heat, cover and simmer for 25 minutes or until rice and lentils are tender and most of the liquid is absorbed.

**3.** Stir in parsley, and salt and pepper to taste. Top each serving with some fried onions. **Makes 4 main-course servings, 8 side-dish servings**.

## Whole Grain Rice

Whole grain rice cooks faster than regular brown rice and has more fibre than white. Combined with fibre- and iron-rich lentils, rice makes a complete source of protein.

## Basmati

Basmati is an aromatic rice, mainly imported from India or Pakistan. Rinse in cold water before using.

Any long grain rice (white or brown) can be used in this recipe.

PER SERVING (SIDE DISH):

180 calories

8 g protein

3 g total fat
   1 g saturated fat
   0 mg cholesterol

31 g carbohydrate
   4 g dietary fibre

318 mg sodium

388 mg potassium

GOOD: Iron
EXCELLENT: Folate

**MAKE AHEAD:** Best when just made but can be covered and refrigerated for up to one day.

# Spanish Rice with Coriander

*Fresh coriander gives this traditional recipe an updated flavor. If it's unavailable, add 2 tsp (10 mL) ground cumin or curry powder along with the tomatoes.*

| | | |
|---|---|---|
| 3 cups | water or vegetable stock | 750 mL |
| 1½ cups | long grain rice | 375 mL |
| 2 tsp | olive oil | 10 mL |
| 1 | medium onion, chopped | 1 |
| 2 | cloves garlic, minced | 2 |
| 3 | medium tomatoes, chopped | 3 |
| 1 | sweet green pepper, chopped | 1 |
| ¼ tsp | red pepper flakes | 1 mL |
| 1 cup | frozen green peas | 250 mL |
| ¼ cup | each chopped fresh coriander and parsley | 50 mL |
| | Salt and pepper | |

**1.** In large saucepan, bring water to boil; add rice. Reduce heat, cover and simmer for 20 minutes or until rice is tender and liquid absorbed.

**2.** In large nonstick skillet, heat oil over medium heat; cook onion for 3 minutes or until tender.

**3.** Add garlic, tomatoes, green pepper and red pepper flakes; cook, stirring occasionally, for 5 minutes.

**4.** Stir in cooked rice, peas, coriander, parsley, and salt and pepper to taste; cook, stirring, for 1 minute. **Makes 6 servings**.

**MAKE AHEAD:** Spanish Rice can be covered and refrigerated for up to one day or frozen for up to one month.

### Variation
For color and variety, use half a sweet green pepper and half a yellow pepper in this Spanish rice.

### Canned Tomatoes
Drained canned tomatoes, chopped (1 to 1½ cups/250 to 375 mL), can also be used in this recipe instead of the fresh.

*Per Serving:*

228 calories
6 g protein
2 g total fat
   0.4 g saturated fat
   0 mg cholesterol
46 g carbohydrate
   3 g dietary fibre
34 mg sodium
308 mg potassium

GOOD: Folate
EXCELLENT: Vitamin C

# Chinese Vegetable Fried Rice

## What's in a Serving?

Canada's Food Guide to Healthy Eating recommends we have 5 to 12 servings of grain products and 5 to 10 servings of fruits and vegetables per day. One cup (250 mL) of cooked rice equals two servings of grain in the Food Guide.

One of my servings of Chinese Vegetable Fried Rice is what I think an adult would eat for a main course, and would equal two servings of grains, three servings of vegetables and one serving of meat under the Food Guide.

### Nutritional Note

To reduce sodium, omit ham (which adds 393 mg sodium per serving) and oyster sauce (which adds 643 mg sodium per serving).

*PER SERVING:*

362 calories
17 g protein
9 g total fat
   2 g saturated fat
   124 mg cholesterol
54 g carbohydrate
   3 g dietary fibre
1103 mg sodium
590 mg potassium

GOOD: Vitamin A; Iron
EXCELLENT: Vitamin C; Folate

---

*This is such a great way to use up leftover rice that I try to have leftovers. Oyster sauce adds extra flavor; sesame oil and soy sauce could be added instead. For a vegetarian dish, omit ham. Add tofu if desired.*

| | | |
|---|---|---|
| 1 tbsp | vegetable oil | 15 mL |
| 2 cups | diced zucchini | 500 mL |
| 1 cup | sliced celery | 250 mL |
| 4 cups | cold cooked rice* | 1 L |
| 1/4 lb | diced cooked ham | 125 g |
| 1 | sweet red pepper, diced | 1 |
| 2 | eggs, lightly beaten | 2 |
| 1 1/2 cups | bean sprouts (4 oz/125 g) | 375 mL |
| 1/3 cup | oyster sauce | 75 mL |
| 1/2 cup | chopped green onions | 125 mL |

**1.** In large nonstick skillet, heat oil over high heat; stir-fry zucchini and celery for 2 minutes.

**2.** Add rice; stir-fry for 1 minute.

**3.** Add ham and red pepper; stir-fry for 1 minute.

**4.** Make a well in centre; stir in eggs for 30 seconds.

**5.** Add bean sprouts; stir-fry for 1 minute or until eggs are set. Stir in oyster sauce. Sprinkle with green onions. **Makes 4 servings**.

* About 1 1/3 cups (325 mL) uncooked parboiled long grain rice yields 4 cups (1 L) cooked.

**MAKE AHEAD:** Fried rice can be covered and set aside for up to one hour.

# Wild Rice Pilaf

*A combination of wild, brown and white rice looks attractive. Smoky bacon adds extra flavor to this entertaining dish. If you don't have brown rice, use half wild and half white.*

| | | |
|---|---|---|
| 2 | slices bacon, diced | 2 |
| 1 | onion, diced | 1 |
| ½ cup | wild rice | 125 mL |
| 3 cups | water or chicken stock | 750 mL |
| ½ cup | brown rice | 125 mL |
| ½ cup | long grain white rice | 125 mL |
| ¼ cup | chopped fresh parsley | 50 mL |
| 2 tbsp | chopped fresh basil | 25 mL |
| | Salt and pepper | |

**1.** In saucepan, cook bacon over medium heat for 3 minutes; add onion and cook, stirring, until tender, about 5 minutes.

**2.** Rinse wild rice under cold running water; drain. Add water to bacon and onion in saucepan; stir in wild rice and bring to boil. Add brown rice; cover and simmer for 15 minutes.

**3.** Add white rice; cover and simmer for 25 minutes or until tender.

**4.** Stir in parsley, basil, and salt and pepper to taste. **Makes 8 servings**.

## Wild Rice Pilaf with Lemon and Raisins

Omit fresh basil. Add ½ cup (125 mL) raisins and 1 tsp (5 mL) grated lemon rind; stir in with parsley.

*PER SERVING:*

135 calories
4 g protein
1 g total fat
   0.4 g saturated fat
   1 mg cholesterol
27 g carbohydrate
   2 g dietary fibre
30 mg sodium
105 mg potassium

**MAKE AHEAD:** Through step 3, but reduce cooking time from 25 minutes to 10 minutes; remove from heat and let cool. Refrigerate for up to one day. Reheat in 325°F (160°C) oven, covered, for 25 to 30 minutes or until hot.

# Rice with Black Beans and Ginger

*This absolutely delicious recipe is a favorite of my husband. Use Chinese fermented black beans (not the black turtle beans). I use Chinese bottled black bean sauce made with whole beans. Serve with fish, chicken or meats.*

| | | |
|---|---|---|
| 1 tbsp | vegetable oil | 15 mL |
| 1 tbsp | minced fresh garlic | 15 mL |
| 1 tbsp | chopped onion or shallots | 15 mL |
| 1 tbsp | minced gingerroot | 15 mL |
| 1 cup | long grain rice | 250 mL |
| 2 cups | boiling water | 500 mL |
| ¼ cup | black bean sauce (made with whole beans) | 50 mL |
| 1 | green onion, chopped | 1 |

**1.** In heavy or nonstick saucepan, heat oil over medium heat; cook garlic, onion and ginger for 1 minute, stirring.

**2.** Add rice and water; simmer, covered, for 20 minutes or until rice is tender. Stir in black bean sauce and green onion. **Makes 4 servings**.

**MAKE AHEAD:** Rice can be covered and refrigerated for up to two days.

*PER SERVING:*

220 calories

5 g protein

4 g total fat
    0.4 g saturated fat
    0 mg cholesterol

41 g carbohydrate
    1 g dietary fibre

31 mg sodium

126 mg potassium

---

**FAST-COOKING CARBOHYDRATES**

Cooking these is as easy as boiling water.

| Grain Products | Minutes cooking time |
|---|---|
| Rice noodles | 2 |
| Pasta (fresh) | 3 |
| Couscous (instant) | 3 |
| Rice, instant | 5 |
| Rolled oats, quick-cooking | 5 |
| Pasta (dried) | 8-10 |

For up to 25 minutes of cooking time, consider bulgur, rice, barley, kasha and quinoa.

# Lemon Parsley Rice Pilaf

*This is a favorite dish of mine. Grated lemon rind adds a delicious flavor to this rice. Serve with fish, chicken or meat. (Pictured opposite page 97.)*

| | | |
|---|---|---|
| 1 tsp | vegetable oil | 5 mL |
| 1 cup | chopped onion | 250 mL |
| 1½ cups | long grain white or brown rice | 375 mL |
| 3 cups | chicken or vegetable stock | 750 mL |
| | Grated rind of 1 lemon | |
| 1 tbsp | lemon juice | 15 mL |
| ½ cup | coarsely chopped fresh parsley | 125 mL |
| | Pepper | |

**1.** In heavy saucepan, heat oil over medium heat; cook onion for 5 minutes or until softened.

**2.** Stir in rice, then stock; bring to boil. Reduce heat, cover and simmer for 20 minutes for white, 40 minutes for brown, or until rice is tender.

**3.** Stir in lemon rind and juice, parsley, and pepper to taste. **Makes 8 servings**.

**MAKE AHEAD:** Pilaf can be covered and refrigerated for up to three days; reheat gently.

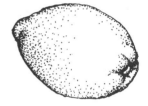

---

**COMPARE**

High-carbohydrate, low-fat, low-sodium grains and legumes

| 1 cup (250 mL) cooked: | Calories | Protein (g) | Fibre (g) |
|---|---|---|---|
| Macaroni | 198 | 7 | 2 |
| Bulgur | 151 | 6 | 8 |
| Couscous | 201 | 7 | 2 |
| Rice, white, parboiled | 200 | 4 | 1 |
| Rice, brown, long grain | 217 | 5 | 3 |
| Barley | 192 | 4 | 9 |
| Lentils | 230 | 18 | 9 |
| Kidney beans (red) | 224 | 15 | 17 |
| Quinoa | 159 | 6 | 2 |

*PER SERVING:*
154 calories
5 g protein
1 g total fat
   0.3 g saturated fat
   0 mg cholesterol
30 g carbohydrate
   1 g dietary fibre
295 mg sodium
168 mg potassium

# Bulgur with Red Onion and Pimiento

## Roasted Red Peppers

Bake sweet red peppers in 400°F (200°C) oven for 20 to 30 minutes, turning once or twice, or until blackened and blistered. Scrape skin from peppers; discard seeds and coarsely chop.

## Bulgur and Cracked Wheat

Both are made from wheat berries. Bulgur is cooked first, then dried, then cracked. Cracked wheat is made from wheat berries that are cracked then milled. They are available from health food stores and provide very high amounts of fibre. Use in salads or as you would rice and pasta.

*Pimientos or sweet red peppers are a colorful and flavorful addition to rice, pasta and grain dishes. In the fall, when sweet red peppers are not too expensive, roast them to substitute for the canned or bottled pimientos or sweet red peppers. Regular cooking onions can also be used instead of red onions. (Pictured opposite page 64.)*

| | | |
|---|---|---|
| 1 tbsp | olive oil | 15 mL |
| 1 cup | thinly sliced red onion | 250 mL |
| 1 cup | bulgur or cracked wheat | 250 mL |
| 2 cups | boiling water | 500 mL |
| 1 tbsp | lemon juice | 15 mL |
| ½ cup | chopped canned pimientos or bottled sweet red peppers | 125 mL |
| ½ cup | chopped fresh parsley or basil | 125 mL |
| ½ tsp | dried basil | 2 mL |
| | Salt and pepper | |

**1.** In small skillet, heat oil over medium heat; cook onion, stirring often, for 10 minutes or until tender.

**2.** Meanwhile, in saucepan, combine bulgur and water; simmer, covered, for 20 minutes or until liquid is absorbed.

**3.** Add onions, lemon juice, pimientos, parsley, dried basil and salt and pepper to taste. **Makes 4 servings**.

*PER SERVING:*

171 calories

5 g protein

4 g total fat
   1 g saturated fat
   0 mg cholesterol

32 g carbohydrate
   7 g dietary fibre

14 mg sodium

225 mg potassium

GOOD: Vitamin C; Folate; Iron

**MAKE AHEAD:** Bulgur can be covered and refrigerated for up to two days.

# Bulgur Pilaf with Shrimp and Snow Peas

*Quick and easy to make, this pilaf is golden yellow like paella —a perfect choice for a special Friday night supper. Serve with a tossed salad and fresh bread.*

| | | |
|---|---|---|
| 1 tsp | vegetable oil | 5 mL |
| 1 | onion, chopped | 1 |
| ¼ tsp | each turmeric and pepper | 1 mL |
| Pinch | cayenne pepper | Pinch |
| 1½ cups | bulgur or cracked wheat | 375 mL |
| 3½ cups | hot vegetable stock | 875 mL |
| ½ tsp | saffron threads | 2 mL |
| ½ lb | snow peas, trimmed | 250 g |
| ½ lb | cooked peeled large shrimp | 250 g |
| ½ cup | chopped fresh parsley | 125 mL |
| 2 | medium tomatoes, chopped | 2 |
| | Salt | |
| | Lemon wedges | |

**1.** In large nonstick skillet, heat oil over medium heat; cook onion, turmeric, pepper and cayenne, stirring occasionally, for 5 minutes or until onion is softened.

**2.** Add bulgur, vegetable stock and saffron; bring to boil. Reduce heat to low; simmer, covered, for 15 minutes or until liquid is absorbed.

**3.** Meanwhile, in pot of boiling water, cook snow peas for 1 minute. Drain and rinse under cold water; drain again.

**4.** To bulgur mixture, add snow peas, shrimp, parsley and tomatoes; cook over medium heat, tossing gently, for about 3 minutes or until hot. Season with salt to taste. Garnish each plate with lemon wedge. **Makes 4 servings**.

**MAKE AHEAD:** Pilaf can be covered and refrigerated for up to four hours; reheat gently.

### Rice Pilaf with Shrimp and Snow Peas

If bulgur or cracked wheat is not available, substitute 1 cup (250 mL) long grain rice and reduce stock to 2 cups (500 mL); cook for 20 minutes.

### Nutritional Note

For someone on a cholesterol-restricted diet, substitute cubes of cooked boneless chicken breast or Marinated Baked Tofu (recipe page 191) for the shrimp.

*Per Serving:*

334 calories
26 g protein
4 g total fat
    1 g saturated fat
    118 mg cholesterol
52 g carbohydrate
    13 g dietary fibre
675 mg sodium
625 mg potassium

Good: Vitamin A
Excellent: Vitamin C; Folate; Iron

# Quinoa-Stuffed Peppers

*This quinoa mixture is delicious as a stuffing for sweet peppers —red, green or purple—or on its own. I keep dried sliced Chinese mushrooms on hand and often use them when I don't have fresh ones.*

| | | |
|---|---|---|
| ½ cup | quinoa | 125 mL |
| 4 | sweet green peppers | 4 |
| 1 tsp | vegetable oil | 5 mL |
| 1 | medium onion, chopped | 1 |
| 8 | mushrooms, quartered (or ¼ cup/50 mL dried mushrooms*) | 8 |
| 1 cup | corn kernels | 250 mL |
| 2 tbsp | minced fresh coriander or parsley | 25 mL |
| 1 tbsp | sodium-reduced soy sauce | 15 mL |
| 2 tsp | sesame oil | 10 mL |
| 2 tsp | chopped fresh garlic | 10 mL |
| Pinch | red pepper flakes | Pinch |
| ¼ cup | fresh whole wheat bread crumbs (see page 193) | 50 mL |

**1.** Rinse quinoa under cold water; drain. In saucepan, bring 1 cup (250 mL) water to boil; stir in quinoa. Reduce heat, cover and simmer for 15 minutes or until water is absorbed and quinoa is transluscent.

**2.** Cut off ½ inch (1 cm) from tops of green peppers; remove seeds. In large saucepan of boiling water, cook peppers for 5 minutes or until tender-crisp. Remove and drain upside down.

**3.** In skillet, heat oil over medium heat; cook onion until tender. Stir in mushrooms, quinoa, corn, half the coriander, soy sauce, sesame oil, garlic and red pepper flakes; stuff into peppers.

**4.** Sprinkle with bread crumbs and remaining coriander. Bake in greased 8-inch (2 L) square baking dish in 350°F (180°C) oven for 30 minutes or until heated through. **Makes 4 servings.**

\* If using dried mushrooms, soak in hot water for 5 minutes; drain, discard tough stems and slice.

**MAKE AHEAD:** Through step 3, covered and refrigerated for up to four hours.

## Quinoa Pilaf

Prepare quinoa mixture, but omit bread crumbs and green peppers.

## Quinoa

Quinoa (pronounced keen-wah) is available at health food stores. It is higher in iron than most other grains and has high-quality protein. Cooked, it puffs up to four times its dry volume.

*PER SERVING:*

202 calories

7 g protein

5 g total fat
  1 g saturated fat
  0 mg cholesterol

36 g carbohydrate
  5 g dietary fibre

148 mg sodium

560 mg potassium

GOOD: Folate; Iron
EXCELLENT: Vitamin C

*Not Great — Needs More Additions Mushrooms etc.*

# Barley and Corn Casserole

*This recipe is the result of a conversation I had with editor Kirsten Hanson, who told me that corn and barley is a nice combination. This dish goes well with any meats, fish or poultry or as part of a meatless meal. Be sure to save any leftover cobs of corn — it's easy to cut off kernels to use here.*

| | | |
|---|---|---|
| 1 tbsp | vegetable oil | 15 mL |
| 1 | onion, chopped | 1 |
| 1 tbsp | minced fresh garlic | 15 mL |
| 1 cup | finely chopped carrots | 250 mL |
| 1 cup | pearl or pot barley | 250 mL |
| 3 cups | vegetable or chicken stock | 750 mL |
| 2 cups | corn kernels | 500 mL |
| ½ cup | chopped fresh parsley | 125 mL |
| | Salt and pepper | |

**1.** In heavy flameproof casserole, heat oil over medium-high heat; cook onion, garlic and carrots for 4 minutes or until onion is softened. Stir in barley; pour in stock. Cover and bake in 350°F (180°C) oven for 1 hour.

**2.** Stir in corn, parsley, and salt and pepper to taste. Bake for another 5 minutes or until heated through and barley is tender. **Makes 8 servings**.

**MAKE AHEAD:** Casserole can be covered and refrigerated for up to two days. To reheat, add ½ cup (125 mL) stock or water and warm in microwave or oven.

| COMPARE | |
|---|---|
| **Corn kernels (1 cup/250 mL)** | **Sodium (mg)** |
| frozen | 29 |
| canned | 559 |

### Barley
Barley is a good source of soluble fibre—the same kind that is in oat bran and kidney beans and may help to reduce blood cholesterol.

### Cooking Tip
Thaw frozen corn kernels under hot water, then drain well before using in this recipe.

*PER SERVING:*

155 calories
4 g protein
2 g total fat
  0.2 g saturated fat
  0 mg cholesterol
32 g carbohydrate
  6 g dietary fibre
250 mg sodium
216 mg potassium

EXCELLENT: Vitamin A

# Bean and Sausage Casserole

*A bit of kielbasa sausage adds a lot of flavor to this nutrient-packed dish. Serve with a green salad or coleslaw and fresh bread.*

## Bean Casserole

Making this dish without sausage reduces the fat to 9 g per serving.

Recipe made with cooked dried beans instead of canned reduces sodium to 372 mg per serving.

## Dried Beans

Instead of using canned beans, you can cook dried beans.

One pound (500 g) dried beans (about 2 cups/500 mL) equals 5 to 6 cups (1.25 to 1.5 L) of cooked beans. Cooked beans freeze up to 6 months.

One can (19 oz/540 mL) beans equals 2 cups (500 mL) drained beans.

| | | |
|---|---|---|
| 1 tsp | olive oil | 5 mL |
| 3 cups | coarsely chopped onions or leeks (white parts only) | 750 mL |
| 3 | cloves garlic, minced | 3 |
| 1 | can (19 oz/540 mL) navy (white pea) beans, drained | 1 |
| 1 cup | shredded low-fat Cheddar-style cheese | 250 mL |
| ½ cup | chopped kielbasa sausage (2 oz/60 g) | 125 mL |
| 2 | tomatoes, chopped* | 2 |
| ¼ tsp | dried rosemary | 1 mL |

### Topping

| | | |
|---|---|---|
| 1 cup | fresh whole wheat bread crumbs (see page 193) | 250 mL |
| 2 tbsp | chopped fresh parsley | 25 mL |
| 2 tsp | olive oil | 10 mL |
| 1 | clove garlic, minced | 1 |

**1.** In nonstick skillet, heat oil over medium heat; cook onions and garlic, stirring occasionally, for about 5 minutes or until tender, adding water if necessary to prevent scorching.

**2.** Remove from heat; stir in beans, cheese, sausage, tomatoes and rosemary. Spoon into gratin dish or 10-inch (25 cm) quiche dish.

**3.** Topping: Combine bread crumbs, parsley, oil and garlic; sprinkle over bean mixture.

**4.** Bake in 350°F (180°C) oven for 20 minutes or until heated through. **Makes 4 servings**.

\* If you don't have any fresh tomatoes, substitute 2 cups (500 mL) drained chopped canned tomatoes.

*Per Serving:*

341 calories
21 g protein
13 g total fat
   5 g saturated fat
   25 mg cholesterol
38 g carbohydrate
   9 g dietary fibre
802 mg sodium
560 mg potassium

Good: Iron
Excellent: Folate; Calcium

**MAKE AHEAD:** Through step 3, covered and refrigerated for up to three hours.

# Potato, Bean and Tomato Stew with Basil

*✓ Good* (handwritten)

*This fast and easy main dish is gentle on the budget, full of flavor and packed with nutrients. It is also delicious with fresh rosemary instead of basil. (Pictured opposite page 161.)*

| | | |
|---|---|---|
| 1 tbsp | olive oil | 15 mL |
| 1 | medium onion, chopped | 1 |
| 2 | large cloves garlic, minced | 2 |
| ½ tsp | paprika | 2 mL |
| 3 | large tomatoes, coarsely chopped* | 3 |
| ¼ cup | chopped fresh basil (or ½ tsp/2 mL dried) | 50 mL |
| ½ tsp | dried oregano | 2 mL |
| 2 | medium potatoes, peeled and diced | 2 |
| 1 cup | water or vegetable stock | 250 mL |
| 1 | can (19 oz/540 mL) chick-peas, drained | 1 |
| | Salt and pepper | |
| ½ cup | chopped fresh parsley | 125 mL |

*(handwritten) used canned tomatoes + 3 fresh*

*(handwritten) 2 cans Kidney Beans drained*

**1.** In large heavy saucepan, heat oil over medium heat; cook onion until tender, about 5 minutes.

**2.** Add garlic, paprika, 2 of the tomatoes, basil (if using dried) and oregano; simmer, stirring often, for 5 minutes.

**3.** Add potatoes and water; cover and boil for 5 minutes, stirring occasionally. Add chick-peas; reduce heat and simmer for 5 minutes or until potatoes are tender.

**4.** Add remaining tomato, basil (if using fresh), and salt and pepper to taste; heat for 1 minute. Serve garnished with parsley in large shallow bowls. **Makes 3 main-course servings**.

*\* Instead of fresh tomatoes, you can use 1 can (28 oz/796 mL) tomatoes, undrained.*

**MAKE AHEAD:** Through step 3, covered and refrigerated for up to two days. Reheat gently before step 4.

### Legumes

Legumes are dried beans, peas and lentils. They have more protein than any other vegetable and are an alternative to meat. Served with a grain product such as bread, they form a complete protein.

Legumes are low in fat, high in fibre, iron and calcium. Dried beans are a good source of Vitamin E.

*PER SERVING:*

334 calories
13 g protein
7 g total fat
   1 g saturated fat
   0 mg cholesterol
58 g carbohydrate
   8 g dietary fibre
293 mg sodium
906 mg potassium

GOOD: Vitamin A; Iron
EXCELLENT: Vitamin C; Folate

# Winter Vegetable Curry with Couscous

*This is one of my favorite winter meals. I like to make a lot and can quite happily eat it for a few days.*

**Nutritional Note**

A delicious and painless way to increase fibre in your diet is to add cooked lentils or beans to salads, soups, casseroles, stews or tacos. Both are low in fat and very high in fibre.

**Couscous**

I think of couscous as a grain but it is actually a very fine (grain-like) pasta made from Durum wheat semolina.

Most couscous sold in Canada is the quick-cooking, or instant, type and is the fastest of all the grains to prepare. You can buy it at most supermarkets, but it is much less expensive at health food stores. If you can't find it, use rice or bulgur.

| | | |
|---|---|---|
| 1 tbsp | olive or vegetable oil | 15 mL |
| 1 | red or cooking onion, cut into wedges | 1 |
| 1 tbsp | curry powder | 15 mL |
| 1 tsp | ground cumin | 5 mL |
| ¼ tsp | cinnamon | 1 mL |
| 2 tbsp | minced gingerroot | 25 mL |
| 1 tsp | minced fresh garlic | 5 mL |
| ¼ tsp | red pepper flakes (optional) | 1 mL |
| 1½ cups | vegetable stock or water | 375 mL |
| 2 tbsp | lemon juice | 25 mL |
| 2 | carrots, sliced | 2 |
| 2 cups | cubed (about 1-inch/2.5 cm) peeled sweet potato | 500 mL |
| 2 cups | cauliflower florets | 500 mL |
| 1 | small zucchini (8-inch/20 cm), cut into chunks | 1 |
| 1 | can (19 oz/540 mL) chick-peas, drained and rinsed | 1 |
| ¼ cup | chopped fresh coriander or parsley | 50 mL |
| | Salt and pepper | |

## Couscous

| | | |
|---|---|---|
| 1½ cups | water | 375 mL |
| 1 tbsp | olive or vegetable oil | 15 mL |
| 1½ cups | couscous | 375 mL |
| | Salt and pepper | |

**1.** In large saucepan, heat oil over medium heat; cook onion for about 3 minutes or until softened. Add curry powder, cumin, cinnamon, ginger, garlic, and red pepper flakes (if using); cook, stirring often, for 1 minute.

**2.** Add stock, lemon juice, carrots and sweet potato; bring to boil. Reduce heat, cover and simmer for 8 minutes. Add cauliflower and zucchini; cook for 5 minutes or until vegetables are tender.

**3.** Stir in chick-peas, coriander, and salt and pepper to taste.

**4.** Couscous: Meanwhile, in saucepan, bring water and oil to boil; stir in couscous. Cover and remove from heat; let stand for 5 minutes. Fluff with fork; season with salt and pepper to taste. Serve vegetable curry over hot couscous. **Makes 6 servings**.

**MAKE AHEAD:** Through step 3, covered and refrigerated for up to two days.

*PER SERVING:*

386 calories
13 g protein
7 g total fat
   1 g saturated fat
   0 mg cholesterol
70 g carbohydrate
   7 g dietary fibre
331 mg sodium
561 mg potassium

GOOD: Iron
EXCELLENT: Vitamin A; Vitamin C; Folate

# Quick and Easy Spiced Couscous

*A hint of cinnamon and allspice is delicious in couscous. This is nice with curries, chicken, lamb or pork.*

| 2 cups | chicken stock | 500 mL |
| 1½ cups | couscous | 375 mL |
| ¼ tsp | each pepper, allspice and cinnamon | 1 mL |
| Pinch | salt | Pinch |
| 1 tbsp | soft margarine or butter | 15 mL |

**1.** In saucepan, bring chicken stock to boil; stir in couscous, pepper, allspice, cinnamon and salt. Remove from heat; cover and let stand for 5 minutes.

**2.** Using two forks, fluff couscous. Stir in butter. **Makes 6 servings**.

**MAKE AHEAD:** Couscous can be covered and refrigerated for up to one day; reheat, covered, in oven or microwave.

### Couscous with Tomato and Basil

Prepare Spiced Couscous. Stir in 1 small finely chopped tomato and ¼ cup (50 mL) chopped fresh basil along with butter.

*PER SERVING:*

203 calories
8 g protein
3 g total fat
   1 g saturated fat
   0 mg cholesterol
36 g carbohydrate
   2 g dietary fibre
292 mg sodium
162 mg potassium

# Crustless Vegetable Quiche

*Not only is this lighter in fat and calories than a traditional quiche, it is much faster and easier to make.*

***Sunday Brunch***

- Crustless Vegetable Quiche
- Asparagus and Mushroom Salad (page 78)
- Rhubarb Bran Muffins (page 203)
  OR
  Lemon Poppyseed Muffins (page 202)
- Apricot Orange and Fig Compote (page 235)
- Gingerbread Cake (page 212)

***Nutritional Note***

Compare:

| *1 serving* | *Fat (g)* |
|---|---|
| Traditional Quiche Lorraine | 48 |
| This recipe | 9 |

*Per Serving:*

170 calories
11 g protein
9 g total fat
   3 g saturated fat
   120 mg cholesterol
13 g carbohydrate
   3 g dietary fibre
279 mg sodium
636 mg potassium

Good: Vitamin C; Calcium; Iron
Excellent: Vitamin A; Folate

| | | |
|---|---|---|
| 1 tbsp | soft margarine or butter | 15 mL |
| ½ cup | fine fresh bread crumbs | 125 mL |
| 1 cup | sliced mushrooms | 250 mL |
| 1 cup | chopped zucchini | 250 mL |
| 3 cups | chopped fresh spinach leaves | 750 mL |
| 2 | eggs | 2 |
| 2 | egg whites | 2 |
| 1 cup | low-fat milk | 250 mL |
| 2 | green onions, chopped | 2 |
| ¼ cup | crumbled feta cheese | 50 mL |
| ¼ cup | chopped fresh parsley | 50 mL |
| 2 tbsp | chopped fresh basil (or 1 tsp/ 5 mL dried) | 25 mL |
| Dash | hot pepper sauce | Dash |
| 2 | medium tomatoes, sliced | 2 |

**1.** Spread 1 tsp (5 mL) of the margarine in 10-inch (25 cm) quiche dish or glass pie plate; sprinkle bottom and sides evenly with bread crumbs.

**2.** In large nonstick skillet, melt remaining margarine over medium heat; cook mushrooms and zucchini, stirring, for 5 to 7 minutes or until tender and liquid has evaporated. Add spinach; cook, stirring, for 2 minutes or until wilted.

**3.** In large bowl, beat together eggs and egg whites; add milk. Stir in onions, cheese, parsley, basil, hot pepper sauce and spinach mixture.

**4.** Spoon into prepared dish; top evenly with tomato slices.

**5.** Bake in 350°F (180°C) oven for 40 to 50 minutes or until firm to the touch and knife inserted in centre comes out clean. **Makes 4 servings**.

**Make Ahead:** Through step 3, covered and refrigerated for up to two hours.

# Marinated Baked Tofu

*This is one of the very best ways to cook tofu. It's really delicious baked in this mixture of ginger and soy sauce.*

| 10 oz | extra-firm tofu | 300 g |
|---|---|---|
| 2 tbsp | sodium-reduced soy sauce | 25 mL |
| 1 tbsp | dark sesame oil | 15 mL |
| 1 tbsp | minced gingerroot | 15 mL |

**1.** Cut tofu into slices slightly larger than ½ inch (1 cm) thick.

**2.** In 8-inch (2 L) square glass baking dish just large enough to hold tofu in single layer, combine soy sauce, sesame oil and gingerroot. Arrange tofu in dish, turning to coat both sides with mixture. Let marinate for 15 to 30 minutes.

**3.** Bake in 375°F (190°C) oven for 20 minutes, turning after 10 minutes. **Makes 4 servings.**

**MAKE AHEAD:** Through step 2, covered and refrigerated for up to 24 hours. Or through step 3, covered and refrigerated for one day; reheat or eat cold.

---

### Buying and Storing Tofu

Check the expiry or best-before date on packaged tofu. If you buy from an open tub, the fresher and whiter the tofu, the better the taste. The clearer the liquid, the fresher the tofu, and fresh tofu has little smell.

For stir-fries, salads and soups, buy the firm or extra-firm type. Buy soft tofu for blending, using in a dip, salad dressing or pie filling, or stirring into puréed food for toddlers.

Tofu should be kept submerged in water and the water should be changed daily. Fresh tofu keeps for about one week in the refrigerator.

---

### ABOUT TOFU

Tofu is made from soybeans and is rich in protein, iron and calcium, although tofus vary: some have three times as much calcium as others. For calcium-packed tofu, choose one that contains calcium sulphate or calcium chloride (those made with magnesium sulphate have less calcium). To top off its nutritional benefits, tofu is low in saturated fats and calories. And because it's made from a vegetable (not animal) product, it's cholesterol-free. If you're lactose intolerant, don't use dairy products or don't mix dairy and meat, consider tofu's versatility.

*PER SERVING:*

139 calories
12 g protein
10 g total fat
  1 g saturated fat
  0 mg cholesterol
4 g carbohydrate
  2 g dietary fibre
252 mg sodium
193 mg potassium

---

EXCELLENT: Calcium; Iron

*Good*
*Needs more sauce.*

# Vegetable Tofu Stir-Fry

*Serve this flavorful dish over rice, noodles, bulgur or couscous.*

| | | | |
|---|---|---|---|
| ¾ lb | firm-style tofu *could use less* | 375 g |
| 4 tsp | cornstarch | 20 mL |
| 2 tbsp | vegetable oil | 25 mL |
| 1 | medium onion, chopped | 1 |
| 1 | carrot, thinly sliced | 1 |
| 2 | stalks celery, sliced | 2 |
| 1 | sweet red or yellow pepper, cut into chunks | 1 |
| 1 cup | frozen peas | 250 mL |
| 1 cup | diced zucchini *used Broccoli* | 250 mL |
| 4 | green onions, chopped | 4 |
| 3 | cloves garlic, minced *2 -* | 3 |

## Tofu Marinade

| | | | |
|---|---|---|---|
| ⅓ cup | rice or cider vinegar | 75 mL |
| 2 tbsp | sodium-reduced soy sauce | 25 mL |
| 2 tbsp | sesame oil | 25 mL |
| 1½ tsp | granulated sugar | 7 mL |
| ¼ tsp | red pepper flakes *used ⅛ could use more* | 1 mL |

**1.** Tofu Marinade: In bowl, combine vinegar, soy sauce, sesame oil, sugar and red pepper flakes. Cut tofu into ½-inch (1 cm) cubes; add to marinade. Cover and marinate in refrigerator for 1 hour, stirring occasionally.

**2.** Drain tofu marinade into small dish; stir in cornstarch, mixing well.

**3.** In large nonstick skillet, heat oil over high heat; stir-fry onion, carrot and celery for 3 minutes. Add red pepper, peas, zucchini, green onions and garlic; stir-fry for 3 minutes or until tender-crisp. Add tofu; stir-fry for 1 minute.

**4.** Whisk cornstarch mixture; add to pan and cook for 1 minute or until thickened. **Makes 4 servings**.

**MAKE AHEAD:** Through step 1 for up to 24 hours.

## Tofu

Tofu, made from soybeans, is an excellent source of vegetable protein, and most kinds are also an excellent source of calcium. If firm-style tofu is unavailable, place regular tofu in sieve over bowl, weigh down and drain for one hour or overnight.

## Nutritional Note

To reduce the fat to 14 g per serving, use only 1 tbsp (15 mL) each of vegetable oil and sesame oil. In any case, the amount of saturated fat is low.

## Garnish

Top with ¼ cup (50 mL) chopped unsalted roasted peanuts if desired.

PER SERVING:

334 calories
17 g protein
21 g total fat
    3 g saturated fat
    0 mg cholesterol
24 g carbohydrate
    6 g dietary fibre
316 mg sodium
591 mg potassium

EXCELLENT: Vitamin A; Vitamin C; Folate; Calcium; Iron

Summer Shrimp and Tomato Pasta (page 160)

# Tomato, Eggplant and Zucchini Gratin

*Try to use the long, narrow Japanese eggplant or very small eggplants. In this type of Mediterranean dish, all the vegetables traditionally would be first sautéed in oil. This method is faster to prepare and much lower in fat.*

| | | |
|---|---|---|
| 1 tbsp | olive oil | 15 mL |
| 1 | onion, sliced | 1 |
| 3 cups | sliced mushrooms (½ lb/250 g) | 750 mL |
| 2 | cloves garlic, minced | 2 |
| 4 | medium tomatoes, chopped | 4 |
| ½ tsp | dried marjoram | 2 mL |
| ¼ tsp | dried thyme | 1 mL |
| | Salt and pepper | |
| 2 | zucchini or small yellow summer squash (4 oz/125 g each) | 2 |
| 2 | small eggplant (4 oz/125 g each) | 2 |
| 1 cup | fresh bread crumbs | 250 mL |
| ⅓ cup | freshly grated Parmesan cheese | 75 mL |

**1.** In nonstick skillet, heat 1 tsp (5 mL) of the oil over medium-high heat; cook onion, mushrooms, garlic and 2 tbsp (25 mL) water, stirring, for 3 minutes or until softened.

**2.** Add tomatoes, marjoram, thyme, and salt and pepper to taste; cook for 20 minutes or until thickened, stirring often.

**3.** Slice zucchini and eggplant diagonally into ¼-inch (5 mm) thick slices. Toss eggplant with remaining oil.

**4.** Spread ½ cup (125 mL) tomato sauce in 13- x 9-inch (3 L) glass baking dish. Layer with half of the zucchini, eggplant and sauce; repeat layers.

**5.** Mix bread crumbs with cheese; sprinkle over top. Bake, uncovered, in 400°F (200°C) oven for 35 minutes or until bubbling. **Makes 4 main-course servings**.

**MAKE AHEAD:** Through step 4 for up to one hour.

## Bread Crumbs

Make fresh bread crumbs by crumbling 2 slices of day-old bread in a food processor. Or rub bread over a grater.

Make your own dry bread crumbs by letting bread dry completely before processing into fine crumbs. Packaged dried bread crumbs are very fine and not as nice as fresh bread crumbs for a topping.

## Fresh Herbs

If fresh herbs are available, use 2 tbsp (25 mL) chopped fresh marjoram and 1 tbsp (15 mL) chopped fresh thyme in the Gratin.

## Fall Dinner

- Italian Chick-Pea and Pasta Soup (page 67)
- Tomato, Eggplant and Zucchini Gratin
- Tossed Salad Greens with Yogurt Herb Dressing (page 87)
- Baked Pear Bread Pudding (page 224)

*PER SERVING:*

167 calories
8 g protein
7 g total fat
   2 g saturated fat
   7 mg cholesterol
22 g carbohydrate
   5 g dietary fibre
226 mg sodium
704 mg potassium

GOOD: Vitamin A; Vitamin C; Folate; Iron

# Apricot-Raisin Muesli

*You can save money by making your own muesli cereal. Use any combination of your favorite dried fruits and nuts. Sometimes I toast the rolled oats, and occasionally I use toasted oat bran. Serve with fresh fruit and milk or yogurt.*

| | | |
|---|---|---|
| 2 cups | rolled oats (not instant) | 500 mL |
| ½ cup | toasted wheat germ | 125 mL |
| ½ cup | oat or wheat bran | 125 mL |
| ½ cup | chopped dried apricots | 125 mL |
| ¼ cup | raisins or chopped figs | 50 mL |
| ¼ cup | chopped brazil nuts or almonds, toasted | 50 mL |
| 1 tsp | cinnamon | 5 mL |

**1.** Spread rolled oats on baking sheet; toast in 400°F (200°C) oven for 5 minutes. Let cool.

**2.** In large jar or airtight container, combine oats, wheat germ, bran, apricots, raisins, nuts and cinnamon; mix well. **Makes 8 servings, ½ cup (125 mL) each.**

## Fibre

Adults need 25 to 35 grams of fibre a day. One of the best ways to get this much fibre is to start the day by eating whole grain cereals. Read cereal boxes and choose ones with at least four grams of fibre per serving. Then for lunch, choose whole wheat pasta, and for supper, have whole grain or brown rice.

## Vitamin E

Wheat germ is an excellent source of Vitamin E, an important antioxidant which may help to reduce heart disease. There is some concern that people on a very low-fat diet may not have an adequate amount of Vitamin E in their diet.

## To Toast Nuts

Spread on baking sheet and bake in 350°F (180°C) oven for 5 minutes or until golden.

*PER SERVING:*

178 calories
8 g protein
5 g total fat
   1 g saturated fat
   0 mg cholesterol
31 g carbohydrate
   5 g dietary fibre
3 mg sodium
353 mg potassium

GOOD: Folate; Iron

**MAKE AHEAD:** Store at room temperature for up to one month.

# BREADS, MUFFINS, CAKES AND COOKIES

Cornmeal Pancakes with
Jalapeño Peppers and Ginger

Apple Cinnamon Whole Wheat Pancakes

Upside-Down Apple Pancake

Banana Blender Pancakes

Citrus Double-Bran Muffins

Jalapeño Cornmeal Muffins

Lemon Poppy Seed Muffins

Rhubarb Bran Muffins

High Fibre Carrot Bran Muffins

Muesli Soda Bread

Raspberry Pecan Tea Bread

Fruit and Fibre Squares

Light Lemon Squares

Orange Hazelnut Biscotti

Apple Cinnamon Cookies

Apricot Streusel Cake

Gingerbread Cake

Pumpkin Spice Cake

Elizabeth Baird's Chocolate
Angel Food Cake

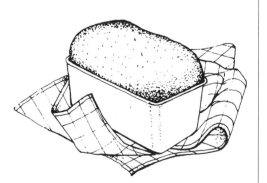

# Cornmeal Pancakes with Jalapeño Peppers and Ginger

*This unlikely combination is surprisingly delightful. Serve for lunch or a light supper and top the pancakes with salsa and yogurt.*

### Double Corn Pancakes

Before turning pancakes, top each one with 1 tbsp (15 mL) kernel corn.

| | | |
|---|---|---|
| 1 cup | cornmeal | 250 mL |
| 1 cup | all-purpose flour | 250 mL |
| 2 tbsp | granulated sugar | 25 mL |
| 1 tbsp | baking powder | 15 mL |
| ½ tsp | baking soda | 2 mL |
| 2 | eggs, lightly beaten | 2 |
| 2 cups | low-fat milk | 500 mL |
| 2 tbsp | vegetable oil | 25 mL |
| 2 tbsp | grated gingerroot | 25 mL |
| 2 tbsp | chopped pickled jalapeño peppers | 25 mL |
| ½ tsp | soft margarine or butter | 2 mL |

**1.** In large bowl, mix cornmeal, flour, sugar, baking powder and baking soda.

**2.** Combine eggs, milk, oil, gingeroot and jalapeño peppers; pour into flour mixture, stirring just until combined.

**3.** Heat nonstick skillet over medium heat until hot; add margarine to lightly grease. Pour in batter, ¼ cup (50 mL) for each pancake; cook until bubbles form on surface and underside is golden brown. Turn and cook just until bottom is lightly browned. **Makes 6 servings of 3 pancakes each.**

*PER SERVING:*

291 calories

9 g protein

9 g total fat
    2 g saturated fat
    78 mg cholesterol

44 g carbohydrate
    2 g dietary fibre

366 mg sodium

233 mg potassium

GOOD: Calcium

**MAKE AHEAD:** Through step 1 for up to one day.

# Apple Cinnamon Whole Wheat Pancakes

*Top these tasty pancakes with yogurt mixed with brown sugar or maple syrup.*

| | | |
|---|---|---|
| ½ cup | all-purpose flour | 125 mL |
| ½ cup | whole wheat flour | 125 mL |
| 1 tbsp | granulated sugar | 15 mL |
| 1½ tsp | baking powder | 7 mL |
| 1 tsp | cinnamon | 5 mL |
| ¼ tsp | baking soda | 1 mL |
| 1 | egg, lightly beaten | 1 |
| 1 cup | low-fat milk | 250 mL |
| ½ cup | grated peeled apple | 125 mL |
| 1 tbsp | vegetable oil | 15 mL |
| ½ tsp | soft margarine or butter | 2 mL |

**1.** In bowl, combine all-purpose and whole wheat flours, sugar, baking powder, cinnamon and baking soda.

**2.** Combine egg, milk, apple and oil; pour into flour mixture, stirring just until combined.

**3.** Heat nonstick skillet over medium heat until hot; add margarine to lightly grease. Pour in batter, ¼ cup (50 mL) for each pancake; cook until bubbles form on surface and underside is golden brown. Turn and cook just until bottom is lightly browned. **Makes 3 servings of 3 pancakes each**.

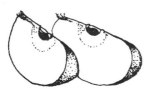

**MAKE AHEAD:** Through step 1 for up to one day.

### Apple Cinnamon Pancakes

You can substitute all-purpose flour for the whole wheat, but pancakes won't be as high in fibre.

### Lower-Fat Baking

Try to use the minimum of high-fat ingredients such as butter, margarine, oil or cream. When possible, I use a liquid vegetable oil such as canola instead of butter, margarine, shortening or lard, because it is lower in saturated fats and is not hydrogenated.

*PER SERVING:*

288 calories
10 g protein
9 g total fat
  2 g saturated fat
  78 mg cholesterol
43 g carbohydrate
  4 g dietary fibre
299 mg sodium
281 mg potassium

GOOD: Calcium; Iron

# Upside-Down Apple Pancake

*Make this fabulous-tasting pancake on the weekend for brunch or breakfast. If you make it in two pie plates, it's easy to turn upside down onto regular plates and looks great. Top with yogurt mixed with a little honey or maple syrup.*

| | | |
|---|---|---|
| 2 tbsp | soft margarine or butter | 25 mL |
| ¼ cup | granulated sugar | 50 mL |
| 2 tsp | cinnamon | 10 mL |
| 3 | medium apples, peeled and sliced | 3 |

**Batter**

| | | |
|---|---|---|
| ⅓ cup | all-purpose flour | 75 mL |
| ½ tsp | baking powder | 2 mL |
| 2 | egg yolks | 2 |
| ⅓ cup | low-fat milk | 75 mL |
| 4 | egg whites | 4 |
| ⅓ cup | granulated sugar | 75 mL |

**1.** In two 9-inch (23 cm) pie plates or one 13- x 9-inch (3 L) baking dish, melt margarine in 400°F (200°C) oven, about 2 minutes.

**2.** Combine sugar and cinnamon; sprinkle evenly over margarine. Bake for 2 minutes or until melted.

**3.** Arrange apple slices in overlapping circles over top; bake for 10 minutes.

**4.** Batter: Meanwhile, in bowl, combine flour and baking powder; blend in egg yolks and milk.

**5.** In large bowl, beat egg whites until white and frothy; gradually beat in sugar until soft peaks form. Fold into milk mixture.

**6.** Spread evenly over apples. Bake for 15 to 20 minutes or until lightly browned.

**7.** Loosen edges with knife; invert onto serving plate. **Makes 6 servings**.

**MAKE AHEAD:** Best served immediately, but fine prepared a few hours in advance and served at room temperature.

## Upside-Down Apple Cake

This pancake can just as easily be called a cake and served for dessert.

*PER SERVING:*

210 calories
5 g protein
6 g total fat
   1 g saturated fat
   75 mg cholesterol
36 g carbohydrate
   2 g dietary fibre
118 mg sodium
137 mg potassium

# Banana Blender Pancakes

*These take two minutes to prepare and taste absolutely delicious. Try topping the pancakes with low-fat yogurt mixed with brown sugar, fresh fruit or traditional maple syrup instead of high-fat butter or margarine.*

| | | |
|---|---|---|
| ½ cup | all-purpose flour | 125 mL |
| ¼ cup | cornmeal* | 50 mL |
| ¼ cup | whole wheat flour | 50 mL |
| 1 tbsp | granulated sugar | 15 mL |
| 1½ tsp | baking powder | 7 mL |
| 1 | egg | 1 |
| 1 cup | low-fat milk | 250 mL |
| 1 tbsp | vegetable oil | 15 mL |
| 1 | banana, diced | 1 |
| 1 tsp | soft margarine or butter | 5 mL |

**1.** In blender or food processor, blend together flour, cornmeal, whole wheat flour, sugar and baking powder.

**2.** Add egg, milk and oil; process until mixed. Stir in banana.

**3.** Heat nonstick skillet over medium heat until hot; add margarine to lightly grease.

**4.** Pour in batter, ¼ cup (50 mL) for each pancake; cook for about 1 minute or until bubbles form on surface and underside is golden. Turn and cook just until bottom is browned. **Makes eight 5-inch (12 cm) pancakes**.

\* Instead of using cornmeal, you can substitute whole wheat flour if desired. The pancakes are also fine made with 1 cup (250 mL) all-purpose flour but won't be as nutritious.

**MAKE AHEAD:** Through step 1 for up to one day.

***Nutritional Note***

For extra fibre and maximum nutrients, have whole fruit rather than juice at breakfast.

*PER PANCAKE:*

121 calories
4 g protein
4 g total fat
   1 g saturated fat
   29 mg cholesterol
19 g carbohydrate
   1 g dietary fibre
78 mg sodium
144 mg potassium

# Citrus Double-Bran Muffins

*Chopped prunes add flavor and keep these delicious muffins moist.*

| | | |
|---|---|---|
| 1 cup | all-purpose flour | 250 mL |
| ½ cup | wheat bran | 125 mL |
| ½ cup | oat bran | 125 mL |
| ½ cup | granulated sugar | 125 mL |
| 1 tsp | baking powder | 5 mL |
| 1 tsp | baking soda | 5 mL |
| ¼ tsp | salt | 1 mL |
| ½ cup | chopped prunes | 125 mL |
| 1 | egg, lightly beaten | 1 |
| 1 cup | buttermilk or soured milk* | 250 mL |
| ¼ cup | vegetable oil | 50 mL |
| | Grated rind of 1 lemon and 1 orange | |
| 1 tbsp | sesame seeds | 15 mL |

**1.** In large bowl, combine flour, wheat bran, oat bran, sugar, baking powder, baking soda and salt. Stir in prunes.

**2.** In separate bowl, mix egg, buttermilk, oil, and lemon and orange rinds. Pour into flour mixture and stir just enough to moisten, being careful not to overmix.

**3.** Spoon into greased nonstick muffin tins. Sprinkle with sesame seeds. Bake in 375°F (190°C) oven for 20 minutes or until tops are firm to the touch. **Makes 12 muffins.**

*To sour milk, add 1 tbsp (15 mL) lemon juice or vinegar to 1 cup (250 mL) milk and let stand for 10 minutes.

## Muffin Exposé

All muffins are not created equal, and it's not only the size that varies. A muffin can be as nutritious as a slice of bread or as frivolous as a piece of cake, with as little as 2 g of fat or as much as 20 g.

When buying muffins, the best bet nutritionally is a low-fat muffin made with whole grains or bran. By regulation, a 40 to 100 g muffin claiming to be low-fat contains no more than 3 g of fat. When you make your own muffins, use whole grains and as little fat as possible.

*Per Muffin:*

163 calories
4 g protein
6 g total fat
  1 g saturated fat
  19 mg cholesterol
24 g carbohydrate
  3 g dietary fibre
218 mg sodium
133 mg potassium

**Make Ahead:** Muffins can be stored in airtight container for up to three days or frozen for up to two weeks.

# Jalapeño Cornmeal Muffins

*Creamed corn makes these muffins very moist, and jalapeño peppers add a zing of flavor. Serve with a main course of chicken or ham or as part of a brunch menu.*

| | | |
|---|---|---|
| 1 cup | cornmeal | 250 mL |
| 1 cup | all-purpose flour | 250 mL |
| 1 tsp | baking powder | 5 mL |
| 1 tsp | baking soda | 5 mL |
| ¼ tsp | salt | 1 mL |
| 2 tbsp | chopped pickled jalapeño peppers | 25 mL |
| 1 | egg, lightly beaten | 1 |
| 1 | can (10 oz/284 mL) creamed corn | 1 |
| 1 cup | buttermilk or soured milk* | 250 mL |
| ¼ cup | vegetable oil | 50 mL |

**1.** In large bowl, combine cornmeal, flour, baking powder, baking soda and salt. Stir in jalapeño peppers.

**2.** In separate bowl, mix egg, corn, buttermilk and oil. Pour into flour mixture and stir just enough to moisten, being careful not to overmix.

**3.** Spoon into greased nonstick muffin tins. Bake in 375°F (190°C) oven for 25 to 30 minutes or until tops are firm to the touch. **Makes 12 muffins.**

\* To sour milk, add 1 tbsp (15 mL) lemon juice or vinegar to 1 cup (250 mL) milk and let stand for 10 minutes.

***Baking Note***
For tender muffins, mix batter as little as possible.

**MAKE AHEAD:** Muffins can be stored in airtight container for up to three days or frozen for up to two weeks.

*PER MUFFIN:*
154 calories
4 g protein
6 g total fat
   1 g saturated fat
   19 mg cholesterol
23 g carbohydrate
   1 g dietary fibre
303 mg sodium
104 mg potassium

# Lemon Poppy Seed Muffins

*If you like a strong lemon flavor, use the rind, or zest, of two lemons in these light muffins.*

| | | |
|---|---|---|
| 1 cup | all-purpose flour | 250 mL |
| 1 cup | whole wheat flour | 250 mL |
| ½ cup | granulated sugar | 125 mL |
| ¼ cup | poppy seeds | 50 mL |
| 1 tsp | baking powder | 5 mL |
| 1 tsp | baking soda | 5 mL |
| ¼ tsp | salt | 1 mL |
| 1 | egg, lightly beaten | 1 |
| ¾ cup | milk | 175 mL |
| ¼ cup | vegetable oil | 50 mL |
| | Grated rind of 1 or 2 lemons | |
| ¼ cup | lemon juice | 50 mL |

**1.** In large bowl, combine all-purpose and whole wheat flours, sugar, poppy seeds, baking powder, baking soda and salt.

**2.** In separate bowl, mix egg, milk, oil, lemon rind and juice. Pour into flour mixture and stir just enough to moisten, being careful not to overmix.

**3.** Spoon into greased nonstick muffin tins. Bake in 375°F (190°C) oven for 25 to 30 minutes or until tops are firm to the touch. **Makes 12 muffins.**

### Whole Wheat Flour

Whole wheat flour is much higher in fibre than all-purpose flour. In many recipes, you can substitute half the amount of all-purpose flour with whole wheat flour. Vitamin E, an important antioxidant vitamin, is found in whole grain cereals and wheat germ.

*PER MUFFIN:*

175 calories

4 g protein

7 g total fat
  1 g saturated fat
  19 mg cholesterol

26 g carbohydrate
  2 g dietary fibre

182 mg sodium

108 mg potassium

**MAKE AHEAD:** Muffins can be stored in airtight container for up to two days or frozen for up to two weeks.

# Rhubarb Bran Muffins

*In this recipe, use Stewed Rhubarb (page 233) or rhubarb stewed with a minimum amount of liquid: just a spoonful or two.*

| | | |
|---|---|---|
| ¾ cup | wheat bran | 175 mL |
| 1 cup | whole wheat flour | 250 mL |
| ½ cup | granulated sugar | 125 mL |
| 2 tsp | cinnamon | 10 mL |
| 1 tsp | baking powder | 5 mL |
| 1 tsp | baking soda | 5 mL |
| ½ cup | raisins | 125 mL |
| 1 cup | stewed rhubarb | 250 mL |
| 1 | egg, lightly beaten | 1 |
| ½ cup | buttermilk or low-fat yogurt | 125 mL |
| ¼ cup | vegetable oil | 50 mL |

**1.** In bowl, combine bran, flour, sugar, cinnamon, baking powder and baking soda; stir in raisins.

**2.** Combine stewed rhubarb, egg, buttermilk and oil; pour into flour mixture and stir just until combined.

**3.** Spoon into greased nonstick muffin tins. Bake in 400°F (200°C) oven for 25 minutes or until tops are firm to the touch. **Makes 12 muffins.**

**MAKE AHEAD:** Muffins can be stored in airtight container for up to two days or frozen for up to two weeks.

## *Pumpkin Muffins*

Substitute 1 cup (250 mL) canned or cooked puréed pumpkin for rhubarb.

## *Applesauce Bran Muffins*

Substitute 1 cup (250 mL) applesauce for rhubarb.

*PER MUFFIN:*

169 calories
3 g protein
6 g total fat
  1 g saturated fat
  18 mg cholesterol
30 g carbohydrate
  4 g dietary fibre
137 mg sodium
202 mg potassium

# High Fibre Carrot Bran Muffins

*These easy-to-make muffins are great for breakfast, snacks or lunch. Grated apple could be substituted for carrot.*

| | | |
|---|---|---|
| 1½ cups | whole wheat flour | 375 mL |
| 1½ cups | high fibre ready-to-eat bran cereal (not flakes) | 375 mL |
| ½ cup | packed brown sugar | 125 mL |
| 1 tbsp | cinnamon | 15 mL |
| 1 tsp | baking powder | 5 mL |
| 1 tsp | baking soda | 5 mL |
| ¼ tsp | salt | 1 mL |
| 1 cup | raisins or chopped dates | 250 mL |
| 1 cup | grated carrots | 250 mL |
| 1¾ cup | buttermilk or soured milk* | 425 mL |
| ¼ cup | vegetable oil | 50 mL |
| 1 | egg, lightly beaten | 1 |
| | Grated rind of 1 lemon or orange | |

**1.** In large bowl, stir together flour, cereal, sugar, cinnamon, baking powder, soda, salt, raisins and carrots.

**2.** Add buttermilk, oil, egg and lemon rind, stirring just until combined.

**3.** Spoon into greased nonstick muffin tins. Bake in 400°F/200°C oven for 20 minutes or until tops are firm to the touch. **Makes 12 muffins.**

\* Instead of buttermilk, you can substitute 1⅔ cups (400 mL) milk mixed with 2 tbsp (25 mL) lemon juice. Let stand for 10 minutes.

### Preparing Muffin Tins

Use nonstick tins; spray lightly over entire pan with nonstick vegetable coating spray.

### Filling Muffin Tins

Fill muffin tins to the top. Depending on the size of your tins, you could get 14 muffins from this recipe.

*PER MUFFIN:*

213 calories
5 g protein
6 g total fat
  1 g saturated fat
  19 mg cholesterol
40 g carbohydrate
  6 g dietary fibre
291 mg sodium
368 mg potassium

GOOD: Vitamin A; Iron

**MAKE AHEAD:** Muffins will keep, wrapped in plastic wrap and refrigerated, for up to two days, or frozen for up to one month.

# Muesli Soda Bread

*This whole wheat, raisin quick bread warm from the oven is a nice treat. You can substitute an equal amount of dried fruit mixture for the raisins. (Pictured opposite page 161.)*

| | | |
|---|---|---|
| 2 cups | whole wheat flour | 500 mL |
| 1 cup | all-purpose flour | 250 mL |
| ½ cup | rolled oats | 125 mL |
| 3 tbsp | granulated sugar | 50 mL |
| 1 tbsp | baking powder | 15 mL |
| 1 tsp | baking soda | 5 mL |
| 1 tsp | salt | 5 mL |
| ¾ cup | raisins | 175 mL |
| 2 tbsp | vegetable oil | 25 mL |
| 1¾ cups | buttermilk | 425 mL |

## Muesli Topping

| | | |
|---|---|---|
| 1 | egg white | 1 |
| 1 tbsp | each rolled oats, wheat germ, oat bran, sunflower seeds and sesame seeds | 15 mL |

**1.** In bowl, combine whole wheat and all-purpose flours, rolled oats, sugar, baking powder, baking soda and salt; stir in raisins.

**2.** Add oil to buttermilk; pour into flour mixture. Stir to make soft dough.

**3.** Turn out onto lightly floured surface and knead about 10 times or until smooth. Place on greased baking sheet; shape into circle about 2½ inches (6 cm) thick. Cut large shallow X on top.

**4.** Muesli Topping: Brush egg white over top of loaf. Combine rolled oats, wheat germ, oat bran, sunflower seeds and sesame seeds; sprinkle over loaf.

**5.** Bake in 350°F (180°C) oven for 65 to 70 minutes or until toothpick inserted in centre comes out clean. **Makes 1 loaf, about 20 slices**.

**MAKE AHEAD:** Best eaten warm from oven, but keeps well for two days.

***Whole Wheat Versus White***

All white flour sold in Canada is enriched with thiamine, riboflavin, niacin and iron. All Canadian baked goods made from white flour are made with enriched flour. If a bread is to be labelled "enriched," it must also have added protein, and may be made with flour also enriched with vitamin $B_6$, folate, pantothenic acid, magnesium and calcium.

The best choices are usually breads made from whole grains: they have more nutrients, flavor, fibre and texture.

*PER SLICE:*

128 calories
4 g protein
3 g total fat
0.4 g saturated fat
1 mg cholesterol
24 g carbohydrate
2 g dietary fibre
239 mg sodium
156 mg potassium

# Raspberry Pecan Tea Bread

*Frozen raspberries make this easy to prepare all year round. Buy the individually frozen raspberries.*

| | | |
|---|---|---|
| 1 cup | granulated sugar | 250 mL |
| ¼ cup | soft margarine | 50 mL |
| 1 | egg | 1 |
| ⅔ cup | milk | 150 mL |
| 1½ cups | all-purpose flour | 375 mL |
| 1 tsp | baking powder | 5 mL |
| ½ tsp | cinnamon | 2 mL |
| ½ cup | chopped pecans | 125 mL |
| 1 cup | raspberries (fresh or frozen, unthawed) | 250 mL |

**1.** Line 8- x 4-inch (1.5 L) loaf pan with foil; grease lightly.

**2.** In large bowl, cream sugar with margarine. Beat in egg, then milk.

**3.** Mix flour, baking powder and cinnamon; beat into egg mixture until blended. Stir in pecans and raspberries.

**4.** Spoon into pan; bake in 350°F (180°C) oven for 60 to 70 minutes or until toothpick inserted in centre comes out clean. Let stand in pan for 3 minutes.

**5.** Transfer foil and tea bread to rack; loosen foil and let cool completely before cutting. **Makes 16 slices.**

**Baking Note**

Soft diet-style tub margarines contain more water than regular soft margarines and are not recommended for baking.

*PER SLICE:*

154 calories

2 g protein

6 g total fat
   1 g saturated fat
   14 mg cholesterol

24 g carbohydrate
   1 g dietary fibre

64 mg sodium

59 mg potassium

**MAKE AHEAD:** Tea bread can be wrapped in foil and stored for up to four days or frozen for up to one month.

# Fruit and Fibre Squares

*Packed with fruit and fibre, these are perfect for a breakfast-on-the-run, lunch-box treat or a quick snack.*

| | | |
|---|---|---|
| 2 cups | bran flakes | 500 mL |
| 1 cup | whole wheat flour | 250 mL |
| ⅔ cup | packed brown sugar | 150 mL |
| 2 tsp | baking soda | 10 mL |
| ½ tsp | salt | 2 mL |
| 1 cup | buttermilk | 250 mL |
| 2 tbsp | vegetable oil | 25 mL |
| 2 | eggs | 2 |
| | Grated rind of 1 orange | |
| 1 cup | chopped dried apricots | 250 mL |
| 1 cup | chopped dates | 250 mL |
| ⅓ cup | chopped almonds | 75 mL |

**1.** In food processor, combine Bran Flakes, flour, sugar, baking soda and salt; process for 1 second.

**2.** Add buttermilk, oil, eggs and orange rind; process until blended.

**3.** Stir in apricots, dates and almonds.

**4.** Spread in greased 13- x 9-inch (3 L) baking dish. Bake in 375°F (190°C) oven for 25 minutes or until tester inserted in centre comes out clean. Let cool before cutting into squares. **Makes 16 squares**.

**MAKE AHEAD:** Wrap individual squares in plastic wrap and store in cookie tin for up to two days, or freeze for up to one month.

### Apricots
Dried apricots and dates are high in fibre and iron.
  For a softer, moister bar, soak apricots in hot water for 10 minutes, then drain.

### Nutritional Note
Instead of spending a large part of your budget and calorie allowance (1,900 a day for an average active woman) on foods such as chips and cookies, spend it on wholesome foods. When buying bread, remember that whole wheat has the same calories as white yet more vitamins and three times the fibre. When baking, add fibre and nutrients by using whole wheat flour (or a half-and-half mixture of whole wheat and all-purpose flour).

*PER SQUARE:*

173 calories
4 g protein
4 g total fat
  1 g saturated fat
  28 mg cholesterol
33 g carbohydrate
  4 g dietary fibre
301 mg sodium
320 mg potassium

# Light Lemon Squares

*This is a light version of a favorite square.*

| | | |
|---|---|---|
| 1 cup | all-purpose flour | 250 mL |
| ¼ cup | granulated sugar | 50 mL |
| ¼ cup | soft margarine | 50 mL |
| 2 tbsp | low-fat yogurt | 25 mL |

## Topping

| | | |
|---|---|---|
| ¾ cup | granulated sugar | 175 mL |
| 2 tbsp | all-purpose flour | 25 mL |
| ½ tsp | baking powder | 2 mL |
| ¼ tsp | salt | 1 mL |
| 1 | egg | 1 |
| 1 | egg white | 1 |
| | Grated rind of 1 large lemon | |
| ¼ cup | lemon juice | 50 mL |
| 2 tsp | icing sugar | 10 mL |

**1.** In food processor or bowl, mix together flour, sugar, margarine and yogurt until just combined.

**2.** Press into 8-inch (2 L) square cake pan lightly coated with cooking spray. Bake in 325°F (160°C) oven for 25 minutes or until golden.

**3.** Topping: In food processor or bowl, combine sugar, flour, baking powder, salt, egg, egg white and lemon rind and juice; mix well.

**4.** Pour over base. Bake for 30 minutes or until top is set.

**5.** Let cool in pan. Sift icing sugar over top. Cut into squares. **Makes 16 squares**.

### Nutritional Note

The traditional lemon square recipe uses ½ cup (125 mL) butter in the base and 2 whole eggs in the topping. Instead, I cut the fat in half.

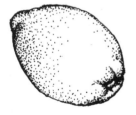

*Per Square:*

115 calories

2 g protein

3 g total fat
  1 g saturated fat
  14 mg cholesterol

20 g carbohydrate
  0.3 g dietary fibre

92 mg sodium

27 mg potassium

**MAKE AHEAD:** Squares can be stored in airtight container for up to one week or frozen for up to two weeks.

# Orange Hazelnut Biscotti

*These crunchy Italian cookies are meant to be dunked in your tea, coffee or hot chocolate.*

| | | |
|---|---|---|
| ¾ cup | coarsely chopped (unskinned) hazelnuts | 175 mL |
| 1½ cups | all-purpose flour | 375 mL |
| 2 tsp | baking powder | 10 mL |
| 2 | eggs | 2 |
| ½ cup | packed brown sugar | 125 mL |
| 2 tsp | vanilla | 10 mL |
| | Grated rind of 1 orange | |
| 1 | egg white | 1 |

**1.** In large bowl, combine nuts, flour and baking powder.

**2.** In separate bowl, beat eggs, sugar, vanilla and orange rind; stir into flour mixture, mixing well to form stiff dough.

**3.** Shape dough into 2 logs about 1-inch (2.5 cm) in diameter. Transfer to ungreased baking sheet.

**4.** Brush tops with egg white. Bake in 350°F (180°C) oven for 25 minutes. Let cool for 5 minutes.

**5.** Slice diagonally into ½-inch (1 cm) thick slices. Arrange on baking sheet. Reduce temperature to 300°F (150°C) and bake for 25 minutes or until crisp and golden. **Makes 36 cookies**.

**MAKE AHEAD:** Biscotti can be stored in airtight container for up to two weeks.

### Almond Ginger Biscotti

Omit hazelnuts, vanilla and orange rind. Substitute ½ cup (125 mL) coarsely chopped unblanched almonds, 1½ tsp (7 mL) ground ginger and 3 tbsp (50 mL) finely chopped crystallized ginger.

*Per Cookie:*

52 calories
1 g protein
2 g total fat
  0.2 g saturated fat
  12 mg cholesterol
8 g carbohydrate
  0.4 g dietary fibre
21 mg sodium
33 mg potassium

# Apple Cinnamon Cookies

*These old-fashioned cookies are favorites in our house.*

| | | |
|---|---|---:|
| ½ cup | soft margarine or butter | 125 mL |
| 1⅓ cups | packed brown sugar | 325 mL |
| 1 | egg | 1 |
| 1½ cups | grated peeled apple | 375 mL |
| 1 cup | raisins | 250 mL |
| ¼ cup | chopped almonds | 50 mL |
| ¼ cup | apple juice | 50 mL |
| 2 cups | whole wheat flour | 500 mL |
| 2 tsp | cinnamon | 10 mL |
| 1 tsp | baking soda | 5 mL |
| ½ tsp | salt | 2 mL |
| ¼ tsp | ground cloves | 1 mL |

**Glaze (Optional)**

| | | |
|---|---|---:|
| 1 cup | icing sugar | 250 mL |
| 2 tbsp | lemon juice | 25 mL |

**1.** In large bowl, cream margarine with sugar until fluffy; beat in egg. Add apple, raisins, almonds and apple juice; mix well.

**2.** In separate bowl, combine flour, cinnamon, baking soda, salt and cloves. Stir into apple mixture; mix well.

**3.** Drop by tablespoonfuls (15 mL) about 2 inches (5 cm) apart onto lightly greased baking sheets. Bake in 375°F (190°C) oven for 10 to 12 minutes or until evenly browned. Let stand on baking sheets for 1 to 2 minutes before removing to racks to let cool.

**4.** Glaze: In small bowl, combine icing sugar and lemon juice until smooth. Spread over each cookie. **Makes 60 cookies**.

**MAKE AHEAD:** Cookies can be stored in airtight container for up to one week or frozen for up to one month.

**Baking Note**

Grated apple adds moistness and flavor to this low-fat cookie.

*PER COOKIE (WITHOUT GLAZE):*

60 calories

1 g protein

2 g total fat
    0.3 g saturated fat
    4 mg cholesterol

11 g carbohydrate
    1 g dietary fibre

62 mg sodium

65 mg potassium

# Apricot Streusel Cake

*This amazingly delicious moist cake has no fat except from the
2% evaporated milk. It's a lovely dessert accompanied by any
fresh fruit, or serve as a coffee cake.*

| | | |
|---|---|---|
| 1 cup | all-purpose flour | 250 mL |
| 1 cup | granulated sugar | 250 mL |
| 1 tsp | baking soda | 5 mL |
| ½ tsp | salt | 2 mL |
| 1 | egg, lightly beaten | 1 |
| ¾ cup | 2% evaporated milk | 175 mL |
| 8 | fresh apricots (1 lb/500g), coarsely chopped, or 1 can (14 oz/398 mL) apricots, drained and coarsely chopped | 8 |

### Topping

| | | |
|---|---|---|
| ¼ cup | packed brown sugar | 50 mL |
| 1 tsp | cinnamon | 5 mL |

**1.** In large bowl, combine flour, sugar, baking soda and salt.

**2.** Add egg and evaporated milk; mix well. Stir in apricots.

**3.** Spread in 8-inch (2 L) square cake pan lightly coated with
cooking spray.

**4.** Topping: Combine brown sugar and cinnamon; sprinkle over
top. Bake in 350°F (180°C) oven for 60 to 70 minutes or until
toothpick inserted in centre comes out clean. **Makes 12 servings**.

***Dessert Topping***

Instead of using high-
fat whipped cream for
a dessert topping, add
sugar to taste to extra-
thick yogurt and flavor
with vanilla, liqueur or
grated lemon rind.
A deliciously low-fat
alternative!

***Cooking Tip***

If using canned
apricots, be sure to
drain them very well.

**MAKE
AHEAD:** Cake can be covered with foil
and stored for three days or frozen
for up to two weeks.

*PER SERVING:*

157 calories

3 g protein

1 g total fat
0.3 g saturated fat
19 mg cholesterol

35 g carbohydrate
1 g dietary fibre

218 mg sodium

188 mg potassium

# Gingerbread Cake

*Grated fresh gingerroot adds an extra flavor dimension to this moist cake, but ground ginger also works well. This cake is delicious topped with stewed sliced apples (see Apple Filling in Apple-Pecan Phyllo Crisps, page 225), or serve with fresh fruit, Microwave Rhubarb Sauce with Ginger (page 233) or ice cream.*

| | | |
|---|---|---|
| ½ cup | packed brown sugar | 125 mL |
| ¼ cup | soft margarine or butter | 50 mL |
| | Grated rind of 1 orange | |
| 1 | egg | 1 |
| 1 | egg white | 1 |
| 1 cup | applesauce | 250 mL |
| ½ cup | fancy molasses | 125 mL |
| ¼ cup | grated gingerroot | 50 mL |
| 1½ cups | sifted cake-and-pastry flour | 375 mL |
| 1 tsp | baking soda | 5 mL |
| 1 tsp | baking powder | 5 mL |
| ½ tsp | salt | 2 mL |

**1.** In bowl and using electric mixer, beat brown sugar, margarine and orange rind until smooth.

**2.** Beat in egg and egg white, beating well after each addition. Mix in applesauce, molasses and ginger until smooth.

**3.** Combine flour, baking soda, baking powder and salt; gradually beat into sugar mixture, beating for 2 to 3 minutes.

**4.** Transfer to 8-inch (2 L) square cake pan. Bake in 350°F (180°C) oven for 40 minutes or until cake pulls away from sides of pan and toothpick inserted in centre comes out clean. Serve warm or cold. **Makes 12 servings.**

**Baking Note**

Instead of using fresh gingerroot, you can add 2 tsp (10 mL) ground ginger and 1 tsp (5 mL) ground cinnamon to the dry ingredients for this cake.

*Per Serving:*

170 calories

2 g protein

4 g total fat
　1 g saturated fat
　18 mg cholesterol

31 g carbohydrate
　1 g dietary fibre

281 mg sodium

202 mg potassium

**Make Ahead:** Cake can be covered with foil and refrigerated for up to four days or frozen for up to two weeks.

# Pumpkin Spice Cake

*Serve this flavorful, moist cake with coffee or for dessert with fruit. Buttermilk and pumpkin purée take the place of fat in this dark, spicy, raisin-studded cake.*

| | | |
|---|---|---|
| 1¾ cups | granulated sugar | 425 mL |
| ¼ cup | soft margarine or butter | 50 mL |
| 1 | egg | 1 |
| ½ cup | buttermilk | 125 mL |
| 1 | can (14 oz/398 mL) pumpkin purée | 1 |
| | Grated rind of 1 orange | |
| 1 tsp | vanilla | 5 mL |
| 1½ cups | all-purpose flour | 375 mL |
| 1½ cups | whole wheat flour | 375 mL |
| 2 tsp | each cinnamon and baking soda | 10 mL |
| 1 cup | raisins | 250 mL |

**Glaze**

| | | |
|---|---|---|
| ¼ cup | icing sugar | 50 mL |
| 1½ tsp | orange juice | 7 mL |

**1.** Grease and flour 10-inch (25 cm) Bundt pan.

**2.** In bowl, beat sugar with margarine; beat in egg until light.

**3.** Beat in buttermilk, pumpkin, orange rind and vanilla.

**4.** Combine all-purpose and whole wheat flours, cinnamon, baking soda and raisins; stir into pumpkin mixture just until combined.

**5.** Pour into pan; bake in 325°F (160°C) oven for 60 to 65 minutes or until toothpick inserted in centre comes out clean. Let cool on rack for 20 minutes; remove from pan.

**6.** Glaze: Blend icing sugar with orange juice; drizzle over cooled cake. **Makes 16 servings.**

**MAKE AHEAD:** Cake can be stored in airtight container for up to two days or frozen for up to one month.

### Nutritional Note

New low-fat dessert products are always being introduced; watch for them in your supermarket. However, don't be fooled. Read the labels carefully.

Many cake mixes claiming to be "low in cholesterol" or "light" require oil to be added, which can make them very high in fat. One "low cholesterol" cake contains 14 grams of fat per serving; that's only one gram less than the regular mix—not a meaningful fat saving. Read the nutrient panel to see how much fat a serving actually contains.

*PER SERVING:*

247 calories
4 g protein
4 g total fat
    1 g saturated fat
    14 mg cholesterol
52 g carbohydrate
    3 g dietary fibre
200 mg sodium
210 mg potassium

EXCELLENT: Vitamin A

# Elizabeth Baird's Chocolate Angel Food Cake

*My friend Elizabeth Baird, food director of* Canadian Living *magazine, made this fabulous cake for my birthday. More flavorful than regular angel food cake, it is still nearly fat-free. Serve with Vanilla Cream (page 239) and fresh berries.*

| | | |
|---|---|---|
| ¾ cup | sifted cake-and-pastry flour | 175 mL |
| 1½ cups | granulated sugar | 375 mL |
| ¼ cup | unsweetened cocoa powder | 50 mL |
| 1½ cups | egg whites (about 11 large eggs), at room temperature | 375 mL |
| 1 tbsp | lemon juice | 15 mL |
| 1 tsp | cream of tartar | 5 mL |
| ½ tsp | salt | 2 mL |
| 1 tsp | vanilla | 5 mL |
| ½ tsp | almond extract | 2 mL |
| | Icing sugar | |

**1.** Onto piece of waxed paper, sift together flour, ¾ cup (175 mL) of the sugar and cocoa. Sift again; set aside.

**2.** In large nonplastic bowl, beat egg whites until foamy. Add lemon juice, cream of tartar and salt; beat until soft peaks form. Gradually add remaining sugar, 2 tbsp (25 mL) at a time, beating until glossy and stiff peaks form.

**3.** Sprinkle with vanilla and almond extract. Sift one-quarter of the cocoa mixture at a time over egg whites, folding in each with rubber spatula.

**4.** Scrape into ungreased 10-inch (4 L) angel food tube pan. Run spatula through batter to eliminate large air pockets; smooth top. Bake in 350°F (180°C) oven for 40 to 45 minutes or until cake springs back when lightly touched.

**5.** Invert pan onto neck of large bottle unless pan has legs attached; let cake hang until cool. Loosen edges with knife; remove cake from pan. Place on plate; place doily over top and dust with icing sugar. Remove doily. **Makes 12 servings**.

**MAKE AHEAD:** Cake can be stored at room temperature for up to two days or frozen for up to one month.

*PER SERVING:*

143 calories

4 g protein

1 g total fat
   0.3 g saturated fat
   0 mg cholesterol

32 g carbohydrate
   1 g dietary fibre

160 mg sodium

65 mg potassium

# DESSERTS

Chocolate Crêpes with Banana Cream Filling and Chocolate Sauce

Chocolate Mocha Ice Cream Pie with Gingersnap Crust

Chocolate Marbled Cheesecake

Orange Chocolate Refrigerator Cake

Lemon Mousse with Raspberry Sauce

Easy Berry Flan

Fresh Plum Flan

Baked Pear Bread Pudding with Honey-Almond Sauce

Apple-Pecan Phyllo Crisps

Pumpkin Pie with Orange Cream

Flaky Pastry

Deep-Dish Pear Pie with Apricots and Ginger

Winter Berry Trifle

Meringues with Lemon Cream

Kiwi Fool

Microwave Rhubarb Sauce with Ginger

Nectarine and Orange Compote

Apricot, Orange and Fig Compote

Berries with Orange Cream

Orange or Lemon Yogurt Cream

Amaretto Custard Sauce

Vanilla Cream

Butterscotch Sauce

# Chocolate Crêpes with Banana Cream Filling and Chocolate Sauce

*This is a fabulous, light dessert. Even though it has a little whipped cream, this fancy dessert is relatively low in fat. It has two egg whites instead of a whole egg and cocoa powder instead of higher-fat chocolate.*

| ½ cup | Chocolate Sauce (recipe follows) | 125 mL |
|---|---|---|

### Chocolate Crêpes

| ⅓ cup | all-purpose flour | 75 mL |
|---|---|---|
| 2 tbsp | unsweetened cocoa powder | 25 mL |
| 1 tbsp | granulated sugar | 15 mL |
| Pinch | salt | Pinch |
| 2 | egg whites, lightly beaten | 2 |
| ⅓ cup | low-fat milk | 75 mL |
| ¼ cup | water | 50 mL |
| 1 tsp | soft margarine or butter | 5 mL |

### Banana Cream Filling

| ⅓ cup | whipping cream | 75 mL |
|---|---|---|
| ⅓ cup | plain yogurt or extra-thick yogurt | 75 mL |
| 2 tbsp | granulated sugar | 25 mL |
| ½ tsp | vanilla | 2 mL |
| 3 | bananas, sliced | 3 |

**Nutritional Note**

For a fat-restricted diet, when making the filling omit whipping cream, use 1 cup/ 250 mL extra-thick yogurt and increase sugar to ¼ cup (50 mL).

**1.** Chocolate Crêpes: In bowl, combine flour, cocoa, sugar and salt; make a well in centre. Add egg whites and whisk lightly to combine. Gradually whisk in milk and water until smooth.

**2.** Heat small nonstick crêpe pan or skillet over medium heat; brush with some of the margarine. For each crêpe, pour in 2 tbsp (25 mL) batter, swirling to cover bottom of pan; pour off any excess. Cook until edges begin to curl and crêpe no longer sticks; turn and cook for 30 seconds. Remove and set aside. Repeat with remaining batter, brushing pan with margarine as necessary.

**3.** Banana Cream Filling: Whip cream; stir in yogurt, sugar and vanilla.

**4.** Assembly: Spread about 2 tbsp (25 mL) filling over one half of each crêpe. Arrange overlapping banana slices over half of filling. Fold uncovered crêpe in half over filling; fold in half again. Arrange on dessert plates; drizzle with chocolate sauce. **Makes 4 servings, 2 crêpes each**.

**MAKE AHEAD:** Through step 2; crêpes can be stacked between waxed paper, wrapped and refrigerated for up to one day or frozen for up to one month.

# Chocolate Sauce

*Chocolate can be part of a healthy diet when you use this low-fat sauce. Drizzle over ice cream, frozen yogurt, or the Chocolate Crêpes.*

| ½ cup | unsweetened cocoa powder | 125 mL |
|-------|--------------------------|--------|
| ⅓ cup | granulated sugar | 75 mL |
| ⅓ cup | water | 75 mL |
| ⅓ cup | corn syrup | 75 mL |
| ½ tsp | vanilla | 2 mL |

**1.** In saucepan, combine cocoa and sugar. Whisk in water and corn syrup.

**2.** Bring to full boil over medium-high heat; boil for 2 minutes, stirring constantly.

**3.** Remove from heat and stir in vanilla. Let cool (sauce will thicken upon cooling). **Makes about 1 cup (250 mL)**.

**MAKE AHEAD:** Sauce can be refrigerated for up to two weeks.

*PER SERVING (INCLUDING SAUCE):*

357 calories
7 g protein
11 g total fat
   6 g saturated fat
   28 mg cholesterol
63 g carbohydrate
   5 g dietary fibre
83 mg sodium
605 mg potassium

GOOD: Iron

**Nutritional Note**
Cocoa is made from roasted cocoa beans with most of the fat (cocoa butter) removed; it is much lower in fat than chocolate but still has all the chocolate flavor.

*PER SERVING (2 TBSP/25 mL):*

90 calories
1 g protein
1 g total fat
   1 g saturated fat
   0 mg cholesterol
21 g carbohydrate
   2 g dietary fibre
10 mg sodium
89 mg potassium

# Chocolate Mocha Ice Cream Pie with Gingersnap Crust

*This easy-to-make dessert tastes delicious and will keep for a few weeks in the freezer.*

| | | |
|---|---|---|
| 20 | gingersnap cookies | 20 |
| 3 tbsp | soft margarine, melted | 50 mL |
| 2 cups | low-fat coffee ice cream* | 500 mL |
| 2 cups | low-fat vanilla ice cream | 500 mL |
| 2 cups | low-fat chocolate ice cream | 500 mL |
| ¼ cup | sliced almonds, toasted | 50 mL |

**1.** In food processor, process cookies into crumbs to make 1½ cups (375 mL). Mix with butter; press onto bottom and slightly up sides of 9-inch (2.5 L) springform pan.

**2.** Bake in 350°F (180°C) oven for 10 minutes or until crisp and brown. Let cool completely; freeze for 10 minutes.

**3.** Soften coffee ice cream; spoon into pie crust, spreading evenly. Cover and freeze for 30 minutes or until firm.

**4.** Soften vanilla ice cream; spread over coffee ice cream. Cover and freeze until firm.

**5.** Repeat with chocolate ice cream; cover and freeze.

**6.** Sprinkle with almonds. **Makes 12 servings**.

* If low-fat coffee ice cream is unavailable, soften 2 cups (500 mL) vanilla ice cream. Dissolve 1 tbsp (15 mL) instant coffee granules in 2 tsp (10 mL) hot water; stir into softened ice cream. Return to freezer for 10 minutes before using.

## Lower-Fat Variations

Although ice cream is called for in the recipe, for the lowest fat content, use a frozen dairy dessert or ice milk, or choose 5% b.f. (butterfat) ice cream. It makes a huge difference in the fat content.

| Recipe made with: | Fat (g)/ serving |
|---|---|
| Frozen Dairy Dessert 1% b.f. | 6.6 |
| Ice Cream 7% b.f. | 11.0 |
| Ice Cream 16% b.f. | 17.5 |

## To Toast Almonds

Bake on baking sheet in 350°F (180°C) oven for 5 to 10 minutes or until lightly browned.

*PER SERVING (USING 1% B.F. FROZEN DAIRY DESSERT):*

- 209 calories
- 5 g protein
- 7 g total fat
  - 1 g saturated fat
  - 9 mg cholesterol
- 33 g carbohydrate
  - 0.3 g dietary fibre
- 149 mg sodium
- 108 mg potassium

**MAKE AHEAD:** Through step 5, covered and refrigerated for up to two weeks.

# Chocolate Marbled Cheesecake

*The secret to the rich taste of this cheesecake is low-fat yogurt, light cream cheese and cocoa.*

| | | |
|---|---|---|
| 4 cups | low-fat yogurt (no gelatin) | 1 L |
| 2 tbsp | graham cracker crumbs | 25 mL |
| 1 cup | light cream cheese (8 oz/250 g) | 250 mL |
| 1½ tsp | vanilla | 7 mL |
| ¾ cup | granulated sugar | 175 mL |
| 1 tbsp | cornstarch | 15 mL |
| 2 | eggs | 2 |
| 2 | egg whites | 2 |
| ¼ cup | unsweetened cocoa powder | 50 mL |

**1.** In cheesecloth-lined sieve set over bowl, drain yogurt in refrigerator for 4 hours or until yogurt is 2 cups (500 mL). Discard liquid.

**2.** Sprinkle graham cracker crumbs evenly in lightly greased 8-inch (2 L) springform pan.

**3.** In bowl, beat together drained yogurt, cream cheese and vanilla. Combine sugar and cornstarch; beat into yogurt mixture.

**4.** Beat in eggs and egg whites one at a time, beating well after each addition. Remove 2 cups (500 mL) to separate bowl; blend in cocoa.

**5.** Spoon half of the white batter into prepared pan. Spoon in chocolate batter, then remaining white batter.

**6.** Without going completely through mixture to bottom of pan, draw knife through batter to make marbled effect.

**7.** Bake in 325°F (160°C) oven for 55 minutes or until edge is set. Remove from oven; immediately run knife around edge of cake to loosen from pan. Let cool completely; remove side of pan. Cover and refrigerate for 4 hours before serving. **Makes 8 servings**.

**MAKE AHEAD:** Cheesecake can be refrigerated for up to two days.

*PER SERVING:*

271 calories
12 g protein
11 g total fat
    6 g saturated fat
    83 g cholesterol
34 g carbohydrate
    1 g dietary fibre
286 mg sodium
370 mg potassium

GOOD: Calcium

# Orange Chocolate Refrigerator Cake

*A little whipped cream added to drained yogurt makes a tasty lower-fat topping.*

| | | |
|---|---|---:|
| 2 cups | low-fat yogurt | 500 mL |
| ⅓ cup | granulated sugar | 75 mL |
| | Grated rind of 1½ oranges | |
| ½ cup | whipping cream, whipped | 125 mL |
| 40 | round chocolate wafers | 40 |
| 2 | oranges, sectioned, or 1 can (10 oz/284 mL) mandarin oranges | 2 |

**1.** In cheesecloth-lined sieve set over bowl, drain yogurt in refrigerator for 4 hours or until yogurt is 1 cup (250 mL). Discard liquid.

**2.** In bowl, mix together drained yogurt, sugar and orange rind; fold in whipped cream.

**3.** Sandwich about half of the mixture between wafers to make log; ice with remaining mixture. Stand toothpicks on top (so cover won't touch cream); cover and refrigerate for 4 hours.

**4.** Garnish with oranges on top and around cake. Slice diagonally to serve. **Makes 8 servings.**

### Tip
If you are in a hurry, buy the extra-thick or Greek-style drained yogurt, or use quark instead of drained yogurt in this recipe.

**MAKE AHEAD:** Cake can be refrigerated for up to one day.

*PER SERVING:*

236 calories
6 g protein
9 g total fat
    4 g saturated fat
    23 mg cholesterol
34 g carbohydrate
    1 g dietary fibre
212 mg sodium
276 mg potassium

GOOD: Vitamin C

# Lemon Mousse with Raspberry Sauce

*This long-time favorite dessert is lightened up by using only half the usual amount of whipping cream and no eggs.*

| | | |
|---|---|---|
| 1 | envelope (7 g) unflavored gelatin | 1 |
| ¼ cup | cold water | 50 mL |
| 1 cup | granulated sugar | 250 mL |
| ½ cup | lemon juice (approx 2½ large lemons) | 125 mL |
| 1 tbsp | grated lemon rind | 15 mL |
| 1 cup | low-fat yogurt | 250 mL |
| ½ cup | whipping cream, whipped | 125 mL |
| | Raspberry Sauce (recipe follows) | |

**1.** In small saucepan, sprinkle gelatin over water; let stand for 1 minute or until softened. Stir over low heat until dissolved.

**2.** In bowl, whisk together sugar, lemon juice, rind and yogurt; whisk in gelatin. Refrigerate until slightly thickened.

**3.** Fold in whipped cream. Spoon into 6-cup (1.5 L) serving bowl or individual sherbet or stemmed glasses. Chill for 2 hours.

**4.** Spoon Raspberry Sauce onto plates; top with scoop of mousse. (Or, spoon sauce over mousse in sherbet glasses.) **Makes 6 servings**.

**MAKE AHEAD:** Through step 3 for up to one day.

## Raspberry Sauce

| | | |
|---|---|---|
| 1 | pkg (300 g) frozen unsweetened raspberries (partially thawed) | 1 |
| 3 tbsp | icing sugar | 50 mL |
| 1 tbsp | lemon juice and/or Grand Marnier | 15 mL |

**1.** In blender, purée raspberries, sugar and lemon juice. Strain through sieve to remove seeds. **Makes 1 cup (250 mL)**.

**MAKE AHEAD:** Sauce can be refrigerated for up to three days.

### Strawberry Sauce

Substitute strawberries for raspberries. Do not strain.

*PER SERVING (NO SAUCE):*
- 227 calories
- 4 g protein
- 8 g total fat
  - 5 g saturated fat
  - 28 mg cholesterol
- 38 g carbohydrate
  - 0.2 g dietary fibre
- 42 mg sodium
- 135 mg potassium

*PER SERVING (2 TBSP/25 ML):*
- 28 calories
- 0.3 g protein
- 0.2 g total fat
  - 0 g saturated fat
  - 0 mg cholesterol
- 7 g carbohydrate
  - 2 g dietary fibre
- 0 mg sodium
- 59 mg potassium

# Easy Berry Flan

*This spectacular dessert is one of my all-time favorites. I make it with any combination of fresh or frozen (unthawed) berries. Making the base is much easier than rolling out pastry. (Pictured on cover.)*

| | | |
|---|---|---:|
| 1½ cups | all-purpose flour | 375 mL |
| ½ cup | granulated sugar | 125 mL |
| 1½ tsp | baking powder | 7 mL |
| ⅓ cup | soft margarine or butter | 75 mL |
| 2 | egg whites | 2 |
| 1 tsp | vanilla | 5 mL |

**Filling**

| | | |
|---|---|---:|
| ½ cup | granulated sugar | 125 mL |
| 2 tbsp | all-purpose flour | 25 mL |
| 3 cups | sliced fresh strawberries | 750 mL |
| 1 cup | fresh blueberries | 250 mL |

**Topping**

| | | |
|---|---|---:|
| 1 cup | halved fresh strawberries and/or blueberries | 250 mL |
| 2 tsp | icing sugar | 10 mL |

**1.** In food processor or bowl, combine flour, sugar, baking powder, margarine, egg whites and vanilla; mix well. Press onto bottom of 11-inch (28 cm) flan pan.

**2.** Filling: In bowl, combine sugar and flour; toss with strawberries and blueberries. Spoon over base. Bake in 350°F (180°C) oven for 60 to 70 minutes or until top is bubbling. Let cool.

**3.** Topping: Arrange berries decoratively over flan. Sift icing sugar over top. **Makes 10 servings.**

## Raspberry and Blueberry Flan

Substitute fresh or individually quick-frozen (unthawed) raspberries for strawberries.

## Bumbleberry Flan

Use at least 3 kinds of berries to make a total of 4 cups (1 L) berries in the filling: strawberries, raspberries, blueberries, boisenberries and/or blackberries.

**PER SERVING:**

237 calories
3 g protein
7 g total fat
  1 g saturated fat
  0 mg cholesterol
42 g carbohydrate
  2 g dietary fibre
133 mg sodium
148 mg potassium

EXCELLENT: Vitamin C

**MAKE AHEAD:** Through step 2, covered and refrigerated for up to 24 hours. Complete step 3 up to one hour before serving.

# Fresh Plum Flan

*This is a lovely fall dessert when plums are in season. In the winter, use 2 cans (each 14 oz/398 mL) plums, thoroughly drained. (Pictured opposite page 224.)*

| | | |
|---|---|---:|
| ¾ cup | granulated sugar | 175 mL |
| ¼ cup | soft margarine or butter | 50 mL |
| 2 | eggs | 2 |
| 1 cup | all-purpose flour | 250 mL |
| 1 tsp | baking powder | 5 mL |
| 1 tsp | grated orange or lemon rind | 5 mL |
| ¼ cup | low-fat milk | 50 mL |
| 2 cups | halved pitted plums | 500 mL |
| ½ cup | packed brown sugar | 125 mL |
| 1 tsp | cinnamon | 5 mL |

**1.** In large bowl and using electric mixer, cream together granulated sugar and margarine; beat in eggs one at a time, beating well after each addition.

**2.** Combine flour, baking powder and orange rind; beat into egg mixture alternately with milk, making three additions of flour and two of milk.

**3.** Turn into greased 10-inch (3 L) springform pan. Arrange plums, cut side down, in circles on top, lightly pushing into batter.

**4.** Combine brown sugar and cinnamon; sprinkle over plums. Bake in 350°F (180°C) oven for 45 to 55 minutes or until top is golden and toothpick inserted into flan comes out clean. **Makes 10 servings**.

## Fresh Pear Flan

Instead of plums, substitute 2 fresh ripe pears, peeled, cored and cut into ¼-inch (5 mm) thick slices. Arrange slightly over-lapping slices in circles on top, lightly pushing into batter.

## Fresh Apple Flan

Instead of plums, use 2 large apples, peeled, cored and cut into ¼-inch (5 mm) thick slices. Arrange slightly overlapping slices in circles on top, lightly pushing into batter.

*PER SERVING:*

222 calories

3 g protein

6 g total fat
  1 g saturated fat
  44 mg cholesterol

40 g carbohydrate
  1 g dietary fibre

106 mg sodium

129 mg potassium

# Baked Pear Bread Pudding with Honey-Almond Sauce

*This recipe is for my friend Alister Spiers, who every fall generously keeps me supplied with pears from his tree. It is also good served with Vanilla Cream (page 239).*

| | | |
|---|---|---|
| Half | large loaf French bread | Half |
| 1½ cups | low-fat milk | 375 mL |
| ½ cup | granulated sugar | 125 mL |
| 1 tsp | almond extract | 5 mL |
| 3 cups | chopped peeled pears | 750 mL |
| 2 | eggs, beaten | 2 |
| 1 tsp | soft margarine or butter | 5 mL |
| 3 tbsp | packed brown sugar | 50 mL |
| 2 tbsp | slivered almonds | 25 mL |

*PER SERVING:*

326 calories
8 g protein
6 g total fat
   2 g saturated fat
   77 mg cholesterol
60 g carbohydrate
   3 g dietary fibre
281 mg sodium
285 mg potassium

**1.** Remove crusts from bread; tear bread into 1-inch (2.5 cm) pieces to make 6 cups (1.5 L). Combine milk, sugar and almond extract; stir in bread cubes and let stand for 10 minutes. Stir in pears and eggs.

**2.** Spread margarine in 8-inch (2 L) square baking dish; pour in mixture, levelling top with spoon. Bake in 350°F (180°C) oven for 40 minutes or until firm to the touch. Sprinkle with brown sugar and almonds; broil for 1 minute or until sugar melts. Serve warm with sauce or topping. **Makes 6 servings**.

**MAKE AHEAD:** Through step 2 for up to four hours.

### Honey-Almond Sauce

| | | |
|---|---|---|
| ¾ cup | low-fat yogurt | 175 mL |
| 2 tbsp | liquid honey | 25 mL |
| ½ tsp | almond extract | 2 mL |

*PER SERVING*
*(2 TBSP/25 mL):*

41 calories
2 g protein
0.5 g total fat
   0.3 g saturated fat
   2 mg cholesterol
8 g carbohydrate
   0 g dietary fibre
22 mg sodium
76 mg potassium

**1.** In small bowl, combine yogurt, honey and almond extract. **Makes ¾ cup (175 mL)**.

**MAKE AHEAD:** Sauce can be refrigerated for up to two days.

# Apple-Pecan Phyllo Crisps

*Once you are familiar with using phyllo pastry, this is a very easy and delicious dessert to make. (Pictured opposite.)*

| | | |
|---|---|---|
| 2 | sheets phyllo pastry | 2 |
| 2 tsp | soft margarine or butter, melted | 10 mL |
| 2 tbsp | chopped pecans, toasted* | 25 mL |
| 1½ tsp | icing sugar | 7 mL |

## Apple Filling

| | | |
|---|---|---|
| ⅓ cup | packed brown sugar | 75 mL |
| | Grated rind of half a lemon | |
| 1 tbsp | lemon juice | 15 mL |
| ½ tsp | cinnamon | 2 mL |
| 3 cups | sliced peeled apples | 750 mL |

**1.** Lay single sheet of phyllo on counter; brush with half of the margarine. Using scissors, cut crosswise into three 5-inch (12 cm) wide strips; fold each strip into thirds to form square shape.

**2.** Using scissors, round off corners and gently mold into muffin cups. Repeat with remaining phyllo to make 6 shells. Bake in 400°F (200°C) oven for 5 minutes or until golden.

**3.** Apple Filling: In heavy skillet, combine sugar, lemon rind, lemon juice and cinnamon; cook over medium heat until bubbly.

**4.** Add apples and cook, stirring often, for 5 minutes or until tender; let cool slightly.

**5.** Spoon into prepared shells. Sprinkle with pecans; sift icing sugar over top. Serve warm or at room temperature. **Makes 6 servings**.

\* Toast pecans in small skillet over medium-low heat for 1 to 2 minutes, stirring.

**MAKE AHEAD:** Through step 2; phyllo crisps can be stored in airtight container for up to three days. Through step 4 for up to six hours.

### About Phyllo

- Packages of phyllo dough containing about 20 paperthin sheets are available at most supermarkets.
- Thaw before using.
- Unwrap package just before using. Cover phyllo with damp tea towel. Use sheets as you need them and recover stack right away to keep from drying out.
- Extra sheets should be thoroughly wrapped and frozen as quickly as possible.

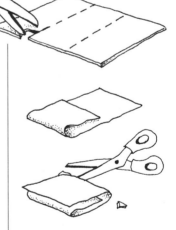

PER SERVING:

132 calories
1 g protein
3 g total fat
    0.4 g saturated fat
    0 mg cholesterol
26 g carbohydrate
    2 g dietary fibre
71 mg sodium
123 mg potassium

# Pumpkin Pie with Orange Cream

*This traditional pie is lightened up by using whole milk instead of cream, a minimum of pastry and an orange cream topping instead of whipped cream.*

| | | |
|---|---|---|
| 2 | eggs, lightly beaten | 2 |
| 2 cups | cooked mashed pumpkin, or 1 can (14 oz/398 mL) pumpkin | 500 mL |
| 1¼ cups | whole milk or 2% evaporated milk | 300 mL |
| ¾ cup | packed brown sugar | 175 mL |
| ½ tsp | each ginger, cinnamon, nutmeg and allspice | 5 mL |
| Pinch | salt | Pinch |
| 1 | unbaked 9-inch (23 cm) pie shell (Flaky Pastry, page 227) | 1 |
| | Orange Yogurt Cream (page 237) | |

**1.** In bowl, beat together eggs, pumpkin, milk, sugar, ginger, cinnamon, nutmeg, allspice and salt. Pour into pie shell.

**2.** Bake in 425°F (220°C) oven for 15 minutes. Reduce heat to 350°F (180°C); bake for 45 minutes or until firm to the touch and knife inserted in centre comes out clean. Serve warm or cold with Orange Yogurt Cream. **Makes 8 servings**.

## Canned Pumpkin

When buying canned pumpkin for this recipe, don't buy pumpkin pie filling, as it is spiced. Instead, just buy plain puréed pumpkin.

## Nutritional Note

Pumpkin is a rich source of iron and beta carotene (Vitamin A).

**Make Ahead:** Pie can be covered and refrigerated for up to three days.

# Flaky Pastry

*This is a tender pastry using a minimum amount of fat. I tried to make a pastry using vegetable oil, which is lower in saturated fat than butter or margarine, but the pastry was too tough.*

| | | |
|---|---|---|
| 1 cup | cake-and-pastry flour | 250 mL |
| ¼ tsp | salt | 1 mL |
| 3 tbsp | hard butter, cut in chunks | 50 mL |
| 3 tbsp | (approx) cold water | 50 mL |

**1.** In bowl, combine flour and salt. With pastry blender or fingers, cut or rub in butter until mixture is crumbly.

**2.** Sprinkle with cold water, tossing with fork to mix. Gather dough together and form into ball. Wrap in plastic wrap and refrigerate for 30 minutes.

**3.** Roll out on lightly floured surface and fit into 9-inch (23 cm) pie plate. **Makes 1 pie shell, enough for 8 servings.**

**MAKE AHEAD:** Through step 3, covered and refrigerated for up to one day.

## Food Processor Pastry

When making pastry in a food processor, it's very important that the butter and water be very cold.

In food processor, combine flour and salt. Add butter and process with on/off motion until mixture resembles coarse crumbs. With processor running, add water all at once through feed tube. Process just until dough starts to clump together. Remove from processor and proceed as with bowl method.

*PER SERVING (⅛ SHELL):*

87 calories
1 g protein
4 g total fat
   3 g saturated fat
   12 mg cholesterol
11 g carbohydrate
   0.4 g dietary fibre
116 mg sodium
16 mg potassium

# Deep-Dish Pear Pie with Apricots and Ginger

*Ginger goes well with pears, but you could substitute one or two teaspoons (5 or 10 mL) of cinnamon instead. Choose ripe yet firm pears as they will keep their shape.*

| | | |
|---|---|---|
| 6 cups | sliced peeled pears (about 7) | 1.5 L |
| ¾ cup | dried apricots, cut in strips | 175 mL |
| | Grated rind of 1 lemon | |
| 2 tbsp | lemon juice | 25 mL |
| 1 tbsp | grated gingerroot (or 1 tsp/5 mL ground) | 15 mL |
| ½ cup | granulated sugar | 125 mL |
| ¼ cup | all-purpose flour | 50 mL |
| | Flaky Pastry (page 227) | |

**1.** In bowl, combine pears, apricots, lemon rind, lemon juice and ginger. Mix sugar with flour; stir into fruit. Pour into deep 9- or 10-inch (23 or 25 cm) pie plate.

**2.** On lightly floured surface, roll out pastry and fit over top. (If pastry isn't large enough, place in centre with fruit showing around edge.) With knife, cut slits in pastry.

**3.** Bake in 425°F (220°C) oven for 15 minutes; reduce heat to 350°F (180°C) and bake for 45 minutes longer or until pastry is golden and filling is bubbling. **Makes 8 servings.**

## Pie Crust Notes

Enjoy just as much flavor but half the fat in a one-crust pie. For a sugar crust, brush top of pastry with milk, then sprinkle with granulated sugar before baking.

## Tip

Use scissors to cut apricots into thin strips.

*Per Serving:*

254 calories

3 g protein

5 g total fat
   3 g saturated fat
   12 mg cholesterol

53 g carbohydrate
   4 g dietary fibre

119 mg sodium

339 mg potassium

**Make Ahead:** Pie can be set aside for up to six hours; serve hot or cold. To reheat, warm in 350°F (180°C) oven for 10 to 15 minutes.

# Winter Berry Trifle

*This light version of a Christmas favorite uses angel food cake, a custard with half the egg yolks and no whipping cream. No one will notice the difference. In fact, after a large meal, they'll like this version better.*

| 1 | angel food cake or light pound cake | 1 |
| --- | --- | --- |
| ½ cup | brandy, dry sherry or raspberry juice | 125 mL |
| 1 | pkg each (300 g each) frozen unsweetened blueberries and raspberries, thawed and drained* | 1 |

## Custard Sauce

| ¾ cup | granulated sugar | 175 mL |
| --- | --- | --- |
| ⅓ cup | cornstarch | 75 mL |
| Pinch | salt | Pinch |
| 4 cups | 2% milk | 1 L |
| 4 | egg yolks, lightly beaten | 4 |
| 2 tsp | vanilla | 10 mL |
| ¼ tsp | cinnamon | 1 mL |

**1.** Custard Sauce: In heavy nonaluminum saucepan, combine sugar, cornstarch and salt; stir in milk. Bring to boil over medium heat; simmer for 2 minutes or until slightly thickened, stirring constantly.

**2.** Whisk about ½ cup (125 mL) into egg yolks; whisk yolks back into sauceapn. Cook, stirring, over low heat for about 1 minute or until thickened; strain into bowl. Stir in vanilla and cinnamon. Place waxed paper directly on surface; refrigerate for at least 2 hours.

**3.** Cut cake into 1-inch (2.5 cm) thick slices. Line bottom of 10-cup (2.5 L) glass bowl with half of the cake; sprinkle with half of the brandy and all of the blueberries. Spoon half of the custard over top. Repeat layers, using raspberries. Cover and refrigerate for 2 hours. **Makes 8 servings.**

\* To use fresh berries, substitute 1½ cups (375 mL) each fresh blueberries and raspberries.

**MAKE AHEAD:** Through step 2 for up to two days. Through step 3 for up to four hours.

### Garnish

Just before serving the trifle, garnish with an array of colorful fruit. Strawberrries, thawed raspberries, peeled sliced kiwifruit and mint leaves would add a festive touch.

*Per Serving:*

372 calories
10 g protein
6 g total fat
    2 g saturated fat
    120 mg cholesterol
69 g carbohydrate
    3 g dietary fibre
207 mg sodium
319 mg potassium

GOOD: Folate; Calcium

# Meringues with Lemon Cream

*I like to serve these for buffets—they taste scrumptious, and are easy to serve and eat. Arrange meringues on large platters and let guests help themselves. (Pictured opposite page 193.)*

## Meringues

| | | |
|---|---|---|
| 6 | egg whites | 6 |
| ¼ tsp | cream of tartar | 1 mL |
| 1½ cups | granulated sugar | 375 mL |
| 1 tbsp | cornstarch | 15 mL |
| | Grated rind of 1 lemon | |
| 1 tsp | vanilla | 5 mL |

## Lemon Cream

| | | |
|---|---|---|
| 2 cups | low-fat yogurt (gelatin free) | 500 mL |
| ⅔ cups | granulated sugar | 150 mL |
| ¼ cup | cornstarch | 50 mL |
| ½ cup | lemon juice | 125 mL |
| ½ cup | water | 125 mL |
| 2 | egg yolks, lightly beaten | 2 |
| | Grated rind of 2 lemons | |
| ½ cup | whipping cream, whipped | 125 mL |

## Garnish

| | | |
|---|---|---|
| 2 cups | sliced strawberries and/or raspberries | 500 mL |

**1.** Meringues: In large bowl, beat egg whites with cream of tartar until soft peaks form. Beat in half the sugar, 1 tbsp (15 mL) at a time, until stiff glossy peaks form. Combine remaining sugar, cornstarch and lemon rind; gradually beat into whites. Beat in vanilla.

**2.** On foil-lined baking sheets, spoon meringue into twelve 4- to 5-inch (10 to 12 cm) rounds and twelve 1½-inch (4 cm) rounds. Using back of spoon, press down on larger rounds to indent and form shells. Bake in 225°F (100°C) oven for 2½ to 3 hours or until firm to the touch and foil peels away easily from meringue. (The smaller rounds will take less time.) Remove foil; let cool on rack.

**3.** Lemon Cream: In cheesecloth-lined sieve set over bowl, drain yogurt in refrigerator for 4 hours or until yogurt is 1 cup (250 mL). Discard liquid.

**4.** In nonaluminum saucepan, mix sugar and cornstarch. Add lemon juice and water; bring to boil, stirring constantly. Reduce heat and simmer gently for 3 minutes or until thickened.

**5.** Whisk a little hot mixture into yolks; gradually stir back into saucepan. Cook over low heat, stirring, for 2 minutes; stir in lemon rind.

**6.** Let cool to room temperature (if in a hurry, stir over a bowl of ice). Stir in drained yogurt. Gently fold in whipped cream.

**7.** Spoon into meringues; top each with small meringue round. Garnish with fruit. **Makes 12 servings**

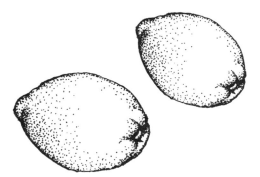

**MAKE AHEAD:** Through step 2; meringues can be stored in airtight container for up to one week. Steps 3 through 6; cover Lemon Cream with plastic wrap and refrigerate for up to one day. Assemble meringues up to two hours before serving.

*PER SERVING:*

239 calories
5 g protein
5 g total fat
  3 g saturated fat
  52 mg cholesterol
45 g carbohydrate
  0.8 g dietary fibre
64 mg sodium
185 mg potassium

GOOD: Vitamin C

# Kiwi Fool

## Cherry Fool

Instead of kiwifruit, substitute 1 package (300 g) frozen sweet dark pitted cherries, thawed and drained; purée. Reduce sugar to 2 tbsp (25 mL) and add 1 tbsp (15 mL) lemon juice. Garnish with cherries.

## Rhubarb Fool

Instead of kiwifruit, substitute 1 recipe Microwave Rhubarb Sauce with Ginger or Stewed Rhubarb (see page 233); purée. Increase whipping cream to ½ cup (125 mL). Garnish with raspberries, strawberries and/or blueberries. **Makes 6 servings**.

### Kiwi for Breakfast
Serve kiwifruit halves in egg cups for an easy-to-eat and different presentation.

*Serve this creamy dessert garnished with sliced kiwifruit and any other fruit such as strawberries or mandarin oranges. Because there is no other fat, this dessert has room for a little whipping cream and it still fits into a healthy diet.*

| | | |
|---|---|---|
| 1 cup | low-fat yogurt (no gelatin) | 250 mL |
| 4 | ripe kiwifruit | 4 |
| ¼ cup | granulated sugar | 50 mL |
| ⅓ cup | whipping cream | 75 mL |

**Garnish**

| | | |
|---|---|---|
| 1 | kiwifruit, sliced | 1 |
| 1 cup | mandarin orange segments or small strawberries | 250 mL |

**1.** In cheesecloth-lined sieve set over bowl, drain yogurt in refrigerator for 3 to 4 hours or until yogurt is ½ cup (125 mL). Discard liquid.

**2.** Cut kiwifruit in half; scoop out fruit and purée in food processor to make about 1¼ cups (300 mL). Stir in sugar and yogurt.

**3.** Whip cream; fold into kiwi mixture.

**4.** Garnish: Serve in stemmed glasses or on dessert plates and top or surround with sliced kiwi and orange segments. **Makes 4 servings**.

*Per Serving:*

237 calories
5 g protein
8 g total fat
    5 g saturated fat
    29 mg cholesterol
38 g carbohydrate
    4 g dietary fibre
55 mg sodium
572 mg potassium

Good: Vitamin A
Excellent: Vitamin C

**Make Ahead:** Through step 3, covered and refrigerated for up to four hours.

# Microwave Rhubarb Sauce with Ginger

*Fresh ginger adds a pleasing flavor to rhubarb sauce. Serve with Gingerbread Cake (page 212) or over frozen vanilla yogurt or strawberries.*

| | | |
|---|---|---|
| 4 cups | chopped rhubarb (1¼ lb/625 g) | 1 L |
| ¾ cup | granulated sugar | 175 mL |
| 1 tbsp | water | 15 mL |
| 4 tsp | minced gingerroot | 20 mL |

**1.** In microwaveable dish, combine rhubarb, sugar, water and gingerroot; cover with lid or vented microwaveable plastic wrap.

**2.** Microwave at High for 4 minutes; stir. Microwave for another 3 minutes or until rhubarb is tender. **Makes 5 servings, ½ cup (125 mL) each.**

### Stewed Rhubarb

Follow Microwave Rhubarb Sauce (gingerroot is optional): In saucepan, combine rhubarb, sugar, water, and gingerroot (if using); cook over medium heat, stirring, until sugar dissolves. Simmer, uncovered and stirring occasionally, for 10 to 15 minutes or until rhubarb is tender.

### Tip

Don't peel the rhubarb, just wash. The skin provides color and I'm sure must have fibre and vitamins. (Discard leaves.)

*Per Serving:*

137 calories
1 g protein
0.2 g total fat
    0 g saturated fat
    0 mg cholesterol
34 g carbohydrate
    2 g dietary fibre
5 mg sodium
260 mg potassium

# Nectarine and Orange Compote

*Poached nectarines spiked with rum and a garnish of orange slices makes a beautiful summer dessert. Add fresh berries or sliced yellow plums to taste. (Pictured on cover.)*

| | | |
|---|---|---|
| 4 cups | water | 1 L |
| ¾ cup | granulated sugar | 175 mL |
| 6 | nectarines | 6 |
| 2 | oranges | 2 |
| 2 tbsp | lemon or lime juice | 25 mL |
| ¼ cup | white rum (optional) | 50 mL |

**1.** In saucepan, bring water and sugar to boil, stirring until sugar dissolves.

**2.** Meanwhile, blanch nectarines in boiling water for 30 to 60 seconds; plunge into cold water to cool. Peel, halve and pit.

**3.** Using zester or vegetable peeler, cut thin strips of rind from one of the oranges; squeeze juice into hot syrup. Add orange rind and lemon juice. Add nectarines (syrup should cover fruit; if necessary cook in batches); simmer for 5 to 8 minutes or until fruit is tender when pierced. Place nectarines in bowl and pour hot syrup over top; let cool.

**4.** Slice remaining orange; halve each slice and add to bowl. Add rum (if using). **Makes 8 servings**.

## Peach and Orange Compote

Substitute peaches for nectarines.

### Nutritional Note

Canada's Food Guide to Healthy Eating recommends we have 5 to 10 servings per day of fruit and vegetables and to choose dark green and orange vegetables and orange fruit more often.

These foods are higher than other vegetables and fruits in certain key nutrients such as Vitamin A and folate. Go for cantaloupes, oranges, mangoes, peaches and papayas.

*Per Serving:*

138 calories
1 g protein
0.5 g total fat
    0 g saturated fat
    0 mg cholesterol
35 g carbohydrate
    2 g dietary fibre
5 mg sodium
280 mg potassium

**Make Ahead:** Compote can be covered and refrigerated for up to one day; serve at room temperature.

# Apricot, Orange and Fig Compote

*I love to have this in the refrigerator on hand for breakfast or dessert. I often add fresh fruit such as grapes, kiwi, banana or berries.*

| | | |
|---|---|---|
| 1 cup | dried figs (about 6 oz/180 g) | 250 mL |
| 2 cups | water | 500 mL |
| 1 cup | dried apricot halves | 250 mL |
| 6 | whole allspice | 6 |
| | Grated rind and juice of 1 lemon | |
| 1 tbsp | liquid honey | 15 mL |
| 2 | oranges, peeled and sliced | 2 |

**1.** Trim off tough ends of figs.

**2.** In saucepan, combine water, figs, apricots, allspice and grated rind and juice of lemon; bring to boil. Cover and reduce heat; simmer for 20 minutes or until fruit is tender. Let cool.

**3.** Stir in honey and oranges. Serve at room temperature or cold. **Makes 8 servings**.

**MAKE AHEAD:** Compote can be stored in refrigerator for up to five days.

**Nutritional Note**

Orange juice is a good source of folate as well as Vitamin C. Folate is required for growth and is especially important during pregnancy, particularly in the first month.

*PER SERVING:*

127 calories

2 g protein

0.4 g total fat
    0.1 g saturated fat
    0 mg cholesterol

33 g carbohydrate
    4 g dietary fibre

6 mg sodium

470 mg potassium

GOOD: Vitamin C

# Berries with Orange Cream

*Spoon this low-fat creamy sauce over juicy fresh strawberries. You'll enjoy it so much you'll want to try it over other fresh berries or sliced fruit or combinations of both. I love this made with Grand Marnier; it's also good with rum or concentrated frozen orange juice.*

| 3 cups | small strawberries | 750 mL |

**Orange Cream**

| ½ cup | 1% sour cream | 125 mL |
| 3 tbsp | granulated sugar | 50 mL |
| 1 tbsp | orange liqueur or rum or concentrated frozen orange juice | 15 mL |
| 1 tbsp | low-fat yogurt | 15 mL |
| ½ tsp | grated orange rind | 2 mL |

**1.** Orange Cream: Combine sour cream, sugar, orange liqueur, yogurt and orange rind; mix well.

**2.** Spoon sauce over individual bowls of berries. **Makes 4 servings**.

**MAKE AHEAD:** Sauce can be refrigerated for up to four days.

*PER SERVING:*

119 calories

4 g protein

1 g total fat
   0.3 g saturated fat
   2 mg cholesterol

24 g carbohydrate
   3 g dietary fibre

30 mg sodium

273 mg potassium

EXCELLENT: Vitamin C

| COMPARE | |
|---|---|
| **1 cup (250 mL) Ice Cream:** | Fat (g) |
| Vanilla 16% b.f. | 24 |
| Vanilla 10% b.f. | 16 |
| Frozen dairy dessert vanilla 1% b.f. | 2 |

# Orange or Lemon Yogurt Cream

*This is delicious over fresh fruit, or as a dessert topping instead of whipped cream. There is a new product on the market called extra-thick yogurt. Use it in this recipe, or, if it isn't available, drain yogurt as in sidebar.*

| | | |
|---|---|---|
| 1 cup | extra-thick yogurt | 250 mL |
| ¼ cup | granulated sugar | 50 mL |
| 1 tsp | grated orange or lemon rind | 5 mL |
| 1 tbsp | frozen orange juice concentrate or lemon juice (optional) | 15 mL |

**1.** Stir together yogurt, sugar, rind and juice (if using). **Makes 1 cup (250 mL).**

**MAKE AHEAD:** Cream can be covered and refrigerated for up to one week.

---

### To Make Your Own Extra-Thick Yogurt

In cheesecloth-lined sieve set over bowl, drain 2 cups (500 mL) low-fat (no gelatin) yogurt in refrigerator for 4 hours or until yogurt is 1 cup (250 mL). Discard liquid.

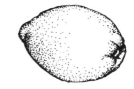

*PER SERVING (2 TBSP/25 ML):*

52 calories
2 g protein
1 g total fat
   1 g saturated fat
   4 mg cholesterol
10 g carbohydrate
   0 g dietary fibre
22 mg sodium
74 mg potassium

---

### ABOUT YOGURT

• Low-fat plain yogurt is very useful in low-fat cooking and often can be substituted for higher-fat ingredients such as sour cream or whipping cream.

• Because yogurt is more acidic than other dairy products, reduce other acidic ingredients such as lemon juice or vinegar when substituting yogurt.

• Stir in yogurt, don't beat or use a food processor or it will liquefy.

• When heating yogurt, to prevent it from separating, mix 1 tbsp (15 mL) cornstarch or flour into 1 cup (250 mL) of yogurt.

• When buying yogurt to drain, be sure to get the kind without any gelatin. You want the kind that has a little liquid on top.

# Amaretto Custard Sauce

*Serve this light sauce over berries or fresh fruit and top with toasted slivered almonds. Or, for a super-fast sauce, stir amaretto (almond liqueur) into slightly softened vanilla ice cream.*

| | | |
|---|---|---:|
| 1 tbsp | granulated sugar | 15 mL |
| 2 tsp | cornstarch | 10 mL |
| 1 cup | 2% milk | 250 mL |
| 1 | egg yolk, whisked | 1 |
| 2 tbsp | amaretto or coffee liqueur | 25 mL |

**1.** In small nonaluminum saucepan, combine sugar and cornstarch; stir in milk. Bring to simmer over medium heat, stirring constantly; reduce heat to low and cook, stirring, for 5 minutes or until thickened slightly.

**2.** Whisk about half of the hot mixture into yolk; whisk back into hot milk mixture. Cook, stirring, over low heat for 2 minutes or until thickened. Remove from heat and stir in amaretto. Let cool. **Makes about 1¼ cups (300 mL).**

### Almond Custard Sauce

Prepare Amaretto Custard Sauce, substituting 1 tsp (5 mL) almond extract for the amaretto.

*Per Serving*
*(2 tbsp/25 mL):*

33 calories
1 g protein
1 g total fat
  1 g saturated fat
  24 mg cholesterol
5 g carbohydrate
  0 g dietary fibre
13 mg sodium
40 mg potassium

**MAKE AHEAD:** Sauce can be covered and refrigerated for up to two days.

# Vanilla Cream

*Thanks go to my friend and fabulous cook Mary Holmes for this low-cal, lower-fat, crème-fraîche-like sauce. It's delicious over fresh berries or any fresh fruit along with Gingerbread Cake (page 212), or with Baked Pear Bread Pudding (page 224) or with any dessert instead of whipped cream. If possible, make it a day in advance because the sauce thickens considerably upon standing.*

| ½ cup | light sour cream | 125 mL |
|-------|------------------|--------|
| ½ cup | 2% milk | 125 mL |
| ½ cup | low-fat or extra-thick yogurt | 125 mL |
| ¼ cup | granulated sugar | 50 mL |
| ½ tsp | vanilla | 2 mL |

**1.** Combine sour cream, milk, yogurt, sugar and vanilla; stir to dissolve sugar. Cover and refrigerate for at least 1 hour. **Makes 1½ cups (375 mL).**

**MAKE AHEAD:** Sauce can be covered and refrigerated for up to three days.

*PER SERVING (2 TBSP/25 ML):*

40 calories
1 g protein
1 g total fat
   1 g saturated fat
   3 mg cholesterol
6 g carbohydrate
   0 g dietary fibre
21 mg sodium
65 mg potassium

# Butterscotch Sauce

*Serve this sauce hot or cold over frozen yogurt, or vanilla, chocolate or coffee ice cream, or with gingerbread, baked apples, poached pears or peaches.*

| | | |
|---|---|---|
| 1 cup | packed light brown sugar | 250 mL |
| ½ cup | 2% evaporated milk | 125 mL |
| 1 tbsp | soft margarine or butter | 15 mL |
| 2 tbsp | light corn syrup | 25 mL |

**1.** In heavy saucepan, combine sugar, milk, margarine and corn syrup; bring to boil over medium heat, stirring often. **Makes 1 cup (250 mL).**

PER SERVING
*(2 TBSP/25 ML):*

145 calories

1 g protein

2 g total fat
    0.4 g saturated fat
    1 mg cholesterol

32 g carbohydrate
    0.1 g dietary fibre

48 mg sodium

146 mg potassium

**MAKE AHEAD:** Sauce can be covered and refrigerated for up to one week.

# CANADIAN DIABETES ASSOCIATION FOOD CHOICE VALUES

People with diabetes have the same nutritional needs as anyone else. A dietitian-nutritionist can show one how to balance the kind and amount of food eaten with activity and/or medication by individualizing a meal plan based on the Canadian Diabetes Association's *Good Health Eating Guide*.

The recipes in this book have had Food Choice Values and Symbols assigned to them according to *Guidelines for Assigning Canadian Diabetes Association Food Choice Values* (Beta Release, Vol. 17, Number 3, September, 1993). By providing these values, people with diabetes and their families can incorporate these recipes into their meal planning accurately.

For more information on diabetes, the Canadian Diabetes Association, or the *Good Health Eating Guide*, contact your local Canadian Diabetes Association Branch. **The following food choice values refer to the main recipes indicated, not to recipe variations which may appear on those pages.**

| Page No. | Recipe (portion size) | Starchy ▢ | Fruits & Veg. ◨ | 2% Milk ◆ | Protein ⊘ | Fats & Oils ▲ | Extra ✚ |
|---|---|---|---|---|---|---|---|
| 34 | Jiffy Salsa Dip ($\frac{1}{16}$ of recipe) | | | | | | 1 |
| 35 | Clam Dip with Herbs (2 tbsp) | | | | $\frac{1}{2}$ | | |
| 36 | Roasted Red Pepper and Fresh Basil Dip (1 tbsp/15 mL) | | | | | $\frac{1}{2}$ | |
| 37 | Roasted Eggplant Dip (1 tbsp/15 mL) | | | | | | 1 |
| 38 | Herbed Cheese Spread ($\frac{1}{16}$ of recipe) | | | | $\frac{1}{2}$ | | |
| 39 | Crostini (3 slices) | 1 | | | | | 1 |
| 40 | Chicken Fingers ($\frac{1}{16}$ of recipe) | | | | $\frac{1}{2}$ | | |
| 41 | Chinese Chicken Balls with Dipping Sauces | | | | | | |
| 41 | • Chinese Chicken Balls – no sauce (1 ball) | | | | $\frac{1}{2}$ | | |
| 41 | • Minted Coriander Dipping Sauce ($\frac{1}{2}$ tsp/2 mL) | | | | | | 1 |
| 41 | • Spicy Apricot Sauce ($\frac{1}{2}$ tsp/2 mL) | | | | | | 1 |
| 42 | Smoked Turkey-Wrapped Melon Balls ($\frac{1}{48}$ of recipe) | | | | | | 1 |
| 43 | Thai Shrimp Salad in Mini Pita Pockets (3 pieces) | $\frac{1}{2}$ | | | $\frac{1}{2}$ | | |
| 44 | Sun-Dried Tomato and Onion Toasts ($\frac{1}{36}$ of recipe) | $\frac{1}{2}$ | | | | | |
| 45 | Fresh Tomato Pizza ($\frac{1}{4}$ of recipe) | 3 | 1 | | 2 | $\frac{1}{2}$ | |
| 46 | Tortilla Pizza Triangles ($\frac{1}{32}$ of recipe) | | | | | | 1 |
| 46 | Tortilla Pizza Triangles ($\frac{1}{8}$ of recipe) (4 pieces) | $\frac{1}{2}$ | | | $\frac{1}{2}$ | | |
| 47 | Goat Cheese and Pesto Tortilla Pizzas ($\frac{1}{8}$ of recipe) | $1\frac{1}{2}$ | | | 1 | $1\frac{1}{2}$ | 1 |
| 48 | Grilled Salmon Ribbons with Sesame and Coriander ($\frac{1}{4}$ of recipe) | | | | 3 | | |
| 48 | Grilled Salmon Ribbons with Sesame and Coriander ($\frac{1}{16}$ of recipe) | | | | 1 | | |
| 49 | Thai Pork Skewers ($\frac{1}{30}$ of recipe) | | | | $\frac{1}{2}$ | | |
| 49 | Thai Pork Skewers ($\frac{1}{48}$ of recipe) | | | | | | 1 |
| 50 | Open-Faced Sandwiches | | | | | | |
| 50 | • Bruschetta ($\frac{1}{4}$ of recipe) | 1 | | | 1 | 1 | 1 |
| 50 | • Greek Salad ($\frac{1}{4}$ of recipe) | $2\frac{1}{2}$ | $\frac{1}{2}$ | | $\frac{1}{2}$ | 2 | 1 |
| 51 | • Smoked Turkey with Asparagus ($\frac{1}{4}$ of recipe) | $1\frac{1}{2}$ | | | 2 | | 1 |
| 51 | • Grilled Chicken Breast with Mango Salsa ($\frac{1}{4}$ of recipe) | $1\frac{1}{2}$ | | | 2 | | 1 |
| 52 | Cheese and Tomato Quesadillas ($\frac{1}{12}$ of recipe) | $\frac{1}{2}$ | | | $\frac{1}{2}$ | $\frac{1}{2}$ | |
| 53 | Spicy Popcorn (1 cup/250 mL) | $\frac{1}{2}$ | | | | $\frac{1}{2}$ | |

The Food Choice Symbols are a copyright of the Canadian Diabetes Association.

The following food choice values refer to the main recipes indicated, not to recipe variations which may appear on those pages.

| Page No. | Recipe (portion size) | Starchy ▢ | Fruits & Veg. ▱ | 2% Milk ◈ | Protein ⌀ | Fats & Oils ▲ | Extra ⚬⚬ |
|---|---|---|---|---|---|---|---|
| 53 | Candied Corn (1 cup/250 mL) | ½ | 1 | | | ½ | |
| 54 | Tofu Blender Drink (¼ of recipe) | | 3½ | | 1½ | ½ | |
| 54 | Hot Spiced Cider (without Calvados or brandy) (1/16 of recipe) (½ cup/125 mL) | | 1½ | | | | |
| 55 | Fruit Spritzers (1 serving) | | 2½ | | | | |
| 56 | White Sangria Punch (⅔ cup/150 mL) | | 1½ | | | | |
| 58 | Curried Cauliflower Soup (1/6 of recipe) (¾ cup/175 mL) | | 1 | 1 | ½ | | |
| 58 | Chilled Cucumber Mint Soup (1/6 of recipe) (¾ cup/175 mL) | | | 1 | | | 1 |
| 59 | Purée of Tomato Soup with Fresh Basil (1/6 of recipe) (½ cup/125 mL) | | ½ | | | ½ | |
| 60 | Broccoli Soup (1/5 of recipe) (1 cup/250 mL) | 1 | | ½ | ½ | | |
| 61 | Leek and Mushroom Soup with Fresh Basil (1/6 of recipe) (1 cup/250 mL) | ½ | | 1 | | ½ | 1 |
| 62 | Hot and Sour Soup (1/8 of recipe) (¾ cup/175 mL) | ½ | | | 1½ | ½ | |
| 63 | Oriental Noodle and Chicken Soup (1/8 of recipe) (¾ cup/175 mL) | 1 | | | 1 | | 1 |
| 64 | Miso Soup with Tofu (¼ of recipe) (¾ cup/175 mL) | | ½ | | ½ | ½ | |
| 65 | Three-Grain Vegetable Soup (1/6 of recipe) | ½ | 1 | | 1 | | |
| 66 | Red Bean and Rice Soup (1/6 of recipe) (1 cup/250 mL) | 1 | ½ | | 1 | | |
| 67 | Italian Chick-Pea and Pasta Soup (¼ of recipe) (1¼ cup/300 mL) | 2 | | | 1½ | | |
| 68 | Carrot and Corn Chowder (1/6 of recipe) | 1 | ½ | 1 | | | |
| 69 | Fish 'n' Vegetable Chowder (¼ of recipe) (1¾ cups/425 mL) | 2 | ½ | 1 | 3 | | |
| 70 | Hearty Scotch Broth (1/8 of recipe) (1 cup/250 mL) | ½ | ½ | | 1 | | |
| 72 | Light Tuna Salad in Tomatoes (⅓ of recipe) | ½ | ½ | | 2 | | |
| 73 | Warm Scallop Salad (1/6 of recipe) | | ½ | | 2 | | |
| 74 | Chick-Pea, Sweet Peppers and Fresh Basil Salad (1/8 of recipe) | 1 | | | | ½ | |
| 75 | Mediterranean Lentil and Bean Salad (1/8 of recipe) | 1 | ½ | | 1 | | |
| 76 | Bulgur Salad with Cucumber and Feta (1/12 of recipe) | ½ | | | | 1 | 1 |
| 77 | Easy Couscous Vegetable Salad (¼ of recipe) | 1 | ½ | | | 1 | |
| 78 | Asparagus and Mushroom Salad (1/6 of recipe) | | | | ½ | ½ | 1 |
| 79 | Green Bean Salad with Buttermilk Dressing (1/6 of recipe) | | ½ | | ½ | ½ | |
| 80 | Salade Composée (¼ of recipe) | 2½ | 1 | | 1½ | 2 | |
| 81 | Thai Cucumber Salad (1/6 of recipe) | | ½ | | | | |
| 82 | Oriental Coleslaw (1/12 of recipe) | ½ | | | ½ | 1 | 1 |
| 83 | Purple Vegetable Slaw (¼ of recipe) | ½ | | | ½ | ½ | 1 |
| 84 | Warm Potato and Tuna Salad (¼ of recipe) | 2½ | | | 2 | | 1 |
| 85 | Tossed Green Salad with Asian Vinaigrette (1/8 of recipe) | | | | | ½ | 1 |
| 86 | Tomato Basil Dressing (1 tbsp/15 mL) | | | | | ½ | |
| 87 | Yogurt Herb Dressing (1 tbsp/15 mL) | | | | | ½ | |
| 88 | Mustard Garlic Vinaigrette (1 tbsp/15 mL) | | | | | 1 | |
| 90 | Chinese Chicken Burgers (¼ of recipe) | | | | 3½ | | 1 |
| 91 | Grilled Chicken Breast Burger with Sautéed Onions and Sun-Dried Tomatoes (¼ of recipe) | 2 | 1 | | 4 | | |
| 92 | Jamaican Jerk Chicken (¼ of recipe) | | 1 | | 4½ | | |
| 93 | Herb and Buttermilk Barbecued Chicken (1/6 of recipe) | | | | 3½ | | 1 |
| 94 | Sherry Chicken Breast Stuffed with Zucchini and Carrots (1/6 of recipe) | | ½ | | 4 | | |
| 96 | Hoisin Sesame Chicken Platter (1/6 of recipe) | | 1 | | 4 | | |
| 97 | Chicken and Snow Peas in Black Bean Sauce (¼ of recipe) | | 1 | | 4 | | |
| 98 | Asian Chicken (1/6 of recipe) | 3½ | | | 3½ | | 1 |
| 99 | Asian Sauce (1 tbsp/15 mL) | | ½ | | | | |
| 100 | Barbecued Curried Chicken Breasts (1/6 of recipe) | | 1 | | 4 | | |
| 101 | Chicken and Vegetable Stew with Parsley Dumplings (¼ of recipe) | 4 | 1 | | 4 | | |

The following food choice values refer to the main recipes indicated, not to recipe variations which may appear on those pages.

| Page No. | Recipe (portion size) | Starchy | Fruits & Veg. | 2% Milk | Protein | Fats & Oils | Extra |
|---|---|---|---|---|---|---|---|
| 102 | Turkey Vegetable Casserole ($\frac{1}{8}$ of recipe) | $1\frac{1}{2}$ | $\frac{1}{2}$ | $\frac{1}{2}$ | $2\frac{1}{2}$ | | |
| 104 | Roast Turkey with Sausage, Apple & Herb Stuffing ($\frac{1}{14}$ of recipe), light | | | | 4 | | |
| 104 | Roast Turkey with Sausage, Apple & Herb Stuffing ($\frac{1}{14}$ of recipe), dark | | | | 4 | | |
| 105 | Sausage, Apple and Herb Stuffing ($\frac{1}{14}$ of recipe) | $\frac{1}{2}$ | | | $\frac{1}{2}$ | | 1 |
| 106 | Giblet Gravy ($\frac{1}{4}$ cup/50 mL) | | | | $\frac{1}{2}$ | $\frac{1}{2}$ | 1 |
| 107 | Lemon Pepper Turkey Loaf ($\frac{1}{4}$ of recipe) | $\frac{1}{2}$ | | | $3\frac{1}{2}$ | 1 | |
| 108 | Thai Barbecued Turkey Scaloppine ($\frac{1}{4}$ of recipe) | | | | 4 | | 1 |
| 110 | Fish Mediterranean ($\frac{1}{4}$ of recipe) | | | | $3\frac{1}{2}$ | | 1 |
| 110 | Steamed Ginger Fish Fillets ($\frac{1}{4}$ of recipe) | | | | 2 | | 1 |
| 111 | Lemon Tarragon Sole Fillets ($\frac{1}{4}$ of recipe) | | | | 3 | | 1 |
| 112 | Baked Breaded Fish Fillets with Almonds ($\frac{1}{4}$ of recipe) | $\frac{1}{2}$ | | | $3\frac{1}{2}$ | | |
| 113 | Lemon Sesame Tuna Fillets ($\frac{1}{4}$ of recipe) | | | | $5\frac{1}{2}$ | | |
| 114 | Barbecued Trout with Light Tartar Sauce ($\frac{1}{4}$ of recipe) | | | | $5\frac{1}{2}$ | | 1 |
| 115 | Barbecued Salmon Fillets ($\frac{1}{4}$ of recipe) | | | | 5 | | |
| 116 | Baked Whole Salmon Stuffed with Mushrooms and Artichokes ($\frac{1}{12}$ of recipe) | | $\frac{1}{2}$ | | $3\frac{1}{2}$ | | |
| 117 | Creamy Dill Sauce (1 tbsp/15 mL) | | | | | | 1 |
| 118 | Shrimp and Chicken Jambalaya ($\frac{1}{8}$ of recipe) | 3 | 1 | | 5 | | 1 |
| 119 | Spicy Scallops ($\frac{1}{4}$ of recipe) | | $\frac{1}{2}$ | | $2\frac{1}{2}$ | | |
| 120 | Salmon Salad Fajitas ($\frac{1}{4}$ of recipe) | $1\frac{1}{2}$ | 1 | | $1\frac{1}{2}$ | 2 | |
| 123 | Garlic-Soy Marinated Beef Strips ($\frac{1}{6}$ of recipe) | | $\frac{1}{2}$ | | $2\frac{1}{2}$ | | |
| 124 | Beef and Asparagus Stir-Fry ($\frac{1}{4}$ of recipe) | | 1 | | 3 | | |
| 125 | Beef Fajitas ($\frac{1}{3}$ of recipe) | $3\frac{1}{2}$ | | | 3 | $2\frac{1}{2}$ | |
| 126 | Hoisin-Garlic Flank Steak ($\frac{1}{4}$ of recipe) | | $\frac{1}{2}$ | | $3\frac{1}{2}$ | | |
| 127 | Burgers with Creamy Tomato Pickle Sauce ($\frac{1}{4}$ of recipe) | 2 | $\frac{1}{2}$ | | 3 | $1\frac{1}{2}$ | |
| 127 | Burgers with Creamy Tomato Pickle Sauce ($\frac{1}{4}$ of recipe using light mayonnaise) | 2 | $\frac{1}{2}$ | | 3 | 2 | |
| 128 | Meat Loaf with Herbs ($\frac{1}{4}$ of recipe) | | 1 | | $3\frac{1}{2}$ | | 1 |
| 129 | Beef Filet Roasted with Mustard Peppercorn Crust ($\frac{1}{8}$ of recipe) | | | | 4 | | 1 |
| 130 | Pork Tenderloin Teriyaki ($\frac{1}{6}$ of recipe) | | | | $2\frac{1}{2}$ | | 1 |
| 131 | Lettuce Wrap Pork ($\frac{1}{4}$ of recipe) | | 2 | | $2\frac{1}{2}$ | 1 | |
| 132 | Chalupas without toppings ($\frac{1}{8}$ of recipe) | 6 | | | 3 | | |
| 132 | Chalupas with toppings ($\frac{1}{8}$ of recipe) | 6 | $\frac{1}{2}$ | | $3\frac{1}{2}$ | $\frac{1}{2}$ | |
| 133 | Chick-Pea and Pork Curry ($\frac{1}{4}$ of recipe) | 2 | 1 | | 2 | $\frac{1}{2}$ | |
| 134 | Skillet Sausage and RIce Paella ($\frac{1}{4}$ of recipe) | $2\frac{1}{2}$ | 1 | | 2 | $1\frac{1}{2}$ | |
| 135 | Honey Garlic Roast Pork ($\frac{1}{12}$ of recipe) | | $\frac{1}{2}$ | | 3 | $\frac{1}{2}$ | |
| 136 | Chutney-Glazed Ham ($\frac{1}{12}$ of recipe) | | $\frac{1}{2}$ | | $3\frac{1}{2}$ | | |
| 137 | Lemon Grass Marinated Leg of Lamb ($\frac{1}{8}$ of recipe) | | | | 4 | | |
| 138 | Onions Stuffed with Lamb and Spinach ($\frac{1}{5}$ of recipe) | $\frac{1}{2}$ | 1 | | $1\frac{1}{2}$ | $\frac{1}{2}$ | |
| 139 | Lamb and Feta Pita Pockets ($\frac{1}{4}$ of recipe) | 2 | 1 | | 3 | $1\frac{1}{2}$ | |
| 140 | Moroccan Rabbit Tagine ($\frac{1}{6}$ of recipe) | 1 | $2\frac{1}{2}$ | | 5 | | |
| 142 | Sesame Carrots ($\frac{1}{4}$ of recipe) | | 1 | | | $\frac{1}{2}$ | |
| 143 | Snow Peas with Mushrooms ($\frac{1}{8}$ of recipe) | | $\frac{1}{2}$ | | | $\frac{1}{2}$ | |
| 144 | Sherried Green Beans with Sweet Red Peppers ($\frac{1}{10}$ of recipe) | | $\frac{1}{2}$ | | | $\frac{1}{2}$ | |
| 145 | Green Beans with Herbs and Pine Nuts ($\frac{1}{10}$ of recipe) | | $\frac{1}{2}$ | | | $\frac{1}{2}$ | |
| 146 | Spinach with Lemon and Nutmeg ($\frac{1}{3}$ of recipe) | | | | $\frac{1}{2}$ | | 1 |
| 146 | Cauliflower with Fresh Dill ($\frac{1}{6}$ of recipe) | | $\frac{1}{2}$ | | | $\frac{1}{2}$ | |
| 147 | Ginger Stir-Fried Zucchini ($\frac{1}{4}$ of recipe) | | $\frac{1}{2}$ | | | $\frac{1}{2}$ | |
| 148 | Portobello Mushrooms with Sweet Peppers ($\frac{1}{6}$ of recipe) | | $\frac{1}{2}$ | | | 1 | |

The following food choice values refer to the main recipes indicated, not to recipe variations which may appear on those pages.

| Page No. | Recipe (portion size) | Starchy ▪ | Fruits & Veg. ◪ | 2% Milk ◆ | Protein ⊘ | Fats & Oils ▲ | Extra ◆◆ |
|---|---|---|---|---|---|---|---|
| 149 | Grilled Fall Vegetables (1/6 of recipe) | | 1/2 | | | 1 | |
| 150 | Barbecued Potato Packets (1/4 of recipe) | 2 | | | | 1/2 | |
| 150 | Rosemary Garlic Roasted Potatoes (1/6 of recipe) | 1 1/2 | | | | 1/2 | |
| 151 | New Potatoes with Herbs | 2 | | | | 1/2 | |
| 151 | Buttermilk Mashed Potatoes (1/12 of recipe) | 1 | | | | | 1 |
| 152 | Sweet Potato and Apple Purée (1/12 of recipe) | 1 1/2 | 1/2 | | | 1/2 | |
| 154 | Pasta with Chick-Peas, Tomatoes and Herbs (1/4 of recipe) | 4 | 1/2 | | 1 1/2 | 1 | |
| 155 | Pasta With Tomatoes, Cheese and Jalapeños (1/6 of recipe) | 3 1/2 | 1/2 | | 1 1/2 | 1 1/2 | |
| 156 | Spaghettini with Ham and Cheese (1/4 of recipe) | 3 | | | 3 1/2 | | |
| 157 | Macaroni and Cheese (1/5 of recipe) | 3 | | | 2 1/2 | 1 1/2 | |
| 158 | Light Fettuccine Alfredo with Fresh Herbs (1/3 of recipe) | 4 | | 1/2 | 1 1/2 | 1 | 1 |
| 159 | Linguine with Mushrooms and Green Peppers (1/6 of recipe) | 4 | | 1/2 | 1 | 1 | |
| 160 | Summer Shrimp and Tomato Pasta (1/4 of recipe) | 5 1/2 | 1/2 | | 5 1/2 | | |
| 161 | Linguine with Scallops and Leeks (1/4 of recipe) | 6 | | 1/2 | 4 | | 1 |
| 162 | Pasta Provencal with Tofu (1/4 of recipe) | 3 | 1 | | 2 | 1 | |
| 163 | Singapore Noodles with Pork (1/4 of recipe) | 3 1/2 | 2 | | 1 1/2 | 1/2 | |
| 164 | Jiffy Chinese Noodles (1/8 of recipe) | 1 1/2 | 1 | | | 1/2 | |
| 165 | Make-Ahead Party Thai Noodles (1/8 of recipe) | 1 1/2 | 1/2 | | 1/2 | 1/2 | |
| 166 | Szechuan Beef with Noodles (1/4 of recipe) | 3 | 1 1/2 | | 4 | | |
| 167 | Thai Noodles with Chicken and Broccoli (1/4 of recipe) | 3 | 1 | | 4 | 1/2 | |
| 168 | Singapore Noodle and Chicken Salad (1/6 of recipe) | 1 | 1/2 | | 1 1/2 | 1/2 | |
| 169 | Spicy Noodle Salad (1/8 of recipe) | 1 1/2 | 1/2 | | | 1/2 | |
| 170 | Pasta Salad with Sun-Dried Tomatoes (1/8 of recipe) | 1 1/2 | 1/2 | | | 1 1/2 | |
| 171 | Pasta and Ham Salad with Tomato Basil Dressing (1/4 of recipe) | 2 1/2 | | | 1 1/2 | 1 1/2 | 1 |
| 172 | Seafood Pasta Salad (1/8 of recipe) | 1 1/2 | 1/2 | | 3 | | |
| 174 | Spinach Rice Casserole (1/6 of recipe) | 1 1/2 | 1/2 | | 2 | 2 | |
| 175 | Green Vegetable Risotto (1/8 of recipe) | 1 1/2 | | | 1/2 | 1/2 | 1 |
| 175 | Green Vegetable Risotto (1/4 of recipe) | 3 | | | 1 | 1 | 1 |
| 176 | Indian Rice with Lentils and Mushrooms (1/8 of recipe) | 1 1/2 | 1/2 | | 1/2 | 1/2 | |
| 176 | Indian Rice with Lentils and Mushrooms (1/4 of recipe) | 3 | 1 | | 1 | 1 | |
| 177 | Spanish Rice with Coriander (1/6 of recipe) | 2 1/2 | 1/2 | | | 1/2 | |
| 178 | Chinese Vegetable Fried Rice (1/4 of recipe) | 3 | 1/2 | | 1 1/2 | 1 | |
| 179 | Wild Rice Pilaf (1/8 of recipe) | 1 1/2 | | | | 1/2 | 1 |
| 180 | Rice with Black Beans and Ginger (1/4 of recipe) | 2 1/2 | | | 1 | 1 | 1 |
| 181 | Lemon Parsley Rice Pilaf (1/8 of recipe) | 2 | | | | 1/2 | |
| 182 | Bulgur with Red Onion and Pimiento (1/4 of recipe) | 1 1/2 | | | 1/2 | 1/2 | 1 |
| 183 | Bulgur Pilaf with Shrimp and Snow Peas (1/4 of recipe) | 2 | 1 | | 3 | | |
| 184 | Quinoa-Stuffed Green Peppers (1/4 of recipe) | 1 1/2 | 1 | | 1/2 | 1/2 | |
| 185 | Barley and Corn Casserole (1/8 of recipe) | 1 1/2 | 1/2 | | | 1/2 | |
| 186 | Bean and Sausage Casserole (1/4 of recipe) | 1 1/2 | 1/2 | | 2 1/2 | 1 | |
| 187 | Potato, Bean and Tomato Stew with Basil (1/3 of recipe) | 3 | 1/2 | | 1 | 1/2 | |
| 188 | Winter Vegetable Curry with Couscous (1/6 of recipe) | 4 | | | 1/2 | 1 | 1 |
| 189 | Quick and Easy Spiced Couscous (1/6 of recipe) | 2 1/2 | | | | 1/2 | |
| 190 | Crustless Vegetable Quiche (1/4 of recipe) | 1/2 | 1/2 | | 1 1/2 | 1 | |
| 191 | Marinated Baked Tofu (1/4 of recipe) | | | | 1 1/2 | 1 | 1 |
| 192 | Spicy Vegetable Tofu Stir-Fry (1/4 of recipe) | 1/2 | 1 | | 2 | 3 | |
| 192 | Spicy Vegetable Tofu Stir-Fry (1/4 of recipe with peanuts) | 1/2 | 1 | | 2 | 4 | |
| 193 | Tomato, Eggplant and Zucchini Gratin (1/4 of recipe) | 1/2 | 1 | | 1 | 1 | |
| 194 | Apricot-Raisin Muesli (1/8 of recipe) (1/2 cup/125 mL) | 1 | 1 | | 1/2 | 1/2 | |

The following food choice values refer to the main recipes indicated, not to recipe variations which may appear on those pages.

| Page No. | Recipe (portion size) | Starchy ■ | Fruits & Veg. ▨ | 2% Milk ◆ | Protein ⊘ | Fats & Oils ▲ | Extra ✛✛ |
|---|---|---|---|---|---|---|---|
| | | | | | | FOOD CHOICE PER SERVING | |
| 196 | Cornmeal Pancakes with Jalapeño Peppers and Ginger (⅙ of recipe) | 2 | 1 | ½ | ½ | 1 | |
| 197 | Apple Cinnamon Whole Wheat Pancakes (⅓ of recipe) | 2 | 1 | | ½ | 1½ | |
| 198 | Upside-Down Apple Pancake (⅙ of recipe without honey or maple syrup topping) | ½ | 2½ | | | 1 | |
| 199 | Banana Blender Pancakes (⅛ of recipe) (1 pancake) | 1 | ½ | | | ½ | |
| 200 | Citrus Double-Bran Muffins (1 muffin) (1/12 of recipe) | 1 | 1 | | | 1 | |
| 201 | Jalapeño Cornmeal Muffins (1 muffin) (1/12 of recipe) | 1½ | | | | 1 | |
| 202 | Lemon Poppy Seed Muffins (1 muffin) (1/12 of recipe) | 1 | 1 | | | 1½ | |
| 203 | Rhubarb Bran Muffins (1 muffin) (1/12 of recipe) | 1 | 1½ | | | 1 | |
| 204 | High Fibre Carrot Bran Muffins (1/12 of recipe) (1 muffin) | 1 | 2 | | | 1 | |
| 205 | Muesli Soda Bread (1/20th of loaf) | 1 | ½ | | | ½ | |
| 206 | Raspberry Pecan Tea Bread (1/16 of recipe) | ½ | 1½ | | | 1 | |
| 207 | Fruity and Fibre Squares (1/16 of recipe) | ½ | 2 | | | 1 | |
| 208 | Light Lemon Squares (1/16 of recipe) | ½ | 1½ | | | ½ | |
| 209 | Orange Hazelnut Biscotti (1/36 of recipe) | ½ | | | | ½ | |
| 210 | Apple Cinnamon Cookies (without glaze) (1/60 of recipe) | 1 | | | | ½ | |
| 211 | Apricot Streusel Cake (1/12 of cake) | 1 | 2 | | | | |
| 212 | Gingerbread Cake (1/12 of cake) | ½ | 2 | | | 1 | |
| 213 | Pumpkin Spice Cake (1/16 of cake) | 1 | 3½ | | | ½ | |
| 214 | Elizabeth Baird's Chocolate Angel Food Cake (1/12 of recipe) | ½ | 2½ | | | | |
| 216 | Chocolate Crêpes with Banana Cream Filling and Chocolate Sauce (¼ of recipe) (2 crepes) | ½ | 5 | | | 2 | |
| 217 | Chocolate Sauce (2 tbsp) | | 2 | | | | |
| 218 | Chocolate Mocha Ice Cream Pie with Gingersnap Crust (1/12 of recipe) | ½ | 2½ | | | 1½ | |
| 219 | Chocolate Marbled Cheesecake (⅛ of recipe) | | 2½ | 1 | 1 | 1 | |
| 220 | Orange Chocolate Refrigerator Cake (⅛ of cake) | 1 | 1½ | ½ | | 1½ | |
| 221 | Lemon Mousse (without Raspberry Sauce) (⅙ of recipe) | | 3½ | | | 1½ | 1 |
| 221 | Lemon Mousse with Raspberry Sauce (⅙ of recipe) (2 tbsp/25 mL of sauce) | | 4 | | | 1½ | 1 |
| 221 | Raspberry Sauce (2 tbsp/25 mL) | | ½ | | | | |
| 222 | Easy Berry Flan (1/10 of recipe) | 1 | 2½ | | | 1½ | |
| 224 | Baked Pear Bread Pudding with Honey Almond Sauce (⅙ of recipe) | 1½ | 3 | ½ | | 1 | |
| 224 | Honey-Almond Sauce (⅙ of recipe) | | 1 | | | | |
| 225 | Apple-Pecan Phyllo Crisps (⅙ of recipe) | ½ | 1½ | | | ½ | |
| 226 | Pumpkin Pie with Orange Cream (⅛ of pie) | ½ | 3 | | | 1½ | |
| 227 | Flaky Pastry (⅛ of crust) | ½ | | | | 1 | |
| 228 | Deep-Dish Pear Pie with Apricots and Ginger (⅛ of recipe) | 1 | 3½ | | | 1 | |
| 228 | Fresh Plum Flan (1/10 of recipe) | ½ | 3 | | | 1 | |
| 229 | Winter Berry Trifle (⅛ of recipe) | 2 | 3 | 1 | | ½ | |
| 230 | Meringues with Lemon Cream (1/12 of recipe) | | 4 | 1 | | 1 | |
| 232 | Kiwi Fool (¼ of recipe) | | 3½ | ½ | | 1½ | |
| 233 | Microwave Rhubarb Sauce with Ginger (⅕ of recipe) (½ cup/125 mL) | | 3 | | | | |
| 234 | Nectarine and Orange Compote (without rum) (⅙ of recipe) | | 3½ | | | | |
| 235 | Apricot, Orange and Fig Compote (⅛ of recipe) | | 3 | | | | |
| 236 | Berries with Orange Cream (¼ of recipe) | | 2 | | | ½ | |
| 237 | Orange or Lemon Yogurt Cream (2 tbsp/25 mL) | | ½ | ½ | | | |
| 238 | Amaretto Custard Sauce (2 tbsp/25 mL) | | ½ | | | | |
| 239 | Vanilla Cream (2 tbsp/25 mL) | | ½ | | | | |
| 240 | Butterscotch Sauce (2 tbsp/25 mL) | | 3 | | | ½ | |

# CANADA'S FOOD GUIDE
# TO HEALTHY EATING

Health Canada   Santé Canada

## CANADA'S
# Food Guide
## TO HEALTHY EATING

Enjoy a variety
of foods from each
group every day.

Choose lower-
fat foods
more often.

**Grain Products**
Choose whole grain
and enriched
products more
often.

**Vegetables & Fruit**
Choose dark green and
orange vegetables and
orange fruit more often.

**Milk Products**
Choose lower-fat
milk products more
often.

**Meat & Alternatives**
Choose leaner meats,
poultry and fish, as well
as dried peas, beans and
lentils more often.

Canada

Healthy
Canada

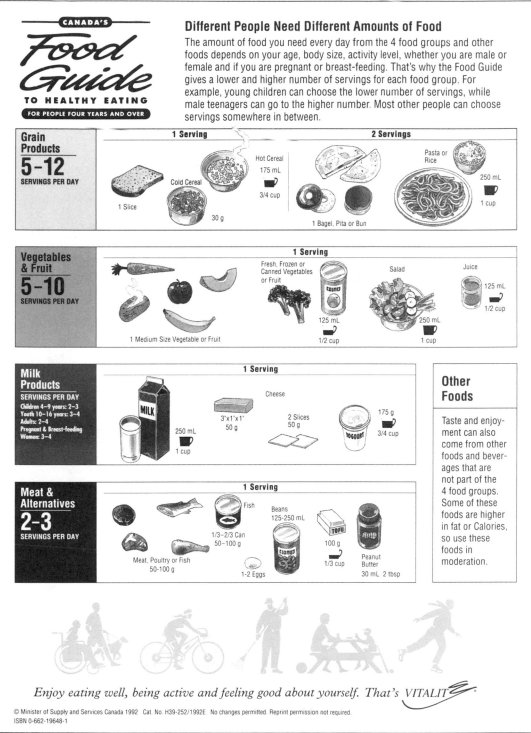

## Different People Need Different Amounts of Food

The amount of food you need every day from the 4 food groups and other foods depends on your age, body size, activity level, whether you are male or female and if you are pregnant or breast-feeding. That's why the Food Guide gives a lower and higher number of servings for each food group. For example, young children can choose the lower number of servings, while male teenagers can go to the higher number. Most other people can choose servings somewhere in between.

**CANADA'S Food Guide TO HEALTHY EATING**
FOR PEOPLE FOUR YEARS AND OVER

### Grain Products
**5-12** SERVINGS PER DAY

**1 Serving**
- 1 Slice
- Cold Cereal 30 g
- Hot Cereal 175 mL 3/4 cup

**2 Servings**
- 1 Bagel, Pita or Bun
- Pasta or Rice 250 mL 1 cup

### Vegetables & Fruit
**5-10** SERVINGS PER DAY

**1 Serving**
- 1 Medium Size Vegetable or Fruit
- Fresh, Frozen or Canned Vegetables or Fruit 125 mL 1/2 cup
- Salad 250 mL 1 cup
- Juice 125 mL 1/2 cup

### Milk Products
SERVINGS PER DAY
Children 4–9 years: 2–3
Youth 10–16 years: 3–4
Adults: 2–4
Pregnant & Breast-feeding Women: 3–4

**1 Serving**
- MILK 250 mL 1 cup
- Cheese 3"x1"x1" 50 g
- 2 Slices 50 g
- YOGOURT 175 g 3/4 cup

### Meat & Alternatives
**2-3** SERVINGS PER DAY

**1 Serving**
- Meat, Poultry or Fish 50-100 g
- Fish 1/3–2/3 Can 50–100 g
- 1-2 Eggs
- Beans 125-250 mL
- TOFU 100 g 1/3 cup
- Peanut Butter 30 mL 2 tbsp

### Other Foods

Taste and enjoyment can also come from other foods and beverages that are not part of the 4 food groups. Some of these foods are higher in fat or Calories, so use these foods in moderation.

*Enjoy eating well, being active and feeling good about yourself. That's VITALIT*

© Minister of Supply and Services Canada 1992   Cat. No. H39-252/1992E   No changes permitted. Reprint permission not required.
ISBN 0-662-19648-1

# INDEX

Quesadillas:
  about, 52
  cheese and tomato, 52
Quiche, vegetable, 190
Quinoa, about, 184
Quinoa-stuffed peppers, 184

# R

Rabbit tagine, 140
Rainbow trout, barbecued, 114
Raisins:
  carrot bran muffins, 204
  muesli, 194
Raspberry:
  flan, 222
  pecan tea bread, 206
  sauce, 221
  trifle, 229
Recipe analysis, about, 26
Red bean and rice soup, 66
Red cabbage slaw, 83
Red snapper, Mediterranean,
  110-11
Rhubarb:
  about, 233
  bran muffins, 203
  fool, 232
  sauce, 233
  stewed, 233
Rice:
  about, 65
  basmati, about, 176
  with black beans and ginger, 180
  Chinese fried, 178
  and kidney bean soup, 66
  pilaf, 179, 181
    with shrimp and snow peas,
      183
  risotto, green vegetable, 175
  and sausage paella, 134
  shrimp and chicken jambalaya,
    118-19
  Spanish, 177
  and spinach casserole, 174
  vegetable salad, 77
  whole grain, about, 176
Rice vermicelli:
  and Asian chicken, 98
  chicken soup, 63
  with pork, 163

Rice, wild. *See* Wild rice
Ricotta cheese, dip, 36
Risotto:
  about, 175
  green vegetable, 175
Roast(ed):
  beef filet, 129
  pork
    loin, 135
    tenderloin, 130
  potatoes, 150
  sweet red peppers, 36, 47, 182
  turkey, 104
  vegetables, 151
Rosemary garlic roasted
  potatoes, 150
Rutabaga:
  about, 65
  chicken stew, 101
  Scotch broth, 70
  and vegetable soup, 65

# S

Salad dressing, 76
  Asian vinaigrette, 85
  coleslaw, 82
  and fat content, 85
  for noodle salad, 169
  mustard garlic vinaigrette, 88
  tomato basil, 86
  yogurt herb, 87
  *See also* vinaigrette
Salade composée, 80
Salad(s):
  asparagus and mushroom, 78
  bulgur with cucumber and
    feta, 76
  chick-pea, sweet pepper and
    basil, 74
  composée, 80
  couscous vegetable, easy, 77
  Greek, 50
  green bean with buttermilk
    dressing, 79
  lentil and bean, 75
  noodle, 169
    and chicken, 168
  Oriental coleslaw, 82
  pasta
    and ham, 171
    seafood, 172

  with sun-dried tomatoes, 170
  plate, 75
  purple vegetable slaw, 83
  scallop, warm, 73
  shrimp, 43
  Thai cucumber, 81
  tossed green, with Asian
    vinaigrette, 85
  tuna, 72
    warm potato and, 84
Salmon:
  canned, salad fajitas, 120
  fettuccine, 158
  fillets, 115
  skewers, 48
  whole stuffed, 116
Salsa, mango, 51
Salt. *See* Sodium
Sandwiches:
  open-face, 50
  smoked turkey, 51
Sangria, 56
Saturated fats, 17
Sauce:
  Asian, 99
  dessert. *See* Dessert sauces
  dill, 117
  dipping, 41
  herb cream, 102-3
  lettuce wrap pork, 131
  Mediterranean fish, 110-11
  microwave, for green beans,
    144
  peanut, 123
  for scallops, 119
  for stir-fry, 124
  tartar, 114
  for Thai noodles, 165, 167
  tomato pickle, 127
Sausage:
  apple and herb stuffing, 105
  and bean casserole, 186
  and rice paella, 134
Scallop(s), 119
  linguine with leeks, 161
  pasta
    salad, 172
    and tomatoes, 160
  salad, 73
  spicy, 119

Tofu:
    about, 191, 192
    buying and storing, 191
    drink, 54
    hot and sour soup, 62
    marinade, 192
    marinated baked, 191
    miso soup, 64
    pasta Provençal, 162
    stir-fry, 192
Tomato pickle sauce, 127
Tomato(es):
    basil dressing, 86
    canned, and pasta, 155
    couscous salad, 77
    eggplant and zucchini gratin,
      193
    how to store, 59
    pasta
      with cheese, 155
      with chick-peas, 154
      Provençal, 162
      with shrimp, 160
    pizza, 45
    potato and bean stew, 187
    quiche, 190
    soup, 59
    Spanish rice, 177
    stuffed with bulgur, 76
    tagine, 140
    tuna salad, 72
    See also Sun-dried tomatoes
Toppings:
    berry, 222
    for chalupas, 132
    dessert, 211
    fat content of, 224
Tortilla(s):
    about, 46
    chalupas, 132
    cheese and tomato quesadillas,
      52
    chips, 46
    fajitas, 125
    pizza, 46, 47
    salmon salad, 120
Trans fatty acids, 17
Trifle, berry, 229
Trout, 114

Tuna:
    fillets, 113
    and potato salad, 84
    salad, 72
    types, 72
Turkey:
    buying, 104, 106
    and chick-pea curry, 133
    cooking times, 104
    fajitas, 125
    ground, about, 107
    leftover, 102
    loaf, 107
    roast, stuffed, 104
    scaloppine, 108
    skewers, 49
    smoked
      melon balls and, 42
      sandwich, 51
    thawing, 104
    vegetable casserole, 102
Turnip:
    about, 65
    oven-baked fries, 151
Tzatziki, 34

V

Vanilla cream, 239
Vegetable(s):
    Canada's Food Guide, 11
    cooking, 147
    couscous salad, 77
    curry with couscous, 188
    and fish chowder, 69
    grilled, 149
    quiche, 190
    roasted, 151
    slaw, 83
    turkey casserole, 102
Vegetarian:
    chick-pea curry, 133
    food, about, 14
    list of dishes, 15
    meal planning, 15
Vermicelli. See Rice vermicelli
Vinaigrette, 73, 170
    Asian, 85
    lemon cumin, 77
    mustard garlic, 88
    sesame, 78

Vitamin(s):
    about, 22-3, 143
    A (beta carotene), 22
    B, 22
    C, 22
    D, 14
    E, 22, 194, 202

W

Warm potato and tuna salad, 84
Water, drinking of, 12
Water chestnuts with Oriental
  pork, 131
Weight control, 24
Wheat germ, muesli, 194
White bean and lentil salad, 75
Whole wheat:
    about, 202
    bran muffins, 203
    muesli soda bread, 205
    pancakes, 197
    vs white bread, 205
Wild rice, pilaf, 179

Y

Yogurt:
    about, 220, 237
    chocolate cheesecake, 219
    cream, 237
    dill sauce, 117
    eggplant dip, 37
    fruit fools, 232
    herb dressing, 87
    herbed cheese spread, 38
    honey-almond sauce, 224
    lemon
      cream, 230-1
      mousse, 221

Z

Zucchini:
    Chinese fried rice, 178
    eggplant and tomato gratin, 193
    fish chowder, 69
    grilled, 149
    and pasta, 156
    quiche, 190
    stir-fry, 147
    tofu, 192
    stuffing for chicken breasts, 94